TOUGH GUY: THE LIFE OF NORMAN MAILER

Richard Bradford

TOUGH GUY
The life of Norman Mailer

BLOOMSBURY CARAVEL
LONDON · OXFORD · NEW YORK · NEW DELHI · SYDNEY

BLOOMSBURY CARAVEL
Bloomsbury Publishing Plc
50 Bedford Square, London, WC1B 3DP, UK
29 Earlsfort Terrace, Dublin 2, Ireland

BLOOMSBURY, BLOOMSBURY CARAVEL and the BLOOMSBURY CARAVEL logo are
trademarks of Bloomsbury Publishing Plc

First published in Great Britain in 2023

A catalogue record for this book is available from the British Library

ISBN: HB: 978-1-4482-1814-1; eBook: 978-1-4482-1816-5

2 4 6 8 10 9 7 5 3 1

Typeset in Perpetua by Deanta Global Publishing Services, Chennai, India
Printed and bound in Great Britain by CPI Group (UK) Ltd. Croydon, CR0 4YY

MIX
Paper from
responsible sources
FSC® C171272

To find out more about our authors and books visit www.bloomsbury.com and sign up
for our newsletters

To Ames

CONTENTS

ABBREVIATIONS AND REFERENCING

In the main text:

'Dearborn' refers to *Mailer: A Biography* by Mary Dearborn (Boston: Houghton Mifflin, 1999).

'Lennon' refers to *Norman Mailer: A Double Life* by J. Michael Lennon (New York: Simon and Schuster, 2013).

'Manso' refers to *Mailer: His Life and Times*, edited by Peter Manso (New York: Simon and Schuster, 1985).

'Mills' refers to *Mailer: A Biography* by Hilary Mills (New York: Empire Books, 1982).

'Rollyson' refers to *The Lives of Norman Mailer* by Carl Rollyson (New York: Paragon House, 1991).

AFM refers to *Advertisements for Myself* by Norman Mailer (New York: Putnam, 1959).

MoO refers to *Mind of an Outlaw* by Norman Mailer (New York: Random House, 2013).

Other in-text references are either set down in full in brackets – especially with newspaper or magazine pieces – or ascribed by abbreviation to fully specified works in the Bibliography.

ACKNOWLEDGEMENTS

Dai Howells has been of great help: diolch yn fawr. Thanks are due also to Penny Stenning. Jayne Parsons, my editor at Bloomsbury, has been enthusiastic and patient as usual; she has worked intrepidly at the production stage, as has Patrick Taylor. I'm grateful to Lisa Verner of Ulster. Amy Burns made it possible. Any errors are my own.

INTRODUCTION

In his Manhattan office a literary agent is concluding a phone-call with his client on her recently delivered novel.

'I'm sorry, but you must realise … Your story is not credible, it's too fantastic, ridiculously improbable. It was supposed to be a realistic portrayal of the world of books but it's as far-fetched as science fiction. No one will publish it.'

The book in question is about a fictitious novelist who visits his most hostile reviewers at their homes, taking with him a pickaxe handle. One has been hospitalised. Drinking at least a bottle of whiskey a day, supplemented by generous amounts of amphetamines and cocaine, he has broken records as a lothario, treating each of his numerous marriages as an incentive for a new regime of rabid infidelity. He subjects virtually all other members of the literary world to abuse, in print and in person, and those courageous enough to attend his parties are often treated to the spectacle of him naked, fulminating on the colossal proportions of his penis. The novel culminates at one of these events, when he partially severs the hand of a literary rival with a samurai sword. After calling an ambulance he decides to finish the job but being unsteady from drink and drugs visits only minor damage to the soft tissue of his victim's side. The media-swamped trial for attempted murder results in him being found not guilty, and some argue that the jury is stacked with compulsive fans of his work.

The story concludes with him being elected as Governor of New York State. His vision alarms even the more radical elements of his party, promising, as he does, to campaign for the public flogging of paedophiles, free medical treatment for the 'illness' of homosexuality, and legalised bear-baiting in Central Park.

Following his lunch the agent thinks of telephoning his client to pacify her and perhaps discuss how this disastrous project might be salvaged.

Fifteen per cent of even a modest advance is still worth fighting for. But then, quite suddenly, he realises that nothing at all can be done. It is not that this monstrosity goes beyond the usual boundaries of fictional credibility. Rather, it comes too close to the truth: the novel might be deemed libellous as a thinly disguised biography of Norman Mailer.

Mailer was boundlessly provocative in his dealings with virtually everyone he knew, including his six wives. Shortly after his first novel, *The Naked and the Dead* (1948), brought him acclaim, he invited the poet Dorothy Parker to his New York apartment for drinks. Parker and her tiny poodle were introduced to Bea, Mailer's pregnant first wife, and Karl, his gigantic, restive German Shepherd. Soon the conversation was suspended while Mailer did his best to restrain Karl, who after taking a sniff at Parker's dog made a frenzied decision to eat it. The incident lodged in Parker's memory, and as reports of Mailer's ostentatiously bad behaviour became commonplace, the boundary between Karl and Mailer began to fade. She is supposed to have been particularly amused by a story that circulated during the early 1960s. Mailer had himself acquired two poodles, and one night after walking them in Central Park New York returned home 'in ecstasy' with his left eye almost out of its socket. He had, he informed his wife, taken on two sailors who had 'accused my dogs of being queer'.

Mailer tried on two occasions to become mayor of New York City. His first attempt in 1960-61 got no further than an inaugural party-lunch for the campaign. Along with the standard assembly of political bigwigs and journalists Mailer invited a considerable number of the city's disenfranchised, notably drunks and figures with criminal records whom he had met during his research, mostly in bars in the less fashionable parts of the metropolis. These were the kind of people whose interests he claimed to represent, but at the party most seemed more interested in the free drink. Several fights broke out, often involving Mailer, and in the early hours he staggered, bloodied, into the kitchen and stabbed his second wife, Adele, twice with a knife. His motive remains open to speculation since all witnesses were drunk, but Adele herself later wrote that when he ran towards her she treated this as another brash machismo performance. She recalled that he looked like a 'crazed bull', and she joined the game as the matador. "*Aja TORO, AJAtoro, aja*", I called, "come on, you little faggot, where's your *cojones*, did your ugly little mistress cut them off...?"' (*The Last Party*, p. 351). She saw it as imbecilic and ludicrous, but not once did she expect that he would actually use the knife. She required emergency surgery – the wound came within a fraction of an inch of her heart – but refused to press charges. Mailer pleaded guilty to a minor charge of assault and was given a suspended sentence.

In 1969 he ran again and came fourth in a field of five. His plans involved turning New York City into the fifty-first state and seeking more devolution than any of the other fifty. The city would, he hoped, fragment into self-governing, village-like communities where everyone would have a say in matters ranging from water fluoridation to capital punishment. Private automobiles would be banned from the streets of Manhattan, residents would have free use of communal bicycles, and non-profit markets would sell fresh vegetables grown in farms surrounding the metropolis.

His vision, as some credited it, had evolved out of his long-term commitment to very un-American notions of socialism, and he now sounds like a trailblazer for radical Green policies. But, like most of Mailer's visionary enterprises, zealotry was matched by farce. Every month would contain one 'Sweet Sunday', during which all incoming and outgoing trains, road traffic, ships and air transport would be banned. To encourage the urban population to sample the organic, unpolluted experience enjoyed by countryfolk, electricity would be turned off too. At one public meeting he was asked by a nonplussed voter how those in cramped apartments, let alone hospitals, would cope without air conditioning when high-summer temperatures hit the 90s. 'On the first hot day the populace would impeach me!' he replied. Following several other anxious enquiries he grew impatient, informing a woman who asked how snow would be cleared without ploughs in midwinter that 'I'd piss on it'. During the 1960/61 election he had petitioned for the recognition of communist Cuba and declared that the new, quasi-independent New York City must form an alliance with Castro's republic, given their similarities.

Mailer had also campaigned regularly against the US support for the South in the Vietnam War. At several meetings he promised to make citizens of the city exempt from conscription, to which counsellors in his own team suggested that even advocating such policies might be seen by the federal government as treasonable. In truth, Mailer's political principles were a shabbily customised version of his personality: rough-house existentialism was his cover for irresponsibility and hedonism, and his pledge to social equitability mitigated bad behaviour. Despite his wealth and status he believed himself to be one of the people.

Opinions vary on his standing as a writer. *The Naked and the Dead* was acclaimed not so much for its intrinsic qualities but rather because it launched a brutally realistic subgenre of military fiction (*Catch-22* and the novel *MASH* are other examples), with the filth, horror and fear of combat rendered in prose that seems to have come from the notebook of an infantryman unconcerned with the tastes and sensitivities of his readers. There is some irony here given that for most of his time in the military Mailer served more as a cook than as a combatant.

After this his reputation as a novelist began to fade. His second, *Barbary Shore* (1951), a naïve, self-absorbed portrait of American left-leaning politics set in a Brooklyn rooming house, achieved the unenviable status of being scorned by almost every critic who reviewed it. *The Deer Park* (1955) was subjected to similar derision, and it is interesting that in 1959 Mailer brought out the slightly bizarre *Advertisements for Myself*. The book is not a novel, but it remains difficult to define it as a branch of non-fiction. 'Personal Ramblings' would be an appropriate subtitle. Quintessential to its character is the section called 'Evaluations – Quick and Expensive Comments on the Talent in the Room'. The 'talent' are Mailer's contemporaries and eminent predecessors on whom he pours a good deal of contempt. Salinger is 'no more than the greatest mind ever to stay in prep school'. Bellow: 'I cannot take him seriously as a major novelist'. Gore Vidal 'is imprisoned in the recessive nuances of narcissistic explorations which do not go deep enough into himself, and so end as gestures and postures'. Of all the women writers of his day: 'I do not seem able to read them … the sniffs I get from the ink of the women are always fey, old-hat, Quaintsy Goysy, tiny, too dykily psychotic, crippled, creepish, fashionable, frigid …'

Advertisements for Myself was transitional. After it, Mailer became a member of the opaquely determined school of New Journalism. He did not give up on novels, but his most-celebrated works are non-fiction books about real people and events in which he allowed himself the inventive licence of a novelist, pretending to seriousness while making things up as he went along. His writing was a mirror of his life. He was in charge of the story, and despite material evidence to the contrary he could manipulate the narrative in a manner that made him unaccountable. It is clear enough that during the post-1950s period he was irked by the judgements of the literary establishment that he had failed as a novelist. Thereafter he existed in the hinterland between writing and 'literary art', resenting those who had achieved fame in the latter and vilifying them in print whenever the opportunity arose. He heaped loathing on Tom Wolfe, author of the bestselling *The Bonfire of the Vanities*, and he hated Gore Vidal, who was the most eminent celebrity to be punched by him in public, once on television and twice at a cocktail parties.

Mailer's contempt for his peers was not as a rule reciprocated. Most treated it as a backhanded compliment. Indeed it seemed almost an insult not to be insulted by Mailer. The generation of American writers who, like Mailer, began to publish in the 1940s resemble, by contrast, a group of precious adolescents. It is not an exaggeration to state that by the 1980s Truman Capote, Gore Vidal, John Updike, Tom Wolfe, Mailer and a number of associates were united in a state of mutual contempt, ameliorated only by backhanded praise. It was not that they fell out or became estranged, because anything faintly resembling friendship had been fraudulent in the first place.

A great deal of wit was expended in these bilious clashes, which often proved as entertaining as the books of the combatants. 'That's not writing, that's typing,' said Capote on Kerouac. Vidal declared of the former that 'He's a full-fledged housewife from Kansas with all the prejudices', and after Capote's death reflected that 'It was a good career move'. The nastiness that infected the American literary community of these years is an appetising spectacle for those with a taste for the grotesque, but Mailer was special. Notably there are few quotable and amusing phrases by him. In works such as 'Evaluations' he hurled indecorous abuse, while in person he more often used his fists. After being punched by Mailer when the two men appeared on the Dick Cavett TV show, Vidal remarked shrewdly, 'Once again words fail you.' The audience in the studio and watching in their homes found this altercation between cultural aristocrats hilarious, but they were unaware of something even nastier going on. Before he hit him Mailer had accused Vidal of 'murdering' Jack Kerouac. Both men were bisexual, and many years earlier Vidal had remarked to Mailer that he'd enjoyed a one-night stand with the hero of Beat writing. In Mailer's view Vidal had caused Kerouac to become a maladjusted 'queer', which would eventually lead to the poet drinking himself to death. During the 1940s and 50s Mailer was outspokenly homophobic, and even when he later came to regard gay people as figures who should be free to follow their inclinations, he harboured a residual sense of homosexuality as a choice, which he respected mainly because of its 'perversity'. This brings us to the topic of Mailer and sex.

Like most men he wanted to sleep with as many women as he could, and as a literary celebrity the opportunities for him to do so were immense. He accepted these readily – but let us set aside moral judgements and consider sexuality as part of his make-up as a writer. His most famous non-fiction work is probably 'The White Negro' (1957), in which he presents the outliers of society – gangsters and black people in particular – as possessed of an energy that is lacking in the law-abiding, white, God-fearing America. A key element of his thesis is that because black people, he claims, have sex more regularly and energetically than white people, they're touched by a visceral entitlement which sad, monogamous, well-behaved Americans should aspire to. It is absurd but it is also a projection of Norman Mailer's sense of himself. His presentation of black people, largely male, as richly rewarded sex maniacs propagated a racist stereotype, but at the same time it was an excuse for his calculated licentiousness. He cheated on all of his six wives, sometimes covering his tracks efficiently but later in life leaving too many clues. Apart from Bea, his first wife, and Norris, his last, he was a habitual wife beater. Vilely, 'The White Negro' also seems to associate sex with violence – aggression resulting in a kind of pleasured male victory. *An American Dream* (1965) is about Stephen Rojack, a war hero, whose exploits during the 1950s and early 60s are a thinly disguised realisation of what his creator wished he could have got away with, were it not for wife-murder being illegal and the American electorate being generally disinclined to vote for psychopaths. Rojack does kill his wife and shortly afterwards has sex with her maid, following his attempt to anally rape her. The book might more accurately have been called *Mailer's American Dream*.

By the 1970s Mailer's standing as a novelist was more a token of his political radicalism than his reputation serious literary writer, but things improved in 1979 with *The Executioner's Song*. It covers the real-life trial and execution by firing squad of Gary Gilmore, an event that marked the reinstatement of the death penalty in the United States after ten years of effective, though not constitutional, abolition. The most astonishing thing about the book is that it won Mailer the Pulitzer Prize for fiction. At no point in the work or during comments to the media does he state that the events described amount to anything other than fully documented facts. He allows himself some freedom for speculation on the thoughts and feelings of the figures involved but then so do many historians and biographers. The sober, measured character of the prose contrasts so strikingly with the nature of the story that most reviewers treated it as a literary cross-breed: real life transported into something that reads like a novel. It was his best book, and he had rehearsed for it in *The Armies of the Night* (1968), on the anti-Vietnam War demonstrations in which he was involved, and *The Fight* (1975), an account of the Muhammad Ali vs. George Foreman World Title bout he covered in Zaire.

Mailer had charted new territory for writers, but his creative endeavours were also touched by the absurd. Throughout his life Mailer saw writing as an escape route from the generally accepted terms and conditions of existence: being answerable for what we do; treating others, women in particular, with respect; telling the truth rather than habitually making things up; refusing to concede that his personal opinion was subjective, and so on. Fiction allows the writer to indulge such fantasies in the world they create, but for Mailer this was not enough. He wanted to inhabit his inventions, to improve on the life that limited his insatiable desire for hedonism without responsibility and unchallenged greatness. His ambition to change the world according to his private compulsions was as much the driving force behind his mixed-genre books as anything resembling an artistic vision.

A hilarious demonstration of this occurred when he made a film called *Maidstone* (1970). In it he appeared as Norman T. Kingsley, a deranged dictatorial figure running for president, but as the film's director he began to treat the rest of the cast and crew in the same maniacal, authoritarian manner as the figure he played. For many it seemed that he was experimenting in the film with the same mixture of reality and invention that he'd pioneered in his books. Those involved were fully aware of the curious parallels between the political ambitions of Norman T. Kingsley and those of the man who had created and now played and directed him, Norman Kingsley Mailer; the latter's attempt to become mayor of and create a quasi-independent New York City had taken place less than a year before. Drugs and alcohol were consumed from breakfast onwards by all involved, and most began to lose any clear distinction between whether they were in a cinematic representation of a political campaign or part of a real one. Towards the end of the filming Mailer ordered a group of his actors to become assassins, but by this point no one seemed certain of their target – the director, or the presidential candidate played by the director? Rip Torn, the respected Hollywood actor, had like many others become unhappy with Mailer the director's capricious, bullying manner, which was disturbingly similar to the politics of Norman T. Kingsley. Torn tried to kill Norman T. by bashing in Mailer's skull with a claw hammer but insisted he had lost any ability to differentiate between acting and attempted murder. Mailer did not call the police because he was responsible for this madcap blurring of what is and what is made up, and he accepted the consequences.

Mailer began his review of Tom Wolfe's *A Man in Full* by recalling his own remarks of 1965 that America had failed to produce a Tolstoy or a Stendhal, a novelist capable of unravelling their country's complexity, and with undisguised satisfaction he went on to conclude that the promise offered by Wolfe was false. Mailer predicted there will never be a Great American Novelist or the Great American Novel ('A Man Half Full', *The New York Review of Books*, 17 December 1998) without fully explaining why this perpetually sought absolute was an impossibility. No other nation longs so despairingly for such a work, because they do not see themselves as sufficiently perplexing, boundless and unfathomable so that only fiction will capture their essence. What Mailer did not seem to realise when he wrote these words, so close to the end of his career and indeed his life, was that inadvertently he was responsible for the nearest that America would get to its ultimate literary aspiration. His life comes as close as is possible to being the Great American Novel; beyond reason, inexplicable, wonderfully grotesque and addictive.

BROOKLYN BOY

Norman Mailer's father, Isaac Barnett 'Barney' Mailer, was born in Lithuania but spent most of his early years in South Africa after his parents, Benjamin and Celia Mailer, emigrated there in 1900 when he was roughly ten years old: exact certifications of dates of birth are not available. They were Jewish, and when they married their country was part of the Czarist Russian Empire in which antisemitism was rife, enshrined in social conventions, pogroms included, and embedded in laws regarding education and political representation which classified Jews as second-class citizens.

Barney was the second of the Mailers' eleven children, and he took a degree at the University of the Transvaal, probably in a science-based discipline; again, there is no documentation. Eventually he trained to become an accountant. We do know that Barney volunteered as a supply officer in the South African army and was stationed in London in 1917 and served briefly in France, though no one is clear as to whether he saw action. After he was demobbed in 1919, he decided not to return to his parents in Johannesburg and instead took the train from London to Liverpool and boarded the White Star liner RMS *Baltic* for New York. The United States was not the more profitable option, given that his mother and father had over the previous three decades established several successful retail and manufacturing businesses in the largest, most rapidly expanding metropolis in Africa. The Jewish community of the city was one of the wealthiest in the world and was largely spared the prejudices found in most parts of Europe and America. Barney would not see his parents again and Celia never recovered from the devastation of her son's sudden, unexplained disappearance.

Circumstantial evidence suggests that his motive was shame, in that during his years following graduation Barney became a compulsive gambler, spending much of his time at racecourses around the city and displaying an extraordinary talent for choosing slow horses and bad jockeys. Eventually he began to steal cash from his father's business to fund his addiction, but he was never expelled from the family home, and until he made his sudden decision to leave for America, it was assumed by his parents that he would return after the war. His sister Anne and her husband, Dave Kessler, lived in New York, and Barney moved in with them after his arrival, but again it is unclear whether he intended to stay in the country. He was certainly not, like most immigrants, in search of a better life. Despite Barney's transgressions his father was willing to provide him with well-paid employment. It would eventually become evident that Barney was for most of his life caught between what he appeared to be and who he was.

Norman spoke of him rarely, and when he did it was of a man who seemed to compel a particular question: was he really my father? The wealthier, non-Africaner white people of South Africa adopted social mannerisms and accents that made them appear to be English (or at least the English who had exported their culture and lifestyle to the Indian Raj). Barney sounded as if he had gone to a British public school and dressed like it too: three-piece handmade suits, black or pearl-grey leather pants, suede gloves more often carried rather than worn, felt hat and umbrella or cane in his *left* hand.

It was this otherworldly persona that drew Fan Schneider to him in 1920. Anne had been taken very ill with flu, which some feared might be the deadly 'Spanish' variant. She, Dave and Barney took the train to Lakewood, a New Jersey sea resort which was thought to be a healthier environment than the densely populated Brooklyn where they lived.

Hyman and Ida Schneider had spent their earliest years in America during the 1890s on New York's Lower East Side. Hyman and his sister Lena ran a sidewalk stand mostly selling soda water and newspapers, along with locally made candy. They worked from four in the morning until well after dark and gave up because their modest profits were depleted by members of the Irish gangs that dominated the district. Stock was stolen daily, and on most days the siblings took home less cash than they'd spent on merchandise. The Irish mobsters also took a regular percentage of profits from every local retailer.

The Schneiders moved to Long Branch, New Jersey, a beach resort which enjoyed the patronage of the American political and social establishment. The Seven Presidents Park is named in honour of the number of the country's leaders who either owned property there or visited regularly, the last being Woodrow Wilson. Hyman and Ida opened a grocery and general store which thrived, and during the years of the First World War invested in rental houses and a hotel in nearby Lakewood. Hyman had also, since the age of sixteen, been a rabbi, and after the family moved to New Jersey he served the local Jewish community as a spiritual leader and teacher of Hebrew, leaving the businesses in the care of his wife and children. Two of their three daughters, Rose and Fanny, or Fan, helped to run the hotel after graduating from high school. Both were bright enough for university, but convention destined them for respectable work in the family businesses followed by marriage. The New Jersey coast around Long Branch had become the home for first- and second-generation immigrant families who found enough entrepreneurial opportunities there for an escape from the crime-riven areas of New York City. Some were Irish, others Italian, but Lakewood was predominantly Jewish. It was certainly not a self-imposed ghetto; more an area in which liberal and Orthodox Jews could feel comfortable with each other and alongside the largely Christian households of the neighbourhood. It resembled a version of the Europe that most would have hoped for but from which they had been forced to flee.

Fan and Barney first met at the Lakewood hotel in 1919. On Saturday nights the carpets would be rolled back in the dining room and residents and others danced to a band, sometimes jazz. Barney was attracted to Fan, but it was she who turned the evening of flirtation into a courtship, asking him to meet her for a walk the next day and then inviting him to come back for card games with her at the family house on Monday. She later commented that he was 'nice, polite and really handsome', by which she meant that she had never come across anyone quite like him before. He was Jewish, and thus a suitable partner, and an American, seemingly, but he was also captivatingly alien. No one had heard an accent quite like his. Talking movies would not involve English actors until the late 1920s, and American aristocrats who had adopted anglicised diction and pronunciation were seldom encountered in Brooklyn or New Jersey. Barney became even more of an enigma when it was discovered in conversation on family histories that the Mailers and Schneiders had, barely three decades before, lived within around thirty miles of each other in Lithuania. The point, which was never explicitly raised, mainly out of politeness to Barney, who appeared unwilling to address it, was why he had chosen to give up a seemingly privileged lifestyle in South Africa for Brooklyn, where he got by doing freelance accountancy work.

Fan and Barney officially announced their engagement in 1920 only six months after they had met. She had been the driving force behind this, he the cautious though not entirely unhappy participant. After he had spent eighteen months in Milwaukee working as an accountant for a large company and saving money for his future with Fan, they were married by two rabbis in Manhattan on 14 February 1922. More than one hundred guests were present and catered for generously at a reception funded by the Schneiders. Eleven months later, on 31 January 1923, their first child, a boy, was born at Monmouth Memorial Hospital. The Schneiders named him, in Hebrew, Nachum Melech, but on his birth certificate his first names appeared as Norman Kingsley; 'King' is a more or less literal equivalent of the Hebrew notion of Melech.

Fan and Barney moved to a respectable area of Brooklyn in 1928, when their son was five. Barney had found regular work with a firm in Manhattan, and Norman enrolled at P.S. [Public School] 181 on 1023 New York Avenue shortly before his sixth birthday.

The Norman Mailer of his infant years has become part of a general myth, and it is difficult to disentangle his own accounts from family legends. According to his aunts and Fan there was a particularly memorable event in 1925, a year before they left for the city. Norman locked himself in the bathroom of their third-floor apartment and howled to relatives, from a third-floor window, 'Goodbye everybody, forever.' The young Mailer was precocious, but one has to wonder if a two-and-a-half-year-old was capable of experiencing existential, potentially suicidal torment, let alone voicing it. According to Mailer's second wife, Adele, he would, as an infant, after bouts of anger, write notes for his mother informing her of his distress, closing with 'Goodbye forever', before walking around the block and leaving Fan in a state of immense panic. He was then a little older: three and a half. One should remember that Adele was a somewhat credulous and potentially unreliable witness to the real Norman Mailer, a man she treated with respect even after he had tried to kill her.

Norman's sister, Barbara Jane, was born in the summer of 1926, and by this point Fan was coming close to what we now understand as being a nervous breakdown, though medical practitioners at the time were sceptical about any forms of mental illness beyond outright lunacy. Her general practitioner, Dr Slocum, advised her to 'pull herself together'. The cause of her distress was Barney. Shortly before they became engaged, when she told him she loved him, he confessed to her that he was a gambler, and she accepted that he, like many others, was inclined towards an innocuous if socially disreputable pastime. In many ways it made him more attractive to her – at least until after they were married, when she found that his hobby was actually a ruinous addiction which had already cost the family enormous amounts of money, but which he had managed to hide. Barney kept two different bank accounts, one for his wife and children and another for his fixation. He drew upon the former to feed the latter.

Up to his early teens Mailer's life involved shifts between the involuntary disclosure of secrets about the true nature of his father's activities and Fan's incessant attempts to spare him the worst effects of these and the truth about them, both in terms of the state of her marriage and the financial plight faced by the family.

In adulthood Mailer was so outspoken on his life and opinions that one might be forgiven for thinking that his exclusive field of interest was himself. But rarely if ever did he talk or write about his years before Harvard, at least expansively. In 1992 he stated in an interview that 'I've never written about Brooklyn in any real way', going on to explain that 'I think that they're [his memories] probably crystals' (George Feeley, *Million: The Magazine about Popular Fiction*, Jan/ Feb 1992). Mailer uses the term 'crystals' quite frequently, without making it clear as to whether they clarify or blur related events. The best we can make of it is that his adolescence involves vivid memories he prefers to keep to himself.

He wrote profusely about Cy Rembor, his cousin, eight years his senior and his hero. Cy was a local star in baseball games, able to hit homers when no one could pick out the ball. Tall, handsome, ever decent, confident and smiling but certainly never arrogant, Cy became a lawyer, and Mailer took him on as his private attorney. He recalled, 'I worshipped him (with enormous funds of love and envy) because he was a hero.' Compared with his memories of Cy, Barney, his father, is recorded as a shifting, ghostly presence of whom he could hardly bear to speak. The closest he came was to remark that 'I had criminal blood in me', and even then, the nature of this inheritance is oblique. Of Fan, 'I still have an image of Mother, her back to me, lighting the candles that sat on the antique cabinet and whispering a prayer in Hebrew. It was one more element in that adult world that baffled but protected me.' (Bill Broadway, 'Norman Mailer: New Advertisements for Himself', *New Millennium Writings*, Spring/Summer 1998).

This is his admission, to an extent, that he was aware of what Fan was desperately trying to protect him from. She encouraged him to write stories, of which we have no record, and praised him exuberantly for his extraordinary intellectual talents. Once, after receiving a less than impressive report from a teacher at P.S. 181, she charged into the school while the master was teaching and instructed him to reconsider his unfair assessment of her beloved genius. She was, of course, a little biased, but less than a year later Mailer was, after objective tests, judged to have an IQ of 170, the highest ever recorded at the school. There is no record of Barney ever showing any interest, let alone pride, in his son's precociousness.

Mailer was spoiled and protected by Fan, an unintended consequence of her attempts to preserve him from the conflicts between herself and Barney. He remembers that once she thought about divorcing him, but her orthodox religious background held her back. 'To her, a divorced woman was a whore.' (Lennon, p29) Cy, later in interviews, said that his cousin was a weak, 'tearful' 'mummy's boy', who became preoccupied with boxing because he was afraid of other youngsters his age. There was no domestic violence in the Mailer household, but Norman had witnessed 'terrible fights', verbal conflicts between his mother and father. His uncle Dave Kessler effectively bailed them out when they faced what amounted to bankruptcy during the post-depression years of the early 1930s. Aside from Barney's work situation becoming ever more precarious, he managed to run up debts of between $5,000 and $10,000 through gambling alone. He lost money to bookmakers after having borrowed it from various kinds of moneylenders, some connected with the gangster fraternity of New York.

Dave set up a small oil service and delivery business called Sunlight Oil Corporation, which was run by Fan and which saved the family from homelessness and destitution. Dave died of asthma when in his fifties, and Mailer was convinced that his had father killed him without resorting to physical violence. On numerous occasions Dave would be obliged to visit his brother-in-law's flat and perform what Mailer later called 'a comedy on the edge of a cliff', meaning that he would present Barney with further evidence that his addiction was ruining the Sunlight company. According to Mailer, 'Barney would reply in his clipped British accent, "I don't know how you can speak to me in that fashion." At which point Dave's asthma would deepen.' In 1959 Mailer reflected that 'I was a physical coward as a child'. (Lennon, pp17-18)Perhaps the sense of fear and anxiety that were ever-present elements of his life and the lives of those closest to him during those early years were transformed later into his bizarre shifts between seemingly uncontrolled bouts of violence, both verbal and physical.

His bar mitzvah was held in the Temple Shaari Zedek in February 1936, and he delivered the first part of his speech according to convention: an opening in which he warmly welcomed friends and relatives to the ceremony, followed by brief references to passages from the Torah that he felt carried special meaning, and a declaration of what being part of the community of Judaism meant. His note of thanks to his parents and relatives was, all assumed, the close, but Mailer offered a coda that caused some surprise. He made it clear that the community he was proud to join was not that which 'with a bent back [would] receive innocently the inhuman Nazis'. (Lennon, p21)

With hindsight we are aware that the pre-war policies of Nazi Germany were a prologue to the programme of extermination of the 1940s, but at the time, in 1936, only those outside the country who closely monitored the introduction of laws forbidding Jew/Gentile marriage and the gradual restrictions imposed on Jews regarding education, employment and citizenship suspected that something more horrific was to come. The Nazis were doing no more than implementing practices that had been commonplace in most Central and Eastern European societies for two centuries, and which had caused the Mailer and Schneider families to leave Lithuania. Mailer later claimed in a conversation with his biographer J. Michael Lennon that he had been instructed by his mother as early as 1932 on the ongoing and forthcoming evils of Nazism. If so, Fan should be complimented as a woman possessed of extraordinary intuition and foresight given that the Nazis did not come to power until 1933. We have no access to the mindset of Mailer aged nine, but we know that as an adult, when he spoke to Lennon, he regarded himself as an inordinate fount of wisdom, on everything.

He also surprised those present at his bar mitzvah by declaring his empathetic relationship with several famous Jews, principally Albert Einstein and Karl Marx. Einstein had been working in various US universities since 1933, particularly Princeton, but despite his being awarded the Nobel Prize for Physics in 1921 he was not well known outside academia until his work was associated with the development of nuclear power and the atom bomb in the 1940s. Few people present would have heard of him. Marx was far better known, of course, but the fact that he was a Jew was for those in attendance either anomalous or of little relevance. All were Jews seeking a decent living in the home of free enterprise, while Marx had committed himself to predicting the downfall of capitalism. Fan's guests might have been impressed by her son's erudition, but even those who knew something of Marx would have treated Mailer's emphasis on his significance as a Jewish thinker as unintentionally humorous.

Mailer would spend most of his life involved in relentless attempts to spread consternation. His bar mitzvah, at least in his recollections of it, was his dress rehearsal. But since we have no trustworthy account from others of what exactly he said we might also see it as a prelude to another feature of Mailer the adult. He would become a chameleon, choosing to bludgeon the truth into what he thought suitable for the occasion, usually involving an attempt to shock.

He was a brilliant pupil, a boy who went far beyond Fan's expectations of her beloved son. There are no records of how Barney felt about

Norman, but he must have been astonished when teachers from the school stated that he was ready for Harvard at the age of fifteen. The admissions tutors at Harvard agreed that he was intellectually suitable but recommended that he should wait for another year before enrolling at one of the most prestigious American universities. They thought that the admission of an individual who looked like a child, from a low-ranking state high school, would cause freshmen from the culture of privilege and private education to treat him as a curiosity and a target for mockery. With little else to do he began to notice other things about his environment, such as being called 'kike' and 'Christ killer' as he boarded the bus for school.

Not once does Mailer or his relatives or peers suggest that he was remotely interested in serious or even popular literature before he went to university. He preferred comics and the kind of illustrated magazines that catered for teenagers with an interest in aeroplanes and guns. He later admitted to enjoying some kinds of prose fiction, notably the variously authored stories of Tarzan's adventures, and Rafael Sabatini, who wrote *Scaramouche* (1921) and *Captain Blood* (1922), historical novels that turn the past into fantasy. But our notion of what actually occurred during these years of his life should be prefaced with an emphatic 'probably'.

His most memorable comments on his pre-Harvard years in Brooklyn involve sex. At thirteen, 'we, in Brooklyn, in my end of Brooklyn, weren't thinking about anything but sex. We wanted to get laid. We wanted to muzzle a girl as they called it, and put our hands on their breasts.' (Lennon, p24) He admits that his and his friend's ambitions came to no more than the purchase of light pornography, such as *Spicy Detective* magazine, which presented readers with 'huge tits poking through gossamer scraps of torn blouse'. Mailer and his friends Arnold Epstein and Harold Kiesel formed a jazz trio, with Mailer on clarinet. Their improvisations would have impressed devotees of the avant-garde since none of them had learned to play their instruments. Their sole motive was to be hired by dance halls on the coast or resorts in the Catskills mountains, where many New York Jews took their summer holidays. They were not, he concedes, particularly interested in music. They wished to meet girls and young women who would dance and listen at their appearances, and their adolescent lust was quaintly tribalist. They wanted only to play where there was an abundance of 'nice Jewish girls' (Lennon, *Conversations with Norman Mailer*, p. 311).

Mailer's admissions are an indication of what life was like for all Brooklyn residents in the 1930s. His particular area was mostly Jewish, though not exclusively. The Mailers and their neighbours in and around Crown Street usually had secure incomes. They could hardly be regarded as being middle class, yet they felt more comfortable with their lot than families only a few blocks away. Few other areas of the broader region of New York City or even the United States as a whole could merit comparison with Brooklyn as a hub for national, economic and racial diversity. Black people from the South had settled there in the 1920s, when manual workers of all races willing to accept wretched wages were sought for the numerous manufacturing industries of the district. Alongside this legacy of the Civil War, Brooklyn comprised an overspill of the worst aspects of Europe during the previous century: large numbers from Ireland had settled there because of the famine; Italians, usually farmers who could no longer make a living, arrived during the same decades; Continental Europeans from Germany had come from defunct imperial homelands that afforded little more than starvation.

Mailer's comments on life in Brooklyn indicate a degree of cosy insularity, a reluctance to move beyond the community made up of his immediate family and other Jews. Importantly, he seems to regard the antisemitic comments received on the streets and public transport an acceptable fact of life because the community was made up of groups variously displaced and dispossessed, and mutual loathing was commonplace. Whoever called him a kike was used to being derided as a mick (Irish), dago or guinea (Italian), heinie or kraut (German), bohunk (Hungarian), and so on. The Irish were hated by the Italians and vice versa, particularly among those from each community involved in minor and major criminality, and black people were treated vilely by all others and rewarded their neighbours with quiet contempt. For once, the Jews were not the particular victims of discrimination. They were involved in an egalitarian culture of tribal abomination.

The Armies of the Night focuses mainly on the protests against the Vietnam War in 1967 in which Mailer was involved. It also presented the late 1960s as a transformative period in twentieth-century American history.

Aside from Vietnam and the Cold War, the United States was undergoing a period of repentance and reform, particularly regarding its routinely sexist and racist prejudices. Most intriguingly Mailer allows into his observations of the present day some recollections of his youth. Notably he referred to himself in the third person. 'He hated this [his past] because modesty was an old family relative, he had been born to a modest family, had been a modest boy, a modest young man, and he hated that, he loved the pride and arrogance and the confidence and the egocentricity he had acquired over the years ...' (Dearlove, p20; quoting Mailer) It is worth reading between the lines here. The Brooklyn of his youth had been a microcosm of America – with all its prisms of injustice and discrimination – that Mailer had taken against for most of his life once he'd made a name for himself as a cultural celebrity. He felt ashamed that as a teenager he had hidden from all the issues that had turned him into the author who punched as often as he debated, the man who battled with as much as he loved women, and the philosopher whose governing maxim involved divisiveness and violence. Among all of this, in the adult Mailer could be detected only a 'fatal taint, a last remaining speck of the one personality he found absolutely insupportable – the nice Jewish boy from Brooklyn'. (Dearlove, p20; quoting Mailer)

Within a mile of the Mailer apartment was a colony of sheds put together from scrap metal and timber which occupied about fifteen acres close to the waterfront and provided shelter for the families who had built them after the recession. Hundreds died there, sometimes from disease caused by lack of fresh water and sanitation issues, others from starvation. By the time Mailer was in his early teens this horrific camp, known as Hooverville or Tin City, was being bulldozed and its residents sent out to hastily assembled public housing projects, a little more respectable in appearance. Mailer would certainly have witnessed it, a hideous, nightmarish exhibition of squalor and humiliation set against the backdrop of New York's skyscrapers, the wealthiest metropolis on the planet. Such contrasts between extravagant hedonism and hellish deprivation would inform the essays of his later existence as a thinker and writer. That he chose to concentrate in his teens upon a future in the Ivy League universities and sought protection with Fan from the world outside their apartment might well later cause him unease. The boy was, for the man, a little of an embarrassment.

2

ODD MAN OUT

For a while Mailer was committed to enrolling at the Massachusetts Institute of Technology (MIT), physically adjacent to Harvard, but a newer institution – mid-nineteenth century – and far more dedicated to science-based teaching and research. He was enthralled by mechanical engineering as the driving force for the improvement of the human condition, and he had a particular affection for aerospace technology, which probably grew out of his juvenile addiction to science fiction. Flying, he believed, was something that would transform America and the rest of the world. He was tireless in his attempts to charm girls of his age in Brooklyn, with only Rhoda Wolf and Phyllis Bradman recorded as the ones he successfully courted, and even then the liaisons went no further than holding hands. They were enthralled by his predictions that air travel would soon be routine and by his promise to play a role in this, but his announcement that quite soon he would be on his way to the prestigious MIT was met with blank stares or puzzlement. But when he mentioned Harvard, the young ladies flickered their eyebrows and smiled in admiration.

There is no precise evidence as to why Mailer chose the older university, but we have to take into account that its reputation as the finishing school for the elect played some part. Until the 1940s, literature and other humanities subjects were a very minor element of the degree programmes at MIT, something of a recreational diversion for science students rather than topics they were expected to take seriously, unlike Harvard where the opposite was the case. The private school students who studied the arts there saw themselves as part of an intellectual nobility, while the scientists were treated as able foot soldiers who would serve industry and the economy. Irrespective of his choice of institution Mailer would have studied science and engineering, but at MIT there would have been little if any opportunity for him to discover in himself a very different vocation, even if it first began as a distraction. Mailer found literature during his undergraduate years, and, had it not been for the Brooklyn girls, he might never have come to notice it.

Mailer excelled in his entry examinations but did not go for a scholarship until his sophomore year, which again he attained easily. During his first year his family drew upon savings and even took out a bank loan to cover his fees. Barney's sister and brother-in-law helped out, and it was a tremendous achievement of theirs to have got him there at all, given the deprivations caused by Barney's continuing chicanery and gambling. The annual $200 tuition fee, plus board and other costs, took the total to around $1,000, almost $100 more than the average median income for the American working man in 1939.

His dorm was Grays Hall, an architectural anomaly that stood out in Harvard Yard mainly for its ugliness. It was opened in 1863 and resembles the tenement buildings of New York City of the same period, in striking contrast to the elegant Georgian manner of the pre-Revolutionary buildings that surrounded it, a style that endured as a means of maintaining something of the grand legacy of the institution. Nonetheless, the interior of Grays was considered luxurious by the standards of the 1930s, with each dorm having a bathroom and running water. Some residents of the older buildings were still expected to queue at outdoor pumps and lavatories.

For most of his time at university Mailer was something of an outsider, a state that was by parts inadvertent or clumsily rehearsed. Consider his clothes. One of his roommates, Richard Weinberg, was from Memphis and certainly not from a higher social class, but he seemed well enough informed about the required conventions of appearance: 'certain kinds of shoes and socks, gray flannel pants, a three-button, single-breasted – as opposed to double-breasted – muted tweed sports coat with a vent in the back and natural shoulders, what today would be described as "preppie". If you didn't wear that, you were immediately classed as an outsider, someone who didn't understand Harvard's ways.' (Manso, p. 41). Fan recalled that she went with Mailer to the clothes store, where 'he selected his own clothes. They were terrible — loud, outlandish. Trousers with orange stripes. It was his idea of how one should dress at Harvard' (Manso, p. 43), implying that he was fully aware that his idea was completely at odds with those shared by everyone else. Along with the loud trousers he favoured bright-green sports jackets with gold trim. After around a year, once the shock effect wore off, he did take to wearing more subdued outfits while retaining features that suited some of his studied eccentricities. He made sure that his flannel trousers had particularly deep cuffs into which he would flick cigarette ash when he lounged in the rooms of friends.

Despite these early exercises in showiness Mailer compartmentalised key elements of his background. He was happy to advertise, sometimes exaggerate, his Brooklyn origins, accent included. In an engineering class he posed a question to his teacher, a distinguished academic from Central Europe, who suggested that he might take some language lessons. Mailer replied, 'Thank you, I agree. Would you recommend German, or perhaps Polish?'

The sports culture of Harvard was mostly the reserve of those who had finessed their academic accomplishments at the major private schools, notably Andover and Exeter. Football was seen as the physical counterpart to intellectual accomplishment. Boat crews were more socially conceited, regarding themselves as the American equals of the Oxford and Cambridge Boat Race, a folk ritual in which the wealthy and privileged of Britain assemble to congratulate themselves on their superiority.

Mailer was keen to impress himself on these cabals but not because he sought social advancement. Quite the opposite. He wanted to stand out as the rough-house Brooklyn boy who was just as self-confident and courageous as the rich kids. In corridors he adopted the habit of lowering his shoulder to block the advance of footballers, but such gestures did not translate into field performances. After two matches for his dorm team, he was dropped. Before Harvard he had had no experience in a boat of any kind, with oars or sail, but he managed to find himself a place as reserve on a junior eight in a race on the Charles River. The captain complimented his new recruit on his physical proficiency during shore-land training but was decent enough not to mention his fears. Sure enough, however, Mailer's shortness of stature, especially his arms, caused the boat to almost turn over given that each of his strokes was out of synchronisation with those of the seven other men, who were close to six feet tall. This marked the end of his career as an oarsman. It was then that he took an interest in boxing, and particularly in building muscles that would enable him to have an impact with an uppercut. His determination to appear impulsive and daring was caused by his fear of being discovered as the boy who had not quite left home.

In September 1939 Mailer had travelled to Cambridge by train with his mother and his neighbour Marty Lubin, also a freshman, and Marty's father. It seemed like he was going to high school again, this time with dormitories, and throughout his years at Harvard Fan made regular visits, bringing him delicately prepared kosher food, collecting his laundry and returning with it washed and ironed by her and their maid. Mailer would meet her for coffee at various places in or around the university, though strategically far away from the scrutiny of fellow students he'd wished to impress as a man who had found his way into the Ivy League without asking for help from others, least of all his caring mother.

Rhoda Wolf remembers that she and Phyllis Bradman were regularly invited to dinner at the Mailers' when Norman was home, and that there was a curious but not disconcerting pantomime atmosphere. They seemed to be there as guarantee of Norman not being allowed to grow up, at least in Fan's view of things. They were both, his mother was aware, his girlfriends, though from the adolescent high school years when sex was not on the agenda, and it seemed almost comical that the two young women were always invited together, which appeared to allay suspicion of competition or envy on their part or libertinism on Norman's: those things were for adults. Mailer, however, flirted salaciously, and undercover, so that his mother wouldn't notice. Wolf: '... we were having lamb chops and were all cutting our meat, and Norman starts pretending that he's not cutting his chop but cutting his penis. He was grinning – he'd always do these things with this dirty-little-boy look: "I'm not serious, I'm just a dirty little boy" – but underneath he *was* serious.' (Manso, p. 45). He was, in Wolf's view, exposing them to the very wicked young man to which his mother remained oblivious.

By his sophomore year in Harvard Mailer was instructing his fellow undergraduates on what sex involved in the real world of Brooklyn, particularly the vocabulary of sensual encounters. 'In Brooklyn we called kissing a girl "getting to first", touching her tits was "second", and putting your hand up her crotch was "a three bagger".' And he demonstrated that these were more than hypotheses. 'I remember one night I went back to my room after a date in Cambridge. My roommate, Marty Lubin, was at his desk studying, and I went by, putting my fingers under his nose. "Get a whiff of this!"' (Manso, p. 57).

In truth Mailer had not had sex, despite a sordid episode in the summer of 1940. In August he and a friend, unnamed, hitch-hiked 130 miles to Scranton, Pennsylvania, hardly an appealing holiday destination. It was an ugly industrialised city that had attracted large numbers of immigrant manual workers in the early decades of the twentieth century, most of whom lived in grim tenement blocks. It was, however, infamous as the city which had the greatest number of brothels per head of population in America. Whole streets were dedicated exclusively to prostitution. What actually happened to him there is scattered across various accounts, none specific, some nuanced and others fictional. He revisited the experience in 'Love-Buds', a short story written in his senior year at Harvard but never published; the character who seems likeliest to be Mailer fails to have sex with the prostitute. His mother's recollection, years later, is movingly ambiguous.

> Norman's hitchhiking trip made me sick. But I always indulged him, because if he felt he was going to write about it, I figured it can't all be imagination, some of it has to be real. So, while I worried, I didn't make a fuss. He was sleeping out in the open on the grass, and he didn't even have a warm sweater with him, just the clothes on his back. I remember he wrote about brushing his finger in the ketchup, and in the fact that he hated ketchup at the time. (Manso, p. 57)

Fan was worried primarily about his sleeping in the open air as a danger to his health, and there is something touchingly hilarious in her literal interpretation of his failure to get beyond 'brushing his finger in the ketchup'.

Marjorie 'Osie' Radin, Mailer's age and the daughter of neighbours of his parents, later commented that

> I remember when he came back his mother wouldn't let him in until he took his clothes off. He had to come in through the basement – she wanted to make sure he was deloused. For him, though, it was an experience, something to write about. (Manso, p. 57)

For Fan the delousing was necessary because she feared he had brought home fleas or other parasites from his time napping in fields or grass verges. One can imagine a smile forming on his face as he pondered a private double entendre similar to the one from dinner with Rhoda Wolf: mother, your little boy is lousy in ways you'd best not imagine.

Up to the end of the 1920s Harvard's admissions policy was meritocratic without overt discrimination. Small numbers of black people had graduated over the previous century, but as the university seemed willing to open its doors to persons of diverse racial background a powerful cohort of white families indicated a reluctance to pay fees for their boys to share classrooms and, God forbid, dormitories with persons of colour. Through the 1920s the president, A. L. Lowell did not bar African Americans from admission to the university, but he did not allow them to reside in freshman halls. Jews were another matter. In 1929 25 per cent of freshmen were Jewish, a far greater proportion than that of the Jewish population of the United States as a whole in this period (roughly 3%), and an indication that the institution was content to blind their biases: to put it bluntly, Jews were less conspicuously different than blacks. But within a year the university authorities ruled upon a tariff of a maximum of 15 per cent of Jews in the entire student population, without making their new policy public. This was later reduced to a *numerus clausus* of 10 per cent, despite objections from a small number of reformers in the governing body.

Mailer's roommates and neighbours in Grays were Richard Weinberg, Marty Lubin and Max Kaufer, and the fact that they came from different regions of the United States while belonging to the same tribe did not concern them. Only later, much later, was it evident to each that they were members of a three-man ghetto.

Irrespective of whether Jews had gone to private or public schools (and it should be noted that at the time the quota of Jews at Andover was 5 per cent of the student population), the fact that they were Jews was recorded on their cards. No reference was made to, say, Episcopalians as opposed to Catholics; in fact, it was taken for granted that students were Christian of whatever denomination, provided they were not designated as Jews. The parallels between this system and the 1930s Nazi policy of separatism, which involved painting '*Juden*' on the walls of houses or businesses of Jews and obliging them to wear the Star of David on their clothes, is notable but misleading. The Nazis aimed for the conspicuous identification of Judaism, largely as a means of inciting prejudice, while the Harvard establishment opted for a polite, well-mannered form of discrimination.

Unlike black people or Latinos, American Jews of European origin were difficult to identify in terms of skin colour of physiognomy, so at Harvard private records were required to ensure that certain 'types' of students lived in a manner that suitably reflected their background and status. For example, some of the oldest dormitories or halls – notably Holworthy, Hollis, Stoughton and Massachusetts – were occupied almost exclusively by men from schools such as Andover and Exeter, and before the 1930s there was no record of Jews being housed in them. It was always the case that Jewish freshmen shared the same dormitory rooms, somewhere else. (see Jerome Karabel's *The Chosen: The Hidden History of Admission and Exclusion at Harvard, Yale and Princeton*, Houghton Mifflin, 2005)

Neither Mailer nor his fellow roommates experienced the kind of verbal antisemitism they'd known before Cambridge, but there was a different form at work in the university; subtle, implicit but far more endemic.

Harry Levin, Jewish, recalled that 'The year I received tenure I was publicly congratulated at the annual meeting of the Modern Language Association as an example of Harvard's broad-mindedness.' (Manso, p. 39). Levin, with darkly comic understatement, comments that the MLA felt it improper to specify the exact nature of this new mood of broad-mindedness, but he adds that 'Jewish students were assigned Jewish roommates. Day to day, one was made to be aware that one was a Jew.' (Manso, p. 39).

Harvard's exclusive social clubs were founded mostly in the nineteenth century and were referred to as Final Clubs, mysteriously so given that members did not have to be in the graduation year to join. They did need to meet various other criteria, principally family wealth, a private school background or sporting prowess. Sometimes those of more modest circumstances and attainments could be nominated by well-established members who thought them suitable material for social advancement; it was a commonplace that, post-graduation, the societies guaranteed a freemasonry of favours in the profitable professions. Mailer and his friends mocked them regularly, particularly regarding the rituals that were thought to take place in their prestigious locations. The infamous and ancient Porcellian Club, for example, always included a boar's head in its nomenclature, which most treated as an admission to rumours regarding ceremonial activities that involved pigs. Much later Mailer reflected that the only students he met who had no direct knowledge of what went on at club meetings were, like him, Jews. He had never met or heard of Jews who had been admitted to the societies because at the time none ever were.

At the close of his freshman year Mailer decided to divide his degree between his major, aeronautical engineering, and English literature, a radical and for some who knew him inexplicable shift. Before Harvard he had cared little about books, but when he arrived, he noticed a striking anomaly in the cultural and social frieze of the institution. His new contemporary Kingsley Ervin described the atmosphere of the place as 'Very eighteenth-century, a mixture of Boston Brahmin and the literary faculty's elegance' (Manso, p. 39). 'Boston Brahmin' referred to the aristocracy of New England, who regarded themselves as the British country nobility on the other side of the Atlantic and treated a literature degree at Harvard as their cultural and intellectual rite of passage.

Literature degrees were a badge of cultural superiority, but some Harvard dons designed courses that seemed radical and insubordinate, advertising the works of John Steinbeck, James T. Farrell, John Dos Passos, Ernest Hemingway and even the morally louche F. Scott

Fitzgerald. Their novels addressed the less agreeable features of present-day America, where corruption was rife, deprivation congenital and violence almost appealing.

For the vast majority of upper-class students, the fictional worlds of Steinbeck, Dos Passos and Hemingway were as alien as science fiction, but for Mailer they offered a bridge between academic study and writing as something other than a hobby. During the year before Harvard, he had developed a mild preoccupation with Hemingway, and in the summer between his freshman and sophomore years he read all of Dos Passos's *U.S.A.* trilogy, Farrell's *Studs Lonigan* novels and Steinbeck's *The Grapes of Wrath*. He had witnessed some of the cruellest aspects of the American hangover from the depression, though Fan had done her best to protect him from its worst consequences. Now, with these writers, he could reinvent himself twofold: as a young man who might have seen the things that Farrell and Dos Passos wrote about – a lie, but a convincing one given his hard-man demeanour and Brooklyn accent – and as a writer who had found a genre, hard realism, that suited his alleged background and experiences.

He heard before the beginning of sophomore year that in some classes students were also allowed to compose their own pieces of prose or verse and recite these to their tutors and fellow students for appraisal. This too was an extraordinarily far-sighted development. 'Creative Writing', as we understand it, did not become a routine feature of university study in British and American universities until the late 1960s.

Robert Gorham Davis was Mailer's first English tutor, and he was made up of complications. He advocated the teaching of contemporary realist fiction, particularly the work of Farrell and Dos Passos which reflected their authors' involvement in left-wing politics; both writers were socialists. Davis himself was at the time a member of the Communist Party, and later, in fear of losing tenure, he testified against colleagues with similar affiliations to the House Un-American Activities Committee. He was also a snob who regarded Mailer as an uninvited guest to the party he was hosting for Boston Brahmins. On the one hand, Mailer wouldn't be shocked by the low-life content of the work selected for his curriculum – he delighted in it – and on the other, he was not from the same social and intellectual clique as Davis and his pupils. Davis took particular satisfaction in unsettling members of his own class. His father was a millionaire Boston banker, and his family traced its roots back to the *Mayflower*. He liked the creations of Farrell et al. but saw their actual embodiments in the protected environment of Cambridge, such as Mailer, as a little de trop.

Davis's comments on the new convert to English are revealing.

> My impression was that Norman wasn't awfully well educated. He was taking engineering courses ... His knowledge of the major figures from the past was pretty slight and superficial ... I'm pretty sure Latin was required for a Harvard BA, though not for a BS, that's a significant difference. (Manso, p. 48)

Davis would, to his credit, continue to support Mailer in his literary enterprises. He helped him become a contributor to the Harvard literary magazine, *The Advocate*, and more importantly played a part in his first non-Harvard publication in the prestigious New York-based *Story* magazine. Yet there remains a sense that he felt his discovery was an American version of Jude the Obscure, undoubtedly talented but déclassé.

The first story Mailer did for Davis's class was called 'He Was Her Man' and remains unpublished, but we know from Mailer that it was heavily inspired by Hemingway. Its closest relative in the Hemingway oeuvre is probably 'The Killers', a very short story about two hitmen who arrive in an Illinois town to kill Ole Anderson, a boxer. Anderson is informed of their presence, but we leave the story without any knowledge of what happens next. Mailer picks up where Hemingway left off by having a man enter a rooming house in the Catskills where the bellhops 'service' the wives of men working in the city. The man climbs the stairs, and the bellhop on the ground floor hears shots fired, goes to the bedroom and finds that the man has shot his wife dead and blown his own face off. The bellhop's friend and colleague who was in bed with the now-dead wife has fled. According to Mailer, Davis praised it but read the ending again, giving gruesome overdramatic emphasis to the bellhop narrator's description of the scene. In his panicked state the narrator becomes obsessed with where the blood spots and bits of brain have landed. Are they in the carpet or still in the humid air he is breathing? 'I could make out where her eyes and mouth had been, but I wondered what had happened to her nose. I couldn't guess whether it was smashed into the carpet, or if it was still floating around. I hoped it was on the ground, because stepping on it was certainly better than breathing it in.' It reads to me like a lost gem, yet Davis's rendition in the classroom ensured that Mailer would never let it go into print even when he had become an acclaimed writer: 'as he [Davis] reread it the class cracked up. Paroxysms of laughter. Gorham Davis can be dour, but even he started giggling. I didn't know what to do. My first impulse was to leave, but I couldn't, since then everyone would know I was the author – stories were always read anonymously. My next impulse was to kill Davis.' (Manso, p. 48).

'He Was Her Man' is less than fifteen hundred words in length, a noir prose-ideogram which has no equal in conventional writing. His next story was five times as long and was a little more à la mode, in the sense that it fell into line with the modernist-realist techniques of Dos Passos, Hemingway and Farrell.

It clearly carried echoes of Mailer's excursion to Scranton, except that the character is not hitch-hiking to lose his virginity in a brothel. Rather, the story marries contemporary realism with a dose of Nietzsche and drizzles of nihilism and crime fiction. In 'The Greatest Thing in the World', Al Groot hitches a ride with three strangers, tells them lies about his past and about how much money he has, wins cash from them in a pool game and refuses to let them try to win it back. They beat him up, drive him away in their car and there is a hint that he is about to be killed. But he forces the door and escapes by jumping from the vehicle, and the story ends.

It would be his first published piece of work. The *Advocate* magazine, founded in 1866, was seen as a ceremony of initiation for the literary elect. It was read by commissioning editors within the most prestigious American publishing houses, who treated it as a showcase for new talent. Wallace Stevens, E. E. Cummings and T. S. Eliot were Harvard undergraduates who made their debuts in it, and it regarded itself as sufficiently lofty to offer non-Harvard figures space for their work, so long as they were deemed as good as in-house contributors: such outsiders included William Carlos Williams, Ezra Pound and Archibald MacLeish.

Initially the editorial board sent Mailer a note praising the piece but regretting that it probably would not be published, which he took as the equivalent of being shown to the tradesman's entrance of a grand Boston residence rather than being allowed in through the front door. Another person he gave it to found fault with the grammar, and Mailer advised her to 'go take a hot running fuck'. (Lennon, p38) He had, like Joyce and Hemingway, deliberately dispensed with the hidebound dress codes of nineteenth-century writing, such as coherent syntax. He judged *The Advocate*'s editors as 'a bunch of snobs, and Brooklyn may go against me', noting also that over the previous decade it had published nothing by Jewish students. (Lennon, p37)

But within a month of his having received the nice-work-but-no-thanks response, new figures on the *Advocate* board of editors – notably John Crockett, Pete Barton and Bowden Broadwater – made it clear to their more conservative associates that the magazine might soon come close to self-caricature. If it did not make room for the kind of hard realism pioneered by figures such as Dos Passos, Farrell and Hemingway, it would continue to be seen as shackled to the fraternity of old-Harvard. Their acceptance of Mailer's story was their battle cry, and they also invited him to become a member of the editorial board. He commented:

> Getting on *The Advocate* was the watershed, and so much happened to me that it's almost like 'before *The Advocate*' and 'after *The Advocate*'. In a sense, my Harvard life began then. (Manso, p. 56)

He goes on to disclose that it was effectively the beginning of Norman Mailer, author. The appearance of 'The Greatest Thing in the World' in the magazine meant it was noticed by the selection committee of *Story* magazine's nationwide contest for the best piece of short fiction by a college student; it won the prize, and was published in *Story*. He won a hundred dollars, two thirds of his sophomore year scholarship. At *The Advocate*'s seventy-fifth anniversary dinner a well-dressed middle-aged man sought him out and introduced himself as Roy Larsen, associate editor of *Time* magazine, informed him that 'I liked your story a lot', and stated he would be willing to consider him as a contributor. Mailer's fellow students were entranced. Marvin Barrett, member of *The Advocate*'s editorial board, rushed up to him and announced that 'Roy Larson likes your story!', as if to assure Mailer that what he had heard was not a daydream. Later in the year Larsen would ask Ted Amussen of Rinehart & Company, one of America's largest trade publishers, to contact Mailer, and they met.

Mailer did not give up on the reckless hitch-hiking excursions that had inspired 'The Greatest Thing'. In the summer following his sophomore year he set off south to Virginia, got to Leesburg and then took a lift to Elizabeth City, North Carolina. 'I was', he recalled, 'picked up by a redneck who'd been up for two nights. He thought he'd give me a ride so that I could help to keep him awake by talking, but I was appalled at the things he was telling me, I was such a prude.' (Manso, p. 56). He adds, 'All the same, I finished the novel when I came back.' This was *No Percentage*, never published but his first attempt at a full-length piece of fiction, almost 90,000 words in draft form. John Farrar of Rinehart looked at it and saw in it a 'young writer's enthusiasm', but rather too much enthusiasm, 'and not worth publishing'. (ibid.)

The events surrounding the novel and the draft itself encompass Mailer's conflicted state. He enjoyed being seen as a man who didn't quite belong, for the simple reason that at Cambridge it allowed him to grab attention as a conspicuous outsider; lower-class, Jewish, recklessly unconventional. At the same time, he enjoyed the opportunities that were made uniquely available via the clubbish elitism of his university. Shortly after he became part of *The Advocate*, he was elected to the Signet Society, a members' association that stressed its difference from the Final Clubs. Affiliates of the latter qualified through their patrician background and inherited wealth, while the Signet was a meritocracy, admitting men and women by virtue of their promise as literary artists. Previous members included T. S. Eliot, Wallace Stevens and Robert Frost, and while Mailer felt exuberant at joining this platform, he was also troubled at trading in his rough-house image for cultural advancement. *No Percentage* fails as a novel because the young man, the 'rich kid', can't decide whether his wish to join the low-life, uninhibited world of ordinary Americans is worth the loss of what he has grown up with. We leave the draft unclear about what he'll decide to do, and so does he. It is clearly enough an inverse reflection of Mailer's dilemma, and the protagonist's failure to arrive at a decision on his persona was acted out by its creator in a sometimes farcical manner.

Kingsley Ervin remarked that 'Any undergraduate who could visibly make it with a woman had quite a bit of cachet', but that an association with *The Advocate* reduced the likelihood of a man losing his virginity to 'no more than 5 percent' (Manso, p. 57). For women students in other Boston colleges, it carried a whiff of prim erudition and artiness. So, in 1941, just after his eighteenth birthday, Mailer visited a prostitute in the city. He wrote to fellow undergraduate George Washington Goethals a 'hilarious letter' describing her as 'an old bag, but he figured he might as well get it over with ... and he described how he had to wash off with Lysol afterwards'. (Manso, p57) Goethals added that 'I'd been laid before coming to college, but I never talked about my sex life. Norman, on the other hand, was always very candid about wanting to have a lot of women.' (ibid.)

Seymour Breslow had rooms close to Mailer during their sophomore year in Dunster House, a fine neoclassical building overlooking the Charles River which appeared to date from the beginning of the eighteenth century. In truth it had been completed in 1930, and Mailer seemed intent on presenting himself as a thoroughly unsuitable resident of these grand, elegant quarters. Breslow: 'He started going out of his way to use four-letter words around this time, and there was greater tendency on his part to emulate what was supposed to be virile and masculine ...' (Manso, p57) Mailer made a point of smoking and drinking conspicuously, despite the fact that he, like his scholarship fellows, could barely afford strong liquor and that the minimum age for the purchase of bottles of any kind of alcohol was twenty-one. Nonetheless, he prominently displayed a bottle of gin on the mantelpiece of his room, explaining to visitors that it was Hemingway's favourite drink.

It is amusing to compare these performances with the account by Hope, wife of his tutor Davis, following his visit to their apartment for cocktails and supper.

> He made a remarkable impression. When his eyes looked at you, you
> just melted ... He had beautiful manners in a nice, natural, kindly way.
> He seemed to be comfortable, not brash or acting overconfident. He
> was grateful to be invited, and he was just right – easy but respectful
> and tactful. (Manso, p. 55)

Hope's husband backs up her impression of their undemonstrative new
young friend: 'he was quiet and modest and very impressive within that
modesty. There was a self-contained quality about him.'

Marvin Barrett, a fellow member of the *Advocate* board, tells of how
Mailer made a point of being, as Davis politely put it, 'self-contained'.
Social events for *The Advocate* and the Signet involved an unspoken
convention of having to appear in formal dress – black tie and dinner
jacket. Mailer consistently arrived in casual, sometimes louche clothes,
as if silently provoking others to reprimand him for his appearance. No
one ever did.

Goethals recalls that Mailer seemed intent on causing disquiet among
the members of the distinguished societies into which he had recently
been welcomed. Despite the fact that he seemed to treat Hemingway
as his hero, Mailer and Goethals wrote a short play which was an
outrageous parody of *For Whom the Bell Tolls*, its intention evidently to
shock and appal those from *The Advocate* who made up the audience.
Mailer played a version of Hemingway and Goethals appeared as Martha
Gellhorn, or Martha Getshorned, his then wife.

> Before the performance I was in the john taking a piss, with my dress
> up. John Crockett came in and literally fell over on the floor in a dead
> faint. And in the play when Martha 'gets horned' I got horned by
> Norman, who was using a large baloney sausage. (Manso, p. 52)

Goethals later added that 'Norman had a habit of segregating his
friends. He made it clear that I, as a *goy*, could never understand
a Jew.' (ibid.) This was not, Goethals explained, an accusation of
quasi-antisemitism. Mailer also 'pulled the same number on Jewish
classmates', who, he insisted, could never really understand his
state of mind because he was '*poor* Jewish', from Brooklyn. WASPs,

middle-class Jews, and even the small number of African Americans then at Harvard – five in total – were a little more privileged than him because, despite their race, their families had done well enough to get them into the Ivy League. Mailer presented himself as belonging to the genuine proletariat.

Robert C. Harrison, another contemporary, observed that 'Norman was incredibly diligent and determined', but 'he was also a bore. Everybody found him boring because he spent most of his time claiming that he was just a poor Jewish boy from Brooklyn.' (Manso, p. 62).

It is difficult to decide on whether, in his eighteenth year, Mailer was an eclectic litterateur desperately seeking a sense of place or an adolescent self-publicist.

In late 1941, roughly eight weeks after Mailer won the national short story contest, two events took place that would shape the rest of his life. The first occurred in late November went he went to a Boston Symphony Orchestra concert with Larry Weiss, a fellow Harvard student, who was meeting a girl there. His date had asked him to bring a friend; she too would be going to the concert with a young woman she knew from college. The other member of the foursome was Beatrice 'Bea' Silverman. Mailer was immediately attracted to her; she had shiny, long brown hair, full lips, glowing grey eyes, a pretty oval face, and was the real-life equivalent of the curvaceous body-lines of the film stars which decorated the wall of Mailer's room. They got on immediately, Mailer admitting to her accusation that, as she later put it, 'he didn't know his ass from his elbow about music', despite pretending to some knowledge of what the orchestra was performing. Bea was studying music at Boston University and was a talented pianist. He was astonished when she agreed to go back with him to his rooms for 'a coffee' – his invitation was, in part, bravado; women guests were strictly monitored – and shortly afterwards he was caught between feeling that his dreams had come true and a slight notion of inferiority. She stayed the night, and at her prompting, they had sex. Despite being the same age she was far more experienced; he'd paid to lose his virginity, while she had enjoyed sex with boys she'd selected for dates.

Very soon Mailer realised that his new girlfriend was an improvement on his rather off-key performances as himself. She was the only woman he had met who could outperform him with expletives. Impressively articulate, Bea was able to pack erudition into well-formed sentences and pepper them with profanities. She was uninhibited about attaching 'fuck', 'scum', 'assholes' and 'cunts' to the fascist politicians and regimes of Europe. But she was much more than a loud-mouthed political polemicist. One afternoon at a café in Boston, two Harvard men, entertaining girls, greeted Mailer but ignored her, as if, like their two dates, she was more an appendage than a person. Bea turned to the table of four, smiled, and enquired 'how often do you fuck?' They were shocked, but one man, amused, replied, 'Tuesdays and Thursdays only.'

Bea was far more daring and outspoken than any of his male friends, and she was beautiful. Just as significantly she was Jewish, the daughter of a Boston butcher; the family lived in a run-down wood-frame house on the edge of town. Bea was an authentic version of what Mailer claimed to be. Her parents were genuinely proletarian Jews, she had read Marx at high school and was an avid supporter of various forms of communism and socialism, partly because she saw capitalism as iniquitous per se, but most of all because she regarded the one socialist country on the globe, the Soviet Union, as posing a threat to Nazism in Continental Europe. Germany and Russia had been at war since June. By the time she met Mailer, the Germans had advanced to within two miles of Leningrad and were fifteen outside Moscow, but the Red Army was holding out against the odds. Bea was aware that Operation Barbarossa had relieved the pressure on Britain but she was far more committed to the Soviets ideologically, believing Marxism in action was the only form of polity that could erase the ingrained prejudices endemic to capitalism: class consciousness, gender inequality, racism and, most significantly for her, antisemitism. This vision of the Soviet Union would later be exposed as a fiction, particularly with regard to Judaism, but for left-wingers in the West during the 1940s and 50s the myth endured. For Mailer, antisemitism was part of his performance as an interloper, a man who didn't belong in Harvard, and he treated it as a counterpart to his allegedly proletarian background.

Adeline Lubell Naiman had been a roommate of Phyllis Silverman, Bea's sister, at Radcliffe. She later worked with Mailer when she was an editor at Little, Brown but knew him only slightly when he was dating Bea: 'Norman was always presenting himself as a Jew … mythmaking … It was his standard riposte, playing the slum child – even though I wouldn't have taken him seriously, because he wasn't a slum child.' (Manso, p63)

Bea politicised Mailer in part by embarrassing him. Every day they spent together he encountered the harsh transparent versions of various ideas that he had been cultivating. She tutored him, showing him that racism, antisemitism and class distinction were by-products of a single system, capitalism, because the latter was rooted in hegemony, the domination of one group by another. Through her his friends began to treat him as someone more than just bitter and rudderless; now he came across as an informed radical. But she certainly did not calm him down. Socially she was just as explosive, and soon they were seen as a double act, though opinions differed on who was the junior and who the senior partner. By Christmas 1941 they were talking about marriage, but at this stage many other things had changed too.

John Crockett, Mailer's associate on *The Advocate*, remembers him as dismissing the possibility of America involving itself in the war in Europe, despite the fact that many Harvard men were campaigning for their country to support Britain if only in terms of supplying arms, and some were giving up their degrees to go north to enlist with the Canadian forces.

The second life-changing event occurred on 7 December, several weeks after Mailer had begun his relationship with Bea, when Japan attacked Pearl Harbor. Roosevelt declared war on Japan the following day and four days later against the Axis powers in Europe, and only then because Hitler pre-empted the president with a declaration against the United States. It is almost certain that the delay was a formality, that it was inevitable that America would join Britain in the conflict across the Atlantic. Nonetheless, while Roosevelt himself favoured immediate involvement, he was aware that he faced opposition in the House of Representatives and Senate, where feelings about sacrificing young men in a conflict that was none of their business had endured since the early years of the First World War. Hitler rescued the president from this dilemma.

Bea felt that a widespread indifference among Americans towards the evils of Nazism reflected similar antisemitic prejudices at home, and once more she felt it necessary to instruct Mailer on this. But he had other things on his mind. He began a journal recording an account of what was happening, exclusively, in the Pacific. His raw material was made up of news reports on events following Pearl Harbor, interspersed with imaginative colourings. He was turning what was publicly known of the war with Japan into a piece of fiction, and its style was a replica of the Hemingwayesque stories he had already completed and published: brutally realistic and emotionally detached. Even though he had no direct experience of what was happening, he treated it as a literary opportunity. Up to December 1941 he had ransacked the more wretched aspects of America and being American for his writing, but this was territory well-trodden by Steinbeck and others.

Mailer was looking for something he could treat as his artistic signature, a stylistic or thematic exemplar that would be his alone, and he settled on what can but be described as ghoulish naturalism.

In his second summer at Harvard Mailer took on a job at the Boston State Hospital, a mental institution in Mattapan, several miles from the university; he did everything from cleaning wards and providing bed-washes to assisting permanent members of staff in restraining patients. He remembers in particular the treatment of a black man who was no more violent or unruly than any other resident but whose skin colour destined him for special brutality. He was kicked to the ground, and even after he lost consciousness the beatings continued. In his later accounts of this Mailer seems less appalled than grotesquely invigorated. He knew of racism and its violent manifestations, and the beating did not shock him – but witnessing it live was something special. Within a day he had placed the event at the centre of a play called *The Naked and the Dead*, a work he quickly abandoned, but soon afterwards the assault re-emerged in his novella-in-progress, *A Transit to Narcissus*. The latter would appear in print in 1978 but only as a curiosity, something that might be of interest to fans of Mailer or scholars who were delving into his past. As a work in its own right it is of slight importance, but it is worth attention as a morbid point of inspiration that Mailer seemed unwilling or unable to dispose of. The more he wrote about the attack on the man the less acceptable it became as literature, but he seemed addicted to this act of violence as inimitable and profound.

Something similar, similarly morbid that is, occurred in November 1942, when the Cocoanut Grove supper club in Boston caught fire. There were thought to be almost 700 people in the building, many of whom were recently enrolled servicemen, in uniform, entertaining their dates. Harvard students were advised to telephone their parents and reassure them that they were safe. The disaster had sidelined news of the war on the wireless, with 492 fatalities recorded the day afterwards. Some were burned to death, others suffocated by smoke, and many crushed in the chaos as everyone fled towards a small number of exit doors. Jack Maher, another Harvard student, remembers that,

> Norman called me that morning. He wanted to go see the bodies they'd laid out in a public place for identification, and he tried to convince me to go along with him, arguing that it was the kind of event that doesn't happen very often and we should take advantage of it ... But I said no thanks ... he later told me [that] what fascinated him was how shrunken the bodies of adults are after they've been thoroughly charred. He described spending several hours going from one body to the next ... I heard all about it – dismembered bodies, trampled bodies, charred bodies. (Manso, p. 71)

Maher tries as best he can to offer a dispassionate recollection of this, but it is impossible to ignore the sense of shock and disgust that seeps through his description of his erstwhile friend's addiction to seeing and then describing what most human beings would choose to avoid. Many 19-year-olds, usually males, harbour voyeuristic inclinations, an unfortunate feature of immaturity, but for Mailer this was tied to his literary ambitions.

Within two months of witnessing the bodies laid out after the Cocoanut Grove fire, he was writing a never-published novella provisionally called 'A Calculus at Heaven'. It was set in the war in the Pacific, with descriptions of military operations borrowed from press reports. Gruesome particulars came from his direct witnessing of the Boston fire.

He remembered the burnt body of a man that he had looked at for quite a time. It had seemed a terrible degradation, as if the man in burning to death had reverted to a prehistoric type. He had been blackened all over, his flesh in shriveling had given the appearance of a black fur, and his features, almost burnt off, had been snubbed and shrunken, so that the man's face in death had only registered a black circle of mouth with the teeth grimacing whitely and out of place in the blackness of the ape ... ('A Calculus at Heaven', February 1943)

And so on for several further, excruciatingly detailed sentences on the effects of fire on human flesh. Mailer became addicted to macabre incidents not simply as a voyeur but as part of his aesthetic credo. He wanted to write about things that would upset people.

Much later, in *Advertisements for Myself*, he confessed that 'I was worrying darkly whether it would be more likely that a great war novel would be written about Europe or the Pacific'. (*AFM* p. 28) A good deal is implied in this observation. In the Orient, American soldiers, virtually all of them Caucasian, would be pitting themselves against servicemen of a different race and skin colour, while in Europe they would be returning to their ancestral homelands, albeit mostly poisoned by authoritarian ideologies. Mailer made the remark decades after publishing his debut novel, leaving time to speculate on what he'd have produced if the setting for the book had been Europe rather than the Pacific. War is not really the subject of *The Naked and the Dead*, any more than in the sense that the enemy, the Japanese, represent a danger to the characters. Its real topic is America, a nation whose tribalist, class-based and psychosexual tensions are crystallised in US servicemen sent somewhere else, somewhere particularly alien.

Mailer graduated in May 1943. His parents and the Kesslers were present but not Bea; admission was limited to family only. He got a B in engineering and As in other courses, literary studies included. He was graded as cum laude, which at Harvard meant that the recipient was within the top 20 to 30 per cent of their class, which sounds impressive until we learn that the grade was in itself subdivided into magna cum laude students (top 10 to 15 per cent) and summa cum laude (top 5 to 1 per cent). Soon, degree classifications would fade into insignificance.

3

PACIFIC GRIM

Mailer had sent a message to Bea that they would celebrate his graduation together as a couple, and two weeks after his family had returned to Brooklyn from Cambridge they met in Boston and took the ferry to Provincetown. The place had begun as a New England fishing village and became by the end of the nineteenth century a summer location for wealthy bohemians and others from Boston looking to rent holiday properties on the beautiful coast of Cape Cod as an escape from the metropolis. Artists and writers enjoyed its atmosphere, as did couples who knew that neither hoteliers nor anyone else would pay attention to their marital status. Mailer and Bea stayed in an inn on the main thoroughfare, Standish Street, which looked like part of a set for a movie about the Revolution. The weather was excellent, and they spent days on the beach, sometimes swimming or enjoying picnics with bread, cheese and wine.

But the academic year was getting shorter, as the services demanded that graduates should be available for the war as soon as possible. Bea had to be back in Boston University by July, and Mailer returned to the family home in Brooklyn.

He was still working on *A Transit to Narcissus*. Fan was perplexed by his reluctance to involve himself in anything that involved a salary, but as ever she indulged her son's inclinations. He insisted, further to her distress, that whatever he undertook would be temporary; that army conscription was inevitable and imminent.

In late December 1943 Mailer and Bea went for a ski trip to North Conway, New Hampshire, a resort with medium slopes favoured by skiers of only moderate ability. There is no evidence that either of them took to the slopes at all, but they certainly planned other events. Three weeks later, on 7 January 1944, they met again in Yonkers to marry in a civil ceremony. No family or anyone else they knew what they were doing; witnesses were officials from the Yonkers City Hall. The wedding ring was made from 'Mexican silver' – a commonplace term for tin – and cost a quarter. They'd agreed on this as part of their revolt against convention.

Much happened in the subsequent weeks. Fan, when informed by her son, had become hysterical and demanded that the marriage be annulled. She had, according to Bea, always seen her son's girlfriend as a gold-digger, which seemed strange given that Bea's family, though working class, were far better off than the Mailers. Bea's mother was equally appalled, mainly because she thought that an earlier suitor, reading medicine, would guarantee her a place in the Boston bourgeoisie. Mailer, as they saw him, was a feckless misfit whose literary ambitions would never bring the couple financial security. Eventually the Mailers and Silvermans entered negotiations and arranged a traditional Jewish ceremony at the Silvermans' home on 18 March, with a rabbi reading out the *Sheva Brachot* (Seven Blessings).

Mailer wrote later to a Harvard friend that getting married to Bea was one of the few things he would 'never regret'. Compared with the many women with whom he later had relationships she came closest to being his soulmate. They agreed to take part in the formal Jewish marriage because they loved and were infuriated by their families by equal degrees. Mailer treated antisemitism as a badge of honour, one of the proofs that the Land of the Free was in truth the enclave of the prejudiced; being forced to remarry Bea in 1944 further complicated his relationship with Judaism. He and Bea were agnostics, but, like other Jewish non-believers, they felt they could abandon God but not their legacy, their tribe.

Norman introduced his Harvard friend Jack Maher to his family in mid-March 1944. Jack and Mailer's sister, Barbara, began to date and wanted to marry. Maher was an agreeable, kind man, who even asked if it would be possible for him to convert to Judaism if, as Barbara warned him, their long-term relationship would present problems with her family. He was a third-generation Irish Catholic from the Midwest. Fan flew into a state of horror and, on being informed of Jack's wish to convert, fell to the floor in their Brooklyn home, faking a heart attack. Barbara knew her mother was not genuinely ill but recognised the strength of feeling that had prompted her performance and ended her relationship with Jack. Mailer was appalled, and though he never spoke with Fan about it, he never quite forgave her. He would never reject his legacy as a Jew, but he was equally aware of how Judaism could in itself exhibit a special brand of insularity and xenophobia, probably caused by a history of persecution.

Mailer received his draft papers three days later but delayed conscription by informing the authorities that he was involved in vital propaganda work, specifically writing a novel that would improve the morale of American readers and that 'had some relevance to the war effort'. There is no record of whether those responsible for the call-up bothered to consider his claim before rejecting it, but on 25 March he was informed that he was now legally obliged to report for duty two days later.

Camp Upton in Suffolk County, Long Island, was his first destination. It was an induction centre for recruits from the metropolitan East Coast and mostly involved the paperwork of registration and the issuing of basic uniforms. After a week Mailer was transferred to Fort Bragg, North Carolina, for five months of basic training. He was enrolled as a private soldier and never spoke of why he denied himself opportunities self-evidently available. A Harvard graduate, especially one who had majored in engineering, would certainly have been offered a commission leading first to the rank of second lieutenant. His salary would have been three times that of a private, his social standing greatly elevated and his uniform seemingly the product of a fashion designer. A degree in a practical science made him a perfect candidate for the Corps of Engineers or Signals, honourable units but far less dangerous than front-line infantry detachments. On top of his Harvard qualification he scored 166 in the IQ test that followed recruitment: 145–160 was generally regarded as the highest-possible level of attainment, and Mailer's brilliance as a mathematician astounded his enrolment officers even more. The purpose of these tests was to identify recruits with special accomplishments, and it is difficult to imagine that a commission in the Intelligence Corps wouldn't have been offered to him.

In his first interview after the publication of *The Naked and the Dead* (Louise Levites, *New York Star*, 22 August 1948), Mailer was asked about his relationship with the officers. 'Oh, you always get to know them. Working for them ... You generally operate on hate, and hate is the best aid to analysis.' He added that 'most of the guys who wrote war novels were working from the top down', by which, he explained, they were officers or newspaper correspondents. 'I literally functioned as a GI. I hated officers. I had the holy sense of importance that a GI has.'

While the novel involves all ranks, he reserves a special degree of contempt for officers, as if military service has provided those who already felt entitled with the opportunity to exercise their worst characteristics.

His novel was widely celebrated as the best representation of what war meant for ordinary soldiers, but we can never be certain if his comments to Levites were a publicity tactic, presenting his GI status as part of his plan for a brutalist piece of fiction, or if he failed to gain a commission for other reasons.

In the end Mailer did not specialise in anything other than basic soldiering: rifle training, marching, the essentials of al fresco survival and so on. He was still unaware of whether he would be sent to Europe or the Pacific, but when news broke of D Day on 6 June, he wrote to Bea that 'my first reaction was disappointment – I wanted to be on the beach', which is slightly ambiguous. If he was destined for the Pacific, he was almost certain to experience several beach landings, given that American forces were already involved in the 'island-hopping' invasions that month by month took them closer to mainland Japan.

The recruits were not officially told the details of their embarkation time or destination, but it became clear enough that they were heading west after they took the train north to New York City and at Penn Station boarded another for a five-day journey to California, specifically San Francisco, and then to Fort Ord, a hundred miles south of the city.

During the long train journey, he wrote an extraordinary letter to Bea, opening with expressions of love and regretting that they would not be able to 'discover Frisco together'. He composed it when he was staying in the King George Hotel a day after the train had arrived, and the bulk of the piece is a description of his journey from the east to the west coast. Before this, all of his writing had been urban, brutalist, but now there are echoes of Thoreau's quasi-mystical relationship with the natural world.

> ... knowing that we were to remain in the dirty coach for three nights and two days, we accepted it as a form of life, vacuous and unending ... But there were recompenses – the scenery. You hear of the vastness of America and yet it is so easily contained in one's mind ...

By 'easily' he does not mean without effort, because in the rest of this long letter he shows how to turn something almost indescribable into very elegant prose. He begins with the 'flat farm lands which continue absolutely without variation for almost a thousand miles. I cannot describe to you darling how queer, how relaxed the sensation is', but he tries, telling of the peculiar experience of watching the same unchanging landscape perhaps for an hour, returning to his book an hour later finding that nothing beyond the window appeared to have altered.

> How differently must these people conceive of distance, for us thirty miles is so much altering scenery, for them it must be so much time, thirty minutes' time, three hours' time. (22 August 1944)

A seemingly inconsequential observation perhaps, but it contains a trace of something more profound and unrehearsed, on what happens to our sense of time and distance in a featureless landscape.

During his westward journey, Mailer wrote to his parents, to Bea's and to his sister, and while the content of these pieces, in terms of places and events, is the same as that of his letters to his wife, the man who addresses Bea could be someone else. Understandably he intersperses sentences to her with touches of intimate affection – 'darling', 'sweets', 'dearest one' and so on – but there is also a sense of Bea as his prototype reader. Throughout, he tries out stylistic moods and variations. We have no record of her replies to him or her remarks on what he had written when he returned to America after the war was over, but we need only to read the letters to find that they are written to two Beas. One was his beloved wife with whom he delighted in confiding impressions variously aesthetic and metaphysical, completely unlike his reports to other correspondents. The other was Bea as a proxy commissioning editor or agent.

Mailer epitomises the term eclectic in that he rarely wrote one book that was remotely similar to anything else he had produced. The only exception to this was his tendency towards self-focused disarrangement. He might continually be speaking in different tongues, but he was always speaking to and of himself. This curious inclination began during 1944 and 1945, when Bea became his audience, and these early letters were a rehearsal for his career as a shifty literary narcissist.

After *The Naked and the Dead* he would try out ideas in first drafts, revise and rewrite, but these preparations for the finished product would always be private exercises. Which is why the letters are so important. His sense of who he was writing to, his intimate alter ego, enabled him to create the models for the characters who would soon populate one of the most widely celebrated Second World War novels.

He wrote to Bea from the King George Hotel in San Francisco:

> ... in the cities God is a reactionary, an anarchic and perverted symbol. In the west, in the heart of the prairie and the foothills God seems to be everywhere, he is the hills and the sky and the battle between light and darkness, he is all the thundering vast music ever written, and in the city he is nothing. He is the frenetic beat of tension, anxiety, city jazz. Nerves snapping, snapping all the time. (22 August 1944)

The outlandish imagery and convoluted syntax hint at Hawthorne, but there is no evidence that Mailer had even read him. A more likely source of inspiration are the writings of the Kabbalah, the esoteric quasi-mystical branch of Judaism. Mailer's reference to 'God' should be treated with scepticism in that he had already distanced himself from orthodox religious beliefs. Mailer's God is a quixotic, privately apprehended version of himself. *The Naked and the Dead* is told in the third person, but frequently Mailer allows the reader intimate access to the silent ruminations of its characters. One of the most disagreeable of these is General Cummings, who is a megalomaniac, his rank as a military commander enabling him to think of himself as omnipotent. He is addicted to the notion of battle as something that would seal the fate of its participants, often hideously, and he frequently compares himself with God. Compare Cummings's interior monologues with letters such as Mailer's above and it is clear enough where and how his character was conceived.

Bea kept all of his letters, and after Mailer returned to the States he consulted them as an aide-memoire for his novel and sometimes reproduced them almost verbatim. When the figures of his fictional platoon advance towards the Japanese on the island of Anopopei, the account of mountainous terrain before them comes from the description of 'then came the mountains' in his letter to Bea as the train passed from the flatlands of the Midwest to Nebraska.

In the novel:

Far in the distance they could see Mount Anaka rising above the island. It arched coldly and remotely from the jungle beneath it, lofting itself massively into the low-hanging clouds of the sky. (p.447)

His report to Bea of the train journey:

And then came the mountains, but with no abruptness my darling … The land rose in Nebraska in little rolls and dales after we were half-way through, and slowly all through the afternoon and into the evening these little hills grew higher and higher …

The passage in the novel closes with:

In the early drab twilight it [the mountain] looked like an immense old gray elephant erecting himself somberly on his front legs … The mountain seemed wise and powerful, and terrifying in its size.

One can almost watch him underlining passages of the correspondence and refreshing them as his description of the landscape where his characters await a firefight with the Japanese.

... and it is something darling to see behind you in the east, the night, and before you the twilight ... nothing but the brown foothills, rolling and rolling, and rolling beside the train. They looked so much like elephants, that color of brown, wrinkled and old, and wise and friendly but aloof. (22 August 1944)

Two months later, after the completion of advanced combat training at Fort Ord, Mailer and other recently recruited infantrymen boarded the USS *Sea Barb* for the Philippines, and by early December he was describing to Bea the colours and sensations of the western Pacific, including an 'island that only existed in mankind's dream ... the greatest conception of the most bejeweled Oriental ... No wonder heaven is so sensual ...' In the novel, 'The island hovered before them like an Oriental monarch's conception of heaven ...'

At one point he seems so captivated by what he had written Bea two years earlier that he hardly bothers to alter it for the novel.

I looked back toward the stern and there was only the gray-black ocean, the gray darkening sky, and the evil churning of the gray-white wake. It was the aspect of the ocean that is always death. There are bits of phosphorescence that swirl in the foam like strong stars against a milky constellation, so that this gray dead ocean looked like a mirror of the night's universe – so unutterably cold, so implicit with dread and death. (December 1944)

In the novel:

After a little while, there was only the gray-black ocean, the darkened sky, and the evil churning of the gray-white wake. Bits of phosphoresce swirled in the foam. The black dead ocean looked like a mirror of the night; it was cold, implicit with dread and death.

While *The Naked and the Dead* is energised by the tensions between individual characters, there are times when Mailer broadens the perspective, depicting a shared state of mind, an all-embracing sense of trepidation, even terror. The above passage typifies this, and many of the novel's early reviewers and critics praised it as the first to present the experience of warfare as something both inexplicable and inescapable. Raymond Rosenthal of *Commentary* saw it as a 'relief' from writing that had 'ducked the reality' of war; Mailer had offered those who had never experienced battle the mood of 'dark fatalism'. This claim is based on the premise that Mailer was capable of capturing and by implication knowing how all of his fellow servicemen felt. Yet it is evident from the interplay between his letters to Bea and the novel that the 'dark fatalism' of *The Naked and the Dead* was based on the particular impressions of Norman Mailer.

Hilary Mills, Mailer's first biographer, researched his life while he was still in his fifties. Bea spoke candidly to her, reporting on how her husband would work all day on the novel, alone in his study but with the file of more than a hundred letters he had sent to her between 1944 and 1946 along with notes he'd brought back from his time in the Pacific theatre. She said nothing, however, of how they spent their time together as a couple, and one has to wonder if the letters in any way resembled the observations he visited upon her. If so, we should commend Bea for her love and patience and feel not much surprise that she eventually suffered a nervous breakdown.

At Fort Bragg Mailer made friends with Clifford Maskovsky, who was about a year younger and when drafted still between high school and college. They remained on good terms, serving in the same units until the surrender of Japan, and Maskovsky recalls that in 1948 'I was flipping through the back pages of *Time* magazine and saw a picture of Norman with a smoking cigarette in his hand – a sort of sophisticated picture – and my first thought was, Oh, my God, Norman's been arrested for rape.' (Manso, p. 74). He looked closer and found that the photograph was a part of the publicity surrounding *The Naked and the Dead*, but his initial reaction was not entirely flippant. One of his most enduring memories of Mailer involved his apparent obsession with the sex lives of his fellow servicemen. Most of these young men would boast about their (often bogus) experiences with girls, but Mailer seemed to have a prurient interest in the exact detail of what others got up to, asking for accounts of foreplay, orgasms – individual or mutual – and the vernacular of sexual activity. He was particularly taken by an Italian immigrant's statement that 'I just get on and off my wife'; he would tap his wife on the shoulder and tell her 'I'm gonna jump you.'

According to Maskovsky, 'Nobody got angry with him', and Mailer's habit of entering notes of these exchanges in a small yellow journal caused amusement rather than offence. He was seen as a harmless pervert. Hence Maskovsky's initial reaction to the photograph: his old friend had seemed to harbour strange inclinations. It was only when he read the novel that he found the idioms and nuances on which Mailer took notes had been revived almost verbatim in the exchanges between its characters. Moreover, he recognised people he'd known in the Pacific from the habits, physical stature and mannerisms of Mailer's inventions. 'I recognized people and felt a great deal of the book was really autobiographical ... I remember looking at *The Naked and the Dead* and thinking: Here they are, dammit. These are the guys from basic [training].' (Manso, p. 76).

Mailer spent the war on the island of Luzon. Mostly he was well behind the front line working for the Intelligence Corps but only as an administrative auxiliary, typing and filing documents, which caused difficulties since he had never been taught to type. On two occasions at most he volunteered for and was assigned to a reconnaissance unit, patrols that would collect information on Japanese artillery emplacements and trenches, which was vital for the planning of offensive operations. He was shot at, or at least he heard the sound of bullets overhead – his unit was shelled and once he stepped on the rotting corpse of a Japanese soldier. He saw action, briefly, and to his credit he limits the combat sequence of the novel to an account of one significant patrol, an honest reflection of his own experiences.

Another private, Isadore Feldman, got to know Mailer well, and although he did not read *The Naked and the Dead* until 1952, he was struck by the similarities between its characters and figures he remembered from seven years earlier. 'There was a lot of Red Matthewson in Red Valsen, for example. Red even looked the way Valsen's described in the book – a raw-boned guy of Swedish extraction.' (Manso, p. 84) Valsen prefigures the rebels of Mailer's writing of the 1950s; classless, anarchic, purposively irresponsible. Feldman describes him as 'a real character, who had been around', and Mailer himself told of how he admired

Matthewson greatly. He was ten years older than most of the other men and had spent much of his life as a hobo, riding railway wagons across the States, making enough money only to feed himself, but he also displayed an instinctive belief in social equality. Leaving school at twelve he had read virtually nothing, but he loathed racism with a commitment one would associate with college-educated liberals. The Red of the novel, like all other characters, is flawed, but one also detects something close to empathy, even affection, in Mailer's treatment of him.

Feldman also tells of Francis 'Fig' Gwaltney. 'I felt he was kind of a snob – Francis Irby Gwaltney *the third* ... he gave the impression that his family owned half of Arkansas, while I later found out that in fact he was real poor', adding that 'I can't really say if there was a character in the book'. There is: Woodrow Wilson, an impoverished Georgian, nostalgic about his youth in the Old South, which involved incessant drunkenness on moonshine whiskey and sex with any woman he was able to charm, irrespective of race. Feldman: 'The one thing in his favor, though, he wasn't a bigot.'

Robert Hearn is sometimes thought to have been based on an officer in Mailer's unit called Lieutenant Horton, forename unrecorded. Feldman does not remember a man called Horton but he vividly recalls what happens to a young officer called Sachs, who had

gotten into a tiff with his captain ... and he'd stood his ground. So the captain saw to it that he went out on every patrol. He'd come in from one and go right out on the next one. That meant he was condemned to death, and eventually he caught one in the butt, and it ranged up through his stomach. He died two days later. I saw him when they brought him in. Just pitiful. (Manso, p. 86)

This is an eerily precise account of the fate of Hearn, who 'stood his ground' against General Cummings and Sergeant Croft, both very unpleasant. They too ensure that he is assigned to patrols which, as Feldman puts it, 'condemned [him] to death'.

Feldman recognised aspects of Mailer, himself and other Jewish servicemen of their unit in two of the novel's characters, Roth and Goldstein, both of whom are victims of the antisemitism that Mailer depicts as endemic to military culture. 'Like Goldstein,' Feldman reflects, 'I was raised Orthodox, but Norman was on the verge of being a rebel, and I can understand that maybe part of his being a rebel was not feeling comfortable as a Jew.' (Manso, p85)

Mailer returned to the States with more than a hundred and fifty pages of notes in his knapsack, many of which contained verbal portraits of men with whom he'd served. Many of the novel's characters are hybrids of the real soldiers, but his mix-and-match method was not adopted to respectfully preserve their anonymity.He constructed charts involving selections from his notes on real characters and their temperamental features and redistributed each as prototypes for the men who would feature in the novel. 'I studied engineering at Harvard and I suppose it was the book of a young engineer.' (Lennon, p. 76)

Mailer admits that Cummings, Hearn and Croft owe least to his documentary notes, and while he does not explain this, it is clear enough that they are embodied abstractions: respectively, maniacal power-hunger, with a hint at repressed homosexuality; East Coast liberalism at its most honourable and ineffectual; and pure murderous sadism. One thing, however, unites the three of them with each of the other characters. Everyone in the novel carries a trace of Norman Mailer, especially those aspects of himself he'd treat with masochistic self-loathing. Cummings is extraordinarily vile, but equally notable is his author's preoccupation with the monster he has created. Mailer does not like him, but he is fascinated by his own ability to bring such a figure to life, a man whose mother encouraged and rejoiced in his childhood artistic and literary talents while his father treated these as feminised activities. Mailer would never be able to reconcile the notion of art, particularly literary art, with something far more instinctive and, if you are a man, brutal. Hearn, the archetypal liberal with socialist inclinations, does not stand a chance against the establishment embodied by the likes of Cummings. Indeed, the quasi-sexual mutual attraction between the General and the Lieutenant is part of some sort of Manichean necessity; good and evil belong together. In 2003 Mailer spoke of the imminent Iraq war: 'Fascism is more of a natural state than democracy. To assume blithely that we can export democracy into any country we choose can serve paradoxically to encourage more fascism at home and abroad.' ('Only in America', *The New York Review*, March 27th, 2003)

Croft is probably the most irredeemably repulsive of Mailer's inventions, and the moment that endures for most readers involves him crushing an injured bird in his massive fist. The helpless creature had been adopted by other soldiers as a token of something close to compassion, but Croft makes it clear that sadism is something that must be unapologetically enjoyed, whether dealing with birds or human beings. Mailer is at once horrified and fascinated by his ability to produce such an individual, and once more we are projected forward into his career as a writer and his strange evolution as a person, to his love–hate relationship with the psychopathic murderer Gary Gilmore. Mailer would not encounter the 'hero' of *The Executioner's Song* until the 1970s, but he was alert to a remarkably similar presence when he invented Sergeant Croft.

On 8 August 1945, Mailer wrote to Bea of his feelings on the bombing of Hiroshima. It is an extraordinary letter. He declares his approval of an instrument that will 'shorten the war ... that will kill under optimum conditions many people in one instance', and goes on to speculate on the possibility of 'humanity destroying itself'.

> There will be another war, if not in twenty years, then in fifty, and if half of mankind survives, then what of the next war – I believe that to survive the world cities of tomorrow will be built a mile beneath the earth. Man then will have escaped his animal heritage ... he will have descended a thousand fathoms nearer to hell.

He closes with a sentence that is poetic and horribly prophetic. 'The next step is religious awe, and the atom bomb looks like the last deity, the final form line of entelechy.'

This is the language of the Cold War at its height fifteen to twenty years after 1945, when people properly understood the nature and effect of nuclear weapons, and when the two superpowers were massively equipped with them and engaged in a stand-off. On 8 August the only news of the Hiroshima bomb came in a brief statement by President Truman, heavy with hyperbole but short on detail. This was all that

Mailer would have known. The Manhattan Project and the test that had first demonstrated the power of the weapon were state secrets. William Laurence's vivid description of what a nuclear explosion looks like was based on his eye-witness role as reporter on the B29 that accompanied the bomb-carrying aircraft to Nagasaki on 9 August, and his article did not appear in *The New York Times* until a week after Mailer had written to Bea. As to the horrific after-effects on the targets of the bombs nothing was known until John Hersey visited what was left of Hiroshima and sent his famous report for publication in *The New Yorker* on 22 August, after Japan had surrendered.

Even if Mailer had backdated his letter and made use of later material for his apocalyptic vision, nothing written by Laurence, Hersey or anyone else comes close to it.

At the end of August Mailer's unit, the 112th, boarded the USS *Lavaca* for Japan and were moored close to the battleship USS *Missouri* in Tokyo Bay where the Japanese signed the surrender documents on 2 September. Maskovsky later reported that they were close enough to see Admiral Nimitz and General MacArthur with binoculars.

Mailer had spent seven months on Luzon and would remain in the army for a further eight as part of the occupation force in Japan. Bored with the routine tasks delegated to private soldiers – cleaning and painting barracks, and acting as labourer on repair and building projects – he volunteered to train as a cook, an activity completely alien to him.

On the face of things he progressed well, because by January 1946 he was promoted to the albeit temporary position of mess sergeant with a command of twenty-four men. He looked forward to being able to return to Brooklyn with three stripes on his arm and wrote to Bea that he had mastered both the skills of a head chef and a position of management in the military. Gwaltney, who had stayed in the same unit since Luzon, disagreed, and informed Mills that 'He was the worst cook who ever lived ... I mean, he was awful. Never did learn to separate the yellows from the whites of the eggs.' Without rancour Gwaltney saw his performances in the kitchen as an extension of Mailer's war that was by parts sad and endearing. 'He was a brave soldier but not a good one,' he recalled, adding that his comrade was famous for falling over and losing any sense of direction when on reconnaissance patrols on Luzon. 'He couldn't see worth a damn. Near-sighted. He wore GI glasses when he read, but not otherwise and he couldn't hit anything with a rifle. It's a miracle Mailer lived through the war.' (Mills, pp. 78–80). In none of the seven photographs taken of him during his time in military service is Mailer wearing glasses, which, as Gwaltney points out, were a necessity he avoided when not reading.

All of this should be taken into consideration in relation to an incident that began on 3 April. The permanent, senior mess sergeant woke Mailer around ten, stated that the kitchen porters, mostly Japanese prisoners, had not cleaned the kitchen, and ordered him to do the job himself. Mailer called the sergeant a 'chickenshit-son-of-a-bitch', or so he informed Bea in a letter soon afterwards. He was not formally charged with insubordination, though the senior sergeant reported to the captain that he had refused to obey orders. According to Mailer's later account the officer was drunk and insisted that he should apologise to the sergeant. He did so, to both of them, and the following day returned to the captain's office and announced that he no longer wished to wear his stripes. The captain robbed him of his moment of honourable rebuttal by stating that he had already decided to demote him to buck private.

This is generally treated as the inspiration for the passage in *The Naked and the Dead* when Hearn 'crawfishes' – that is, humiliates himself – before General Cummings. In the novel Cummings does not only embarrass Hearn, he effectively kills him. Read through this and imagine how Mailer felt as the hopelessly incompetent soldier who cannot run a kitchen, deprived even of the opportunity to avoid official indignity. Hearn certainly does not feel he deserves his fate at the hands of Cummings and Croft, but there is a hint of stoical acceptance about him, and Mailer presents his integrity as the magnet for sadistic figures of authority. Mailer won no awards for bravery or gallantry, but like all others in the Pacific he was presented with campaign and occupation medals. He threw most of them into the sea when sailing home on the USS *Grant*, and gave away his Combat Infantryman's Badge to a soldier who had never faced enemy fire.

He arrived in Seattle in early May, took the train east and was met by Bea at Grand Central, New York. They went first to a hotel in Brooklyn

Heights, had sex throughout their five nights and checked out only because they were running out of money. The Esplendor Bossert Hotel dated from the early twentieth century and was luxuriously appointed and very expensive. For the next two weeks they stayed in the spare room of Mailer's parents' apartment only a block away. His mother was delighted to recreate the atmosphere of looking after her favourite and Bea indulged her, helping out in the kitchen but never encroaching on Fan's performance as matriarch.

Mailer sent Robert Linscott, senior editor of Random House, the typescript of *A Transit To Narcissus* as an example of what he was capable of producing. His proposal was for a book he was about to write, based on his wartime experiences. Linscott replied that the publishing world was awash with war novels variously imminent, in press and recently contracted, and that Mailer would not find a publisher. Next, he contacted Bea's sister Phyllis, who had recently become a junior editor at Little, Brown. They had lunch, got on well, and Phyllis told him as politely as possible that while his projected novel sounded fascinating, all he could expect would be friendly responses until he could offer an editor or agent something on paper.

Bea and Mailer each saw Provincetown as somewhere special. It had been their refuge from their parents, and they had spent time there immediately before returning to the city to marry, in secret. It was, thought Mailer, the perfect place for him to realise his vocation, to produce the novel on America's involvement in the Second World War that would overshadow the rest in what Linscott described as the 'overpublished mass-market'.

Bea had arranged the rental of one of a terrace of beach-front properties known as Crow's Nest Cottages, and they took the train out of the city on the evening of the same day he'd had lunch with Phyllis.

Mailer had already decided to go for documentary realism, specifically a sequence of brief narratives based on document notes he had already collated when overseas along with correspondence he'd asked Bea to file chronologically. He took one of the two rooms downstairs as his study and shifted between diagrams hung on the wall and index-cards on which he entered details as precise as the place and date of birth of even the minor characters. These he also filled with information on hair colour, successes and failures at school, early girlfriends, arguments with and/or affection for parents, even the type of bicycle they rode during childhood and their favourite films and books; though some, he decided, would be barely literate or not go to the movies at all. What is extraordinary about the breadth and particularity of this mass of detail is that only about twenty per cent of it featured at all in the novel. It was as though he was cultivating an intimate familiarity with his characters, from their infanthood onwards, before deciding which aspects of them he would fillet out for their appearance in the book. Virtually all of these men were based on comrades from training and Luzon, but at the same time he hypothesised, turned what he knew into what might have been and extrapolated potential inclinations into something more agreeable or foul. This was a vital feature of his so-called 'Time Machine' technique, where he transports the reader back to periods in his characters' lives well before the army, often to childhood.

With amazing speed, he completed the first draft in little more than four months over the summer of 1946, and at the end of September the couple moved back to Brooklyn, renting an apartment on Remsen Street less than a quarter of a mile from his parents. Two weeks before that he had arranged a meeting with Adeline Lubell-Naiman in Boston. Adeline had been a close friend of Mailer's sister, Barbara, at Radcliffe, had been a roommate of Bea's sister, Phyllis Silverman at the same college and now worked with Phyllis as an editor for Little, Brown. The two women had spoken about Mailer, and Adeline, holding a slightly senior post, agreed to talk with him about the work-in-progress and was surprised when, as they sat down for lunch, he handed her more than two thirds of the projected final draft.

Adeline recalled for Manso that after Mailer returned to Provincetown she read it in her apartment and produced a brief report based on her initial impressions, stating that 'it is going to be the greatest novel to come out World War II and we must publish it'. This she despatched to her boss at Little, Brown, the senior editor Angus Cameron, promising to follow up with a far more detailed appraisal in around a week. She maintained her enthusiasm in this and bulked out her praise with constructive comments on how the work that went into print would improve on the prototype. Cameron read the work and was equally impressed but had reservations. He was a communist sympathiser, though never a member of the party, and he was pleased by Mailer's special brand of radicalism, notably the presentation of lower-class men as having to take responsibility for a war in which they had no interest and an exposure of the military as a reflection of social prejudice and inequality. But at the same time he knew that Little, Brown would face problems when they tried to get it into print. Depictions of crippling injuries, terror and death were acceptable enough, but having the poor young men subjected to these horrors use terms such as 'son-of-a-bitch', let alone 'fuck', would cause it to be banned by the censor.

Despite his instinct to issue a contract, Cameron sent the typescript to the executive vice president, Raymond Everitt, who had worked with the government Office of Information during the war on how publishing would affect public morale. Alfred McIntyre had become a legend as a junior editor by basing a decision to publish purely on sentiment, memorably 'if it brought a tear to my eye'. Now, however, he was president and accountable to his shareholders for the success of Little, Brown's books. Discussions between the three men, sometimes involving Adeline, took place regularly over several weeks until it was agreed they should consult Bernard DeVoto, veteran of the First World War, prize-winning author of books on the grim reality of the American West and civil rights activist. DeVoto's report told them what they already knew: the book was brilliant but unpublishable in its present state. Mailer was shown DeVoto's assessment and recommendations and was infuriated. He was prepared, just, to expunge the worst of the obscenities, but DeVoto, backed by Cameron, Everitt and McIntyre, also insisted that other, more fundamental, parts of the draft required rewriting. Notably DeVoto felt that while the depiction of Cummings and Croft might escape the red pen of the censor, the book in print would probably be widely condemned as non-patriotic, even treacherous. A general officer and a courageous sergeant had been singled out, respectively, as a closet-gay psychopath and a sadist.

Cameron offered Mailer a contract, conditional on the revised version being acceptable to the company after delivery and with a laughably negotiable advance – Adeline told him informally that they had decided to go no further than $300. Without signing anything but leaving his options open, Mailer looked at how he could turn Cummings and Croft into tragic anti-heroes, victims of the dehumanising effects of war rather than its deranged celebrants. He attempted redrafts of key passages involving the two of them, wrote to Adeline as he was doing so and confessed to despair. In one letter he compared the book with the film *With the Marines at Tarawa*, a documentary approved for movie-house viewings by Roosevelt in 1944, against the opinions of all of the president's advisors. In Roosevelt's view the horrifying shots of the mutilated, burnt and decaying bodies of marines on the beaches of Tarawa island would stiffen the resolve of the population by showing them what was really happening to American troops. Why, Mailer asked Adeline, was this film given an Oscar when his brutal and authentic account was being subjected to revisions that would bury the truth beneath the acceptable?

As Mailer toiled with edits that he loathed, he and Bea became aware that Brooklyn had become a minor literary nucleus. Bea invited the man who rented the apartment near them for drinks. They had met on the stairs of Mailer's parents' building and chatted, and she had learned that this neighbour was working on something that, he hoped, would project him from respectable mediocrity to greatness. She introduced her husband, over whiskeys, to Arthur Miller, who told them of his progress with an as yet untitled play, which would become *Death of a Salesman*, and the two men shared stories about their dealings with the literary establishment. The acquaintance lasted barely a week, but Mailer later regarded it as eerily significant; in *Marilyn* he would accuse a man he barely knew as ruining the life of the woman he idolised.

Bea had also met the published and acclaimed poet Norman Rosten, later known as the 'Bard of Brooklyn'. Rosten and his wife, Hedda, would befriend, and sometimes protect, Marilyn Monroe during the final seven years of her life, a period which overlapped with the decline of her marriage to Miller, with whom she had begun an affair in 1952. Mailer would never meet Monroe but he came to regard his time with Miller and Rosten in 1946 as by parts prophetic and otherworldly, confessing that he saw himself as the 'missing link', a rather bizarre justification for his obsession with the actress.

Bea had served as a WAVES officer (Women Accepted for Voluntary Emergency Service), and she and Mailer qualified for the so-called '52-20

Club', a scheme which guaranteed GIs $20 a week for a full year following their return to civilian status. They walked together to the local post office to collect their $40, which amounted to only slightly less than the average annual income in 1946 of $2,600. On top of this Bea had saved more than $2,000 of her service salary; as an officer she was on much more than her husband, and she lived for the duration of the war in rent-free barracks. Mailer had around $800 of his own, banked from his very modest private soldier's income during his time overseas.

Their apartment was comfortable enough but oddly arranged, part of an otherwise dilapidated terrace that had been bought by the government towards the end of the war and converted into accommodation for veterans. The front door opened into their small kitchen, and aside from the bathroom there were two other rooms seemingly available for sleeping and eating or socialising. Mailer could not, he said, work without complete privacy, so they agreed to use their resources to rent, for a tiny amount, a single room, a 'garret' in the roof of a neighbouring building. He would leave for this at 10.00 am every day and not return until mid-afternoon at the earliest.

Mailer and Bea regularly visited his mother, and the two women would listen as he recited passages from his novel-in-progress. Both praised him as a genius, though Fan would routinely throw up her hands and proclaim, 'Norman! The language! How can you?' He was, at the insistence of Little, Brown, excising the 'fucks', but many 'shits' and 'asses' remained. Adeline Lubell told Mills that her seniors saw the project as their necessary contribution to the expanding industry of memorialising the war in books, more a duty than an investment. They planned a print run of only 3,500 with slight but unexceptional publicity and promotion.

Rosten rescued him. They were talking one day on the street, and Mailer complained that in order to get his book into print he would need to turn it into something he did not want to carry his name. Rosten said that his own publishers, Rinehart, were far more open-minded and that he would be happy to recommend him to his editor, Ted Amussen. Mailer did not disclose that Amussen had already turned him down, thanked his friend, and asked him to forward the draft. He also enclosed Adeline's report on it.

Mailer and Rosten took the subway to Rinehart's offices on Madison Avenue, and there a weird exchange took place, with Mailer's advocate introducing his editor to a man whom Amussen already knew and Amussen sparing Rosten any embarrassment by pretending that Mailer was entirely new to him. Amussen said goodbye to the two men and spent the afternoon with Mailer's typescript. He was astonished that the author he had encountered three years earlier had completely transformed himself and was convinced that his employers would gain considerable praise, and money, by publishing the book. There followed an almost farcical rerun of the episodes at Little, Brown, with Amussen's junior colleague William Rainey describing it as 'magnificent', while John Selby, himself a prospective writer and Amussen's senior, recommended that they must not indulge such 'trash'. Amussen bypassed Selby and went straight to the owner of the company, Stanley Rinehart, who agreed that it was a spectacularly unusual work and that Mailer should be offered a contract. Amussen decided on the advance, and Mailer was astonished to find that he would receive $1,250 on signature, before delivery of the completed work. Rinehart too were a little unhappy with the obscenities; 'fuck' became 'fug', but the 'shits' were retained.

A week after signing the contract Mailer asked Amussen to look at another novel, a completed one. Amussen was impressed and indicated that they would publish if it some suggested alterations were made, but soon after that he left Rinehart for another post. Mailer never referred to it and there is no archived copy. All we know of it comes from a remark made by its author to Mills. 'I didn't want to bother [revising it]. I really didn't want to be a writer. I found out how hard it was,' said Bea. (p 94)

Mailer submitted his completed typescript in August 1947. It ran to almost 900 pages, and he was told that it would take at least nine months to get it into print.

4

WAITING FOR FAME

The details of Bea and Mailer's visit to Paris are straightforward enough. They boarded the RMS *Queen Elizabeth* on 3 October 1947 and would use further grants provided by the GI Bill to enrol for the *Cours de Civilisation Française* at the Sorbonne. The rather grand-sounding programme was in truth based on teaching French to American expatriates in order to bring in money for the university, now cash-strapped in the post-war years. Nowhere, however, can we locate anything resembling a motive for their journey, let alone which of them first suggested it.

It is possible that Mailer was reluctant to start another book until *The Naked and the Dead* went to press, but neither he nor Bea stated as much. The rite-of-passage explanation is difficult to take seriously given that while he admired Hemingway as a writer, he showed no interest in the pre-war obsession with Europe that took the majority of the best American writers across the Atlantic. Mailer dropped out of the Sorbonne course in less than a month having learnt enough French to buy food and deal with rental agencies, according to Bea.

> Paris had been a beacon for painters and writers for decades. It is in some sense a must for young artists. But Norman [was] very much an American writer. I don't think he ever wanted to be an expatriate; there is no vagabond streak in him … We were just a bunch of kids enjoying ourselves being young. The war was over and we were in another country. (Interview with Mills, p. 95)

A hint at Mailer's true reason for his visit to Europe can be found in his first piece of journalism published shortly after he returned to America in summer 1948. He wrote 'A Credo for the Living' (1948) while *The Naked and the Dead* was sweeping him from obscurity to fame, and it is evident that the feelings he expresses about global politics predated his time in Paris. He went to the French capital as a means of testing out rather outlandish opinions. In his view, 'Communism was the answer for Western Europe, and it would have been a more satisfactory answer than the mangle of present-day political life there', and he continues:

> It is perfectly ridiculous to assume that if Europe had gone Communist, Russia would have engaged in a war with us. Both Russia and the countries of Western Europe would have had their own crucial problems of reconstruction ... In the process America would have been influenced by what was occurring in Europe, might gradually and peacefully have oriented itself toward socialism. (*The National Guardian,* 18th October, 1948)

On the liner to France he composed a letter to Fig Gwaltney that reads as an unvarnished rehearsal for the essay he would write on his return: 'I've gone quite a bit to the Left ... the leaders of the United States want to go to war ... I don't think Russia is the villain it's made out to be.' (7th October 1948).

Most of the people the Mailers socialised with during their first months in Paris were of the same age, many of the men were also Harvard graduates, and the majority were, like Mailer, ex-servicemen and recently married to women who had also graduated from Ivy League colleges. Few, if any, had made an impact as writers, though they were arts graduates, and the whole network resembled the US East Coast on holiday. Mailer was, as he stated, 'to the Left', and while his new friends were liberals and fascinated by the various forms of political radicalism in post-war Western Europe – the policies enacted by the recently elected British Labour government would have been unimaginable in the States, for example – none but Mailer were outspoken supporters of the Soviet regime. Stanley Karnow and Stanley Geist had attended some of the same Cambridge classes as Mailer. Mark Linenthal, later to become a critic, academic and poet, had read English at Harvard at the same time as Mailer, and Linenthal's then wife, Alice Adams, had met both her husband and Mailer when she was studying at Radcliffe and would earn esteem as a novelist and short-story writer. Kenneth Lynn, later to produce an acclaimed biography of Hemingway, had graduated only shortly before his arrival in Paris in 1947 but friends had given him contact details for Karnow, who introduced him to Linenthal and Mailer. He too was a Harvard man.

The Mailers spent their first three weeks in the Hotel de l'Avenir on rue Madame, close to the Sorbonne. Unknowingly they were following the example of Hemingway, who, with his first wife, Hadley, had initially lived in a slum on arrival in the city. The 'rooms' at the Hotel de l'Avenir were just that, meaning that guests had to share running water, a bathroom and lavatory with all others on the same floor. Unlike Hadley Hemingway, Bea could not tolerate bohemianism, and quite soon the Mailers moved to a modest but comfortable apartment in the same district.

Linenthal: 'Norman and Bea weren't poor and struggling. They'd saved money during the war ... The two of them were living in Montparnasse, a little furnished apartment – a bourgeois apartment, not a bohemian pad.' (Manso, p. 112). They even had enough money to hire a chambermaid from the hotel to do their cleaning and laundry. According to Linenthal, they were the only Americans who could afford to host parties, at which guests would be well provisioned with wine and cocktails. He recalls that Mailer drank, but much less than Bea, who enjoyed having the opportunity to shock and even cause offence.

Geist and his then wife, Eileen Finletter, were friendly with Jean Malaquais, and they introduced the Mailers to him in November 1947. Malaquais was, like Arthur Koestler, a nomadic victim of mid-twentieth-century Europe. Both were Jews from central-eastern areas of the continent, each had experienced in early adulthood the emergence of fascism, espoused left-wing politics, fought against the Falangists during the Spanish Civil War and came to see that Stalin's regime was as totalitarian and inhumane as Hitler's. Mailer stated later in his Preface to Malaquais' The Joker (Doubleday, 1974) that Malaquais 'had more influence on my mind than anyone I ever knew', which was rather like an avowed creationist claiming Darwin as their mentor.

Mailer knew little if anything of Malaquais before they met, but within a few days, through Geist and others, he became entranced by the man's past. Aged eighteen Malaquais had left his home because 'I had the feeling that the end of the world was approaching in Poland', (Obituary by James Kirkup, *Independent*, 6th January, 1999) by which he meant that the 1926 coup led by Marshal Pilsudski was brought about by conflicts between far-right and communist factions, a microcosmic prelude to the state of Europe in the 1930s. He settled in France, become associated with various left-wing radical groups and joined the POUM militia, which fought against Franco's units in Catalonia. In 1939–40 he saw action as a private soldier in the French army, was captured by the Germans and escaped before being transferred from a POW to a concentration camp, which would have been his assured destination as a Jew with a record as a radical anti-fascist. After the war he returned to Paris following periods in Mexico and the United States. Shortly before he and Mailer met Malaquais published the widely acclaimed novel *Planète sans visa*, based mainly on his experience as an exile in Vichy France.

Malaquais had been subjected to the political tensions that had torn Europe and most of the world to pieces, and Mailer saw him as the fountainhead for his own speculations on what might happen next. The trouble was that Malaquais told him the opposite of what he wanted to hear.

In early 1948, shortly after Mailer and Malaquais met, Henry A. Wallace, previously vice president to Roosevelt, formed the Progressive Party, the closest that America would ever come to having a socialist group which would be taken seriously by the political establishment. It was an almost exact replica of Britain's post-war Labour Party, advocating free health care, a welfare state and the nationalisation of utility industries, but in the presidential election of 1948 it gained only 2.4 per cent of the vote. During its albeit brief period as a new presence on the political landscape it became the magnet for a particular type of American, mostly young, educated and with a vision for a new America. Virtually all of Mailer's expatriate friends in Paris supported Wallace, and Mailer himself was remembered as the most outspoken advocate of the Progressives. Malaquais: 'that winter maybe I saw him a dozen times

... I said that in my opinion the Wallace movement was more or less infiltrated by Stalinists, often by proxy, using people like himself ... He reacted as if I were talking gibberish.' (Manso, p. 113). Malaquais was right. Wallace's status as a respectable figure, an ex-vice president, meant that members of the American Communist Party attached themselves to the Progressives as a means of 'infiltrating' the political establishment. By the 1950s this same uneasy relationship between democratic institutions and a one-party ideology offered traction to such communist hunters as Senator McCarthy.

In Spain the militia controlled by the hard-core Soviet faction of the Republicans were as ruthless in their repression of dissident elements of the anti-Franco alliance as they were in defending the Republic against Franco himself. Stalin wanted his representatives to win the war only to annex Spain as part of the totalitarian USSR. By 1938 members of such nonconformist elements as the Catalonia-based POUM, Malaquais included, were being disarmed, arrested and sometimes summarily executed by members of the Russian NKVD. Malaquais recommended to Mailer Koestler's 1940 novel *Darkness at Noon* and not simply for its literary qualities. It was, explained Malaquais, a painfully honest account of the imprisonments and executions that followed Stalin's show trials during the 1930s. This, he pointed out, was the regime that Wallace was urging Americans to embrace as an ally and even treat as an exemplar for social equilibrium. Malaquais told Mailer that the 'communists would exploit him and then they would drop him and cover him with dirt' and for this 'he disliked me very strongly'. (Lennon, p101)

The term 'useful idiot' is often attributed to Lenin, and Mailer was a classic case. He was sufficiently entranced by the idyll of communism to have blinded himself to its authoritarian nature. Like others in the West, he acted as a subversive advocate for a cause he had chosen not to understand. Malaquais: 'He was ... what you might call a fellow traveler – naive, a kind of Boy Scout intellectually and politically ... He seemed eager, touching, romantic. Also – how do you say? – uncouth? His manners were those of a young Brooklyn boy, not eccentric, not bohemian, with fuzzy notions and no culture, as far as I was concerned.' (Manso, p, 113),

In February 1948 the Linenthals introduced Mailer and Bea to a group of Spanish expatriates. Some were veterans of the Civil War and others had relatives or friends imprisoned by the Franco regime or who had gone underground as anti-fascist subversives. Mailer's principal contact was Paco Benet Goitia. He was only ten years old when the Falangists finally defeated the Republicans and was now ostensibly a Paris-based student, while in truth he spent most of his time working as an intermediary between activists in Spain and France and those willing to cross the Pyrenees to conduct operations. The vast majority of the latter were Americans who, like Mailer and the Linenthals, saw Wallace and the Progressives as a guarantee against fascist and extreme right-wing elements in the West. In 1948 Spain was a nonentity, economically, politically and militarily, but for many it invited a moral crusade. They were like the great Spanish hero Don Quixote, tilting at windmills.

Franco censored anything remotely related to politics, and Paco's first initiative was for the Mailers and Linenthals to take across the border pamphlets and leaflets urging sedition and reporting on how Spain had become an anomaly in a continent that had rid itself of fascist Axis powers. Mailer had recently bought a new Peugeot saloon, and he paid for the documents to be placed in its tyres and hidden under seating. Rolls of pesetas and dollars raised by Paco and his associates to fund the subversives were wrapped in condoms and also hidden in the tyres.

By this point Mailer's parents, Fan and Barney, and his younger sister, Barbara, had joined him in Paris. Barbara was dating a young American student, a Marxist, who was also involved with the group of French anti-Francoists. On the liner from New York to Cherbourg an unusual sequence of coincidences had occurred, beginning with Barbara finding herself at a table next to another American girl of a similar age. They introduced themselves and laughed; they were both called Barbara. Barbara Probst too was travelling with her mother, and as the two women chatted Probst asked Fan about the unbound book she was reading. The latter explained that they were the galley proofs of a novel by her son, Norman Mailer, due to appear within a few weeks in the United States. The name rang a bell, and Probst asked the Mailers if Norman was a friend of a recently married couple, Mark and Alice Linenthal, Cambridge graduates whom she had arranged to meet when she reached Paris. She also recalled that Fan insisted that her own mother should read Norman's forthcoming book, repeating again and again that he was 'a genius'. Probst admitted that her first thought was, 'Sure, another Jewish boy who's going to be a great American writer.' The next day, however, Probst borrowed the proofs from Fan, and when reading it on deck was approached by a woman of around the same age as Fan, who asked her how she came to have the galleys. She answered that the proofs belonged to someone else and that the book was 'quite brilliant'. 'I agree,' said the woman, who introduced herself as Mrs Stanley Rinehart. 'My husband is publishing it.' (Manso, p115)

Probst came from a wealthy East Coast family, and her father had arranged for a spacious saloon car with chauffeur to take them from the liner to Paris. She said farewell to the Mailers, assuming that it was unlikely that their paths would cross thereafter, but a week later she found herself at a drinks party at the Linenthals' apartment being introduced to Norman Mailer and his sister whom she'd already met. The guests were mainly expatriate Americans, French and Spanish, all dedicated to a particular cause.

> I was … struck by how many people were there. Norman had already surrounded himself with a vivacious group of Europeans (remember, this was before the book came out), and a lot of them were Spanish politicos. He introduced Barbara [Mailer] and me to Odette and Robert, one of the last people to be in the Maquis, and also to Enrique Cruz Salido, a kid whose father was a well-known Spanish Socialist. It was through Enrique that Norman had met Paco Benet. Paco had gone to Barcelona with the Linenthals and the Mailers, not only to meet people but to help arrange prison escapes. (Manso, p. 115)

The first expedition to Spain took place in early April 1948, when the Mailers and Linenthals drove to Barcelona to distribute money and pamphlets to Paco's contacts. The episode carried the air of the French Resistance of a few years before. Mark Linenthal recalls them being met on the outskirts of the city by three young men who had clearly been informed of the make of the car and its number plate. They exchanged a few words in French, and one of the Spaniards drove the Peugeot into a barn and locked the door. Linenthal: 'We could hear the wheels being removed, and it all took no more than fifteen minutes.' (Manso, p69)

On Paco's instructions they then set off for Madrid, but the people who met them at a designated spot, again on the edge of the city, told them only that the original plan had been aborted and suggested that they check in to a hotel for a few days and act as tourists in case the Guardia Civil had received information about their activities. What about the material still in the tyres? asked Mailer. The Spaniards spoke briefly to each other, drove the car behind a wall close by and worked even faster than their Catalan comrades. Mailer and Linenthal went to a bullfight the following day, an experience sought by many American admirers of Hemingway who were already visiting Spain as cultural missionaries, and the day after that the two couples drove back to France.

Bizarrely Mailer was undertaking this albeit amateur intelligence work while his novel was going through the final stages of production and advance publicity. The final proofs had arrived in late February and he had telegraphed minor corrections back shortly before setting off for Barcelona. Soon after his return he received a letter via Rinehart from John Dos Passos, whom he admired even more than he did Hemingway. Dos Passos had read a review copy of *The Naked and the Dead* and praised its author as 'courageous ... a first-rate novelist'. In May Mailer received clippings from reviews, virtually all of which celebrated his achievements, and he wrote to Gwaltney that while he enjoyed the praise, he felt that only one in five 'understood' what he was trying to do.

His disappointment seems unjustified given that *The New York Times Book Review* called it 'undoubtedly the most ambitious novel to be written about the recent conflict', and in *The New York Times* itself Orville Prescott described it as 'the most impressive novel about the Second World War that I have ever read', going on to praise Mailer's 'brilliant self-assurance' and nominate him as 'a conscientious student of John Dos Passos'. Mailer confessed privately to Bea that the comments that brought him close to jubilation came in *Time* on 20 May, which saw the novel as comparable to Tolstoy's *War and Peace*. Since Harvard Mailer had become preoccupied with the Russian novelists of the nineteenth century, Tolstoy predominately but not exclusively. During his time in Japan while he was planning *The Naked and the Dead*, Mailer made use of the forces library to get hold of as many novels by Tolstoy, Dostoevsky and Turgenev as were available. Much later he disclosed to Peter Manso, his second biographer, that he found in them something lacking from modern, particularly American, writers; that they were prophets. His understanding of Marx was simplistic, but he regarded these Russian writers as his literary counterparts, able to diagnose in the present day a forthcoming apocalypse, and it goes without saying that once the reviews of *The Naked and the Dead* began to roll in, he came to treat himself as their noble successor.

Much later Gore Vidal remembered being in Paris with Truman Capote and Tennessee Williams when news reached the city of this spectacular contender for the title of the Great American Novel. None of them had heard of Mailer and were unaware that the author of this book, along with his friends and family, were around a mile away and receiving the same publicity. Vidal: 'I remember thinking meanly: So, somebody did it.' ('The Norman Mailer Syndrome', *The Nation,* January 2nd, 1960)

Literary agents in America wanted to take him on, and Mailer learned that Lillian Hellman was at the front of the queue contending for the rights to adapt the novel for a Broadway play. Enquiries from Hollywood for film adaptations involved everyone from suspect independent producers to the Warner Brothers.

In the middle of all of this he kept in touch with Paco, who told him that the original Madrid expedition might now be safe but that he should use other drivers, that he and Linenthal were being monitored by Spanish intelligence. At Paco's suggestion Mailer spoke to his sister and Barbara Probst, explained to them the dangers involved, and advised them that they should have nothing to do with it. Both immediately insisted that they would go. 'What pleased me,' said Probst, 'was that he treated me like an adult ... He wondered – what would my [Probst's] Spanish experience be? How would it affect me?' (Lennon, p106) Mailer insisted that he and the two Barbaras, as drivers, would go to Chartres and Mont-St-Michel. He wanted to see how they could control a car, and he took time for the three of them, away from Paris, to talk about the risks that the two women were facing. Two friends of Paco, students, had been arrested as insurgents and were being used as slave labourers to build a monument to Franco in the so-called Valley of the Fallen, commemorating the victory of the Falangist forces. It was not difficult to escape from their internment camp, but anyone who did so could easily be tracked down within what was a police state. Paco and a few associates arranged for false papers to be made and messages sent to the young prisoners informing them of how the pick-up would take place. Probst was still only eighteen, and the two girls hid the forged documents in their luggage, picked up Paco's escapees and performed convincingly as two young students returning to Paris with their boyfriends.

Much later Probst recalled the events of mid-summer 1948 with a mixture of subdued pride and disbelief. Mailer himself had paid a forger to prepare two false driving licences for them, and the 'crazy scheme' involved them waiting just off the road in the car while the two men were being led back to the prison camp from Sunday Mass. 'Nicholas Sanchez Albornoz and Manuel la Mananna ... were at the end of the line, as arranged, and they just fell into our car and we drove off.' (Manso, p. 123). They drove to France after Barcelona, finding that the road had four checkpoints over a distance of twenty miles well inside Spain. They had planned to 'leave them off in the mountains, and they'd walk across the border to France, where we'd pick them up on the other side', but the young men chose to leave the car early. The two girls spent five days in a little town 'where we'd arranged to meet the two guys coming out of the mountains. But they didn't show up ...' In Perpignan they were met by a senior figure in the Spanish Resistance, 'feeling dreadful we'd lost them forever'. In Paris they were overjoyed to learn, via an anonymous note, that shepherds, working for the Resistance, had brought the men into France. They went to the Mailers' apartment to celebrate only to find that two days earlier he and Bea had returned to New York.

We cannot be sure of when Mailer decided to leave – since they had arrived, he and Bea had agreed to treat the visit as open-ended and indefinite – but early July seems the likeliest date. Prior to the Spanish expedition he, Bea, Barbara and Fan had decided to take a holiday in Northern Italy, mainly Lake Como; Barney decided to stay over in Paris. They called at the American Express office in Nice to see if there was any further news on reviews and other coverage. Mailer emerged with a gigantic cardboard box, filled largely with a selection of fan mail forwarded by Rinehart. At the top of the pile was a cable directly from Stanley Rinehart informing him that the novel had been number one on

The New York Times bestseller list for four weeks – it would remain there for a further eleven – and that sales were approaching 70,000. According to Barbara 'Norman opened the cable and giggled', read it to the others, and all four found themselves unable to control their laughter. 'Gee, I'm first on the bestseller list!' Norman gasped. Fan, said Bea, replied that 'If anyone ever told me I'd be crazy enough to come on this trip, I would have told them it was impossible', (Mills, p102) which makes little sense, except as record of a mother's overjoyed incomprehension.

After their return to Paris the five members of the family remembered the period as the happiest they had spent in each other's company. 'The greatest book written since *War and Peace*,' Mailer would repeat, and then laugh at himself, and the rest would join him without mocking his claim. Barbara Probst was at dinner and witnessed the spectacle of Barney shaking off his usually quiet, self-contained persona. He addressed Bea: 'You're going back to America', and glancing at his son, 'Norman's going to be famous, and you're going to have a lot of competition.' Probst recalled that 'Bea paled visibly', and Barney suggested she should invest in a classier wardrobe, get a top-class hairdresser, and become 'glamorous'. (Rollyson, p52) It was well meant, a little vulgar, and an accurate premonition. Mailer's emergence as a celebrity would ruin their marriage.

Mailer and Bea flew from Paris to New York on 20 July, a form of travel which in 1948 testified to success. Ten days later Mailer's parents and Barbara took the liner, second class.

Immediately after his arrival Mailer drafted 'A Credo for the Living', quoted at the opening of this chapter. It was his manifesto as a writer and a man. He would not continue to adhere to its pro-Stalinist mantras, the ludicrous vision of Eastern Europe as an idyll of collectivisation, but that was not its true topic. It was about Norman Mailer. Buoyed up by his new status as a man of vision he wanted to hit back at Malaquais, whom he pretended to respect but resented. After *The Naked and the Dead* Mailer was unwilling to entertain opinions that did not accord with what some saw as his 'fearless honesty' and others his conviction that he was never in the wrong.

5

BACK HOME

On returning to the States, Mailer and Bea first moved into the same decrepit Brooklyn apartment around the corner from his parents where he had worked on his outstandingly successful debut novel. Strangely, for someone so widely celebrated, he spent his first month in the city in a state of anonymity, not even informing the Rinehart office that their star was back and willing to respond to the dozens of journalists who were clamouring for interviews. He did, however, make contact with Lillian Hellman, who had cabled him in France about a Broadway adaptation of the novel. She invited him to her Manhattan apartment, and, according to an interview he gave later, she received him in her bedroom, dressed in a sexy nightgown and showing 'a truly formidable bare breast'. Another visitor called from downstairs and she answered, 'Come on up. What do you think we were doing? Fucking?' In her conversation with Manso Hellman reports their exchange as polite, measured and involving none of the so-called 'sexual electricity' that Lennon claims was 'always ... between them'. (Lennon, p108)

By October Mailer was being welcomed into the New York literary in-crowd, but accounts of his performances at drinks parties differ radically, particularly regarding his dress sense. This began with a Rinehart launch event in late September. Horace Sutton, columnist and travel author, spoke later about how Mailer had arrived in a faded tan jacket and trousers, cotton shirt and no tie 'as if he was thumbing his nose at a prestigious group of critics who were gathering to meet him'. (Mills pp105-6) Afterwards there was a contest between myth and actuality. Lillian Ross wrote in *The New Yorker* that she'd 'heard rumors' that the 'rough and ready' new author made a point of arriving at literary gatherings 'wearing sneakers and an old t-shirt', but when she first met him at such an event, she found him in grey tweed, ironed shirt, red and white striped tie and shined leather shoes.

Sort through the reports on how he presented himself and it is evident that apart from the first party at his publishers, where he was dressed informally but not disrespectfully, he planned his own mythology of Norman the anti-establishment ragamuffin. He told Mills of how he collected his initial royalty cheque of $100,000 from the Rinehart office, walked across the street to a bank and asked to open an account. He was, apparently, met by a junior manager whose 'jaw dropped in disbelief' at the size of the deposit, and who 'took a disdainful look' at a man with so much money who was wearing a sweatshirt and sneakers. He did deposit the first draft of the royalties the day he received them, but the amount was $50,000, not $100,000, and people in the Rinehart office recall that he was wearing a sports jacket, loosely knotted tie and cotton trousers.

Much later in his career as a writer Mailer would tire of novels and begin to offer accounts of the real world, himself included, that were often stranger than fiction. Perhaps this was his rehearsal.

He and Bea spent a few weeks in August with Fig Gwaltney and his recent wife, Ecey, in Arkansas. The two men went fishing regularly and were joined by their wives for picnics, swimming and cold beers, and on his return to New York Mailer heard that Malaquais had arrived to deliver lectures at the New School for Social Research. Connected with New York University, the NSSR was politically unaffiliated, but during the interwar years it had become something of a magnet for European exiles who saw Soviet Stalinism and fascism as equally malign.

Malaquais remembers that one day Mailer visited him at his apartment and 'brought over someone by the name of Devlin, who spoke as if he were reading me the most hackneyed brochures of the Communist party ... The man was a drudge.' (Manso, p129) Charlie Devlin had been one of the figures who encouraged Mailer in his literary enthusiasms before he joined the army, and in 1948 the two of them were closely aligned in terms of their affection for the Soviet Union. Neither had any time for a proper understanding of Marxism or the monstrous nature of Stalin's dictatorship, but anything likely to cause offence or outrage within the American establishment was alluring enough.

For the subsequent six months there was a rerun of the Paris exchanges between Mailer and Malaquais, which took on the air of a farce.

It is likely that quite early on Malaquais realised that Mailer had deafened himself to everything he said. He was not attempting to indoctrinate or bully his friend, but he was dumbfounded by Mailer's apparent reluctance to even discern an idea before rejecting it. Malaquais agreed to do the French translation of *The Naked and the Dead*, for a fee of $2,000. Mailer thought this stingy and added a thousand from his expanding bank account. A few years later Malaquais remarked to Manso that 'his inscription in my copy read: "To Jean and what has been a pleasant relationship until now and will continue, I hope, for years – Norman Mailer." "Until now …", I'm not sure what that means.' He knew exactly what Mailer's ambiguous qualifier meant.

Malaquais was a political purist in that while he maintained a commitment to the beauty of Marxist ideals, he accepted with weary resignation that such blissful utopias would never come about. He was rather like a priest who loved scripture, the Old and New Testaments and the benevolence of the Church but had lost his faith in an afterlife. Feeling that it would be wrong to force his sceptical position on Mailer he recommended to him the books that had led him to it.

Marx's *Das Kapital* is the centrepiece of communist philosophy; Boris Souvarine's *Stalin: A Critical Survey of Bolshevism* (1939) is an exposure of the horrible consequences of the misapplication of Marxist principles; and the *Report of Court Proceedings in the Case of the Anti-Soviet 'Bloc of Rights and Trotskyites'* … (1938) was an entirely falsified account of the show trials of anti-Stalinists during the 1930s compiled by the People's Commissariat of Justice of the USSR. Malaquais also asked Mailer once more to read Koestler's first-hand account of what had happened under Stalin and wondered how Mailer would deal with this competition between utopianism, candour and mendacity. At the end of March 1949 he would find out.

The National Council of (the) Arts, Sciences and Professions (NCASP) was the American counterpart of several European groups such as the World Peace Council (WPC) and the Soviet Peace Conference.

The latter was based in the Soviet bloc, while the WPC had offices in various parts of Western and Eastern Europe. The common cause was the avoidance of armed conflict between what was now two polarised superstates, made up of Western democracies and the areas of Eastern Europe taken over by the Soviet Union. Czechoslovakia was the final central European country to fall to the communists, in 1948, a few months before Mao Zedong's Chinese Communist Party would triumph over the Nationalist government.

The NCASP claimed to be apolitical, but many of its more prominent figures had been outspoken supporters of Wallace's Progressives, including Dorothy Parker, Charlie Chaplin, Arthur Miller, Dashiell Hammett, Lillian Hellman and a large number of eminent academics, some of whom Mailer had known at Harvard. Despite the widespread publicity surrounding the Wallace presidential campaign of 1948 the Progressives gained the lowest ever percentage of votes for an established party. The Republicans, Democrats and a large number of media outlets had insinuated that the Progressives were pro-Soviet and would undermine the United States' position as the defender of democracy. The Progressives had maintained that their only objective was the maintenance of world peace, and their shell-shocked supporters sought reassurance in the NCASP, specifically at the Cultural and Scientific Conference for World Peace which it sponsored and which was due to be held on 25–29 March 1949 at the Waldorf Hotel in New York City. There were almost three thousand delegates from around the world, including the poet Robert Lowell, the Russian writer A. A. Fadeyev and his compatriot the composer Dmitri Shostakovich.

Mailer was advertised as one of the plenary speakers, and he delivered his address on the 26th. The audience, which included Malaquais and Bea, began to cheer him before he mounted the podium. He had over the previous six months become the most outspoken of the new post-war generation of literary writers, peppering every interview supposedly on *The Naked and the Dead* with controversial comments on what was now routinely referred to as the Cold War. Playing on his self-fashioned mythology as an outsider he wore a sweatshirt at the Waldorf, giving the impression that he had come straight from the dockyards. Many in the audience later reported that his face whitened as he prepared himself to speak, and though his address of roughly forty minutes was not recorded, a few passages stuck in the minds of those present, notably his opening announcement that he was a 'Trojan Horse':

> I don't believe in peace conferences. They won't do any good. So long as there is state capitalism, there is going to be war ... both Russia and America are moving radically towards state capitalism ... the differences between them will be cultural differences, minor deviations, and ... there is no future in fighting for one side or the other. (Lennon, p116-7)

If present developments continued 'we would be put in concentration camps', and writers were powerless to arrest this journey towards apocalypse. There was polite applause, a few boos, but the overwhelming mood was perplexity, in that no one was sure of what he was talking about. Norman Podhoretz, a bitter anti-Stalinist, afterwards expressed his belief that Mailer was evidently no longer a 'fellow traveller'. Lillian Hellman, however, was disappointed that he had become a 'Trotskyist' and put this down to the influence of Malaquais, a 'phony'. Irving Howe, an ally of Podhoretz, was confused, describing Mailer's as 'a third camp position – a plague on both your houses', but that at their core his opinions were 'dubious and underdeveloped'. Malaquais found himself utterly dumbfounded and was unable to reply to Bea when she asked him to sum up her husband's position. From the fragments of the speech that we have, we might assume that he was regurgitating passages from Marx's *Kapital* on the ineluctable forces of history, in the manner of a feckless undergraduate preparing a paper half an hour before the seminar. That, however, is a charitable estimation. More likely, what the audience witnessed was the advent of Mailer's signature style as a speaker, and often a writer, with premises shifting apparently at random and rallying cries for this or that marshalled to shock, impress, or simply fill space.

Mailer and Bea had first visited Hollywood shortly before the 1948 election. He had been invited to give a speech at an event held by movie stars who were Progressive Party supporters, the principal purpose of which was to raise money for the so-called Hollywood Ten who had refused to tell a congressional committee whether they were or had been members of the Communist Party. McCarthyism had begun before anyone had even heard of the senator. Stardom of a sort had greeted Mailer on his return from Paris, but he was unprepared for the events that followed his arrival in Los Angeles. The vast majority of those involved in the film industry – notably writers, producers, directors and celebrity actors – were aligned with the liberal left, and the prospect of meeting the celebrated literary newcomer from the East Coast with radical opinions electrified the city. On the evening of their arrival Mailer and Bea were taken from the airport by limousine to the mansion of Gene Kelly. Present were Edward G. Robinson, Shelley Winters, Montgomery Clift, Farley Granger and Burt Lancaster, but these were early arrivals. As Winters later reported, 'Everyone who was anyone was at this party, AND I MEAN EVERYONE, in Hollywood', (Lennon, p111) including Marlon Brando, Hedy Lamarr and John Garfield. Nine months later, in June 1949, Mailer and Bea drove across America with all they owned to settle in Los Angeles for an indefinite period. Their first home there was a rented two-bedroom wood-panelled house in the hills in Laurel Canyon, above Hollywood geographically but well below it socially.

Two weeks before they moved in Billy Wilder began work directing one of the most celebrated films of the twentieth century. Ostensibly, the centrepiece of *Sunset Boulevard* is Norma Desmond, a long-forgotten star from the silent movie era who is hopelessly intent on a comeback. In truth the satirical target is Hollywood itself, a city of fantasies and ludicrous ambitions; hilarious, unless you are part of it. Mailer's year in the city would have provided excellent material for a follow-up. He contacted Malaquais and his wife, asking them to join him. His friend had written screenplays and directed several films in France, the kind of high-art independent productions that LA producers would generally regard as worthless. But Malaquais had the practical experience that Mailer lacked. The house was too small for both couples, so shortly after the Malaquais' arrival they took a five-bedroom, Spanish-style property a street away from the legendary Sunset Boulevard where super-rich Hollywood celebrities had lived for the previous three decades. The Mailers' first child, Susan, was born a few days before the move.

Before leaving New York, Mailer had been in contact with Samuel Goldwyn, probably the most powerful producer in the American movie industry. Goldwyn knew of the impact and sales figures of *The Naked and the Dead* but had not read the book. In his view, if 200,000 people liked the written version even more would want to see it on screen. By the time they arranged to meet him, however, Goldwyn was preoccupied by the idea of an adaptation of Nathanael West's *Miss Lonelyhearts*, on the turmoils of being a newspaper advice columnist.

Malaquais:

Goldwyn met us in his bathrobe. The agent told him that we – or rather I – had a story, so it was up to us to do the talking. Goldwyn stood there making comments, all the while pushing his false teeth back into place ... and a few days later we got the contract for $50,000 to write an original screenplay, with Montgomery Clift and Charles Boyer in view ... (Manso, p. 138)

It was not until they saw a hard copy of the contract that they realised that they'd been signed up to do an adaptation of West's novel and not, as they'd proposed, *The Naked and the Dead*. The next day Goldwyn's assistant showed them three luxuriously appointed offices, available rent-free, where they could work on the screenplay. Why three, they asked? The two main offices were each furnished with a large managerial desk and leather swivel chair plus a smaller desk and chair and a typewriter. In the third there was a couch, a liquor cabinet and a bed. Would they prefer the secretaries to be 'French, Spanish or Italian', they were asked? According to Malaquais their options had nothing to do with nationality or background, but rather which of 'our amorous interests' would be 'catered to'. Much later, in *The Deer Park*, Mailer would cast a cold eye upon Hollywood as a pit of depraved hypocrisy, but from what we know of his time there he was keeping quiet about himself as a participant.

He spent much of his time with Shelley Winters, who had gained a reputation with secondary roles but would not become an A-list star until the 1950s when *A Place in the Sun* won her an Oscar nomination. For a while she shared a house with Marilyn Monroe, but she despised the

Hollywood stereotype of the 'blonde bombshell', despite being blonde and indisputably attractive. Their friendship began in August when Bea gave birth to Susan. 'Norman,' Winters told Manso, 'never sucked up to the power guys.' The house he shared with Jean and Galy Malaquais was, she observed, chosen 'because it looked ramshackle', and when Charlie Chaplin and his wife, Oona, arrived for drinks the taxi driver apologised for taking them to what was self-evidently the wrong address. She also remembers playing tennis with Mailer at the Chaplins' grand residence. 'I had a gingham romper on, not sexy shorts or anything, and blue sneakers instead of white ones. Norman was wearing brown pants and a plaid shirt and basketball sneakers. Everybody else had whites, but we didn't give a shit.'

> Norman, Burt [Lancaster], and I were having dinner at a Mexican restaurant, and Burt left me alone with Norman ... So he came back to my apartment. I had a leopard couch, the whole thing [and] ... I knew that Lancaster was being unfaithful to me with his wife. Norman had great, piercing blue eyes ... back then they were a bit like Paul Newman's. (Manso, p. 141)

Mark Linenthal says that their affair was brief, almost cordial. Winters: 'He's not capable of sleeping with a starlet and using her and then just saying, "that was great, kid. Goodbye." Unlike most men in Hollywood, he's actually a feminist. He sees women as people, not just sex objects.' She was obviously unaware of the fact that while he was seeing her, he had made use of Goldwyn's offer of a secretary – Spanish, and weekends only – and was having an affair with Lois Wilson, also an actress though not quite a starlet. Alice Linenthal believes that the arrival of Susan was the beginning of the end of the Mailers' marriage. 'Bea was pregnant, and Norman was being courted by the Hollywood CP [Communist Party], being treated like a star [and] ... Pretty, sexy girls would come over and sit down and be introduced to "Norman Mailer, the writer" ... The baby was quite imminent, and I remember Norman saying to us rather touchingly, "This is the last time we're ever going to be alone together."' (Manso, p143-4) He meant that while the four of them might meet again, they would not do so as two couples.

The arrangement with Goldwyn collapsed because the producer was well attuned to what would sell to a mass audience and how to sell it. He rejected drafts of the screenplay because Mailer and Malaquais had turned it into a sermon on the destructive vacuousness of the media. Goldwyn acknowledged that this was a commendable theme and one that would guarantee financial losses. According to Malaquais he wanted a story about how 'good sentiments would be rewarded and bad sentiments punished' and said to Norman, 'Mailer, please stop this professional writer shit and start writing.' (Lennon, p122) Mailer treasured this comment as his own customised contribution to the now legendary collection of Goldwynisms – including 'I'll give you a definite maybe' and 'Any man who goes to a psychiatrist ought to have his head examined.'

Mailer and Malaquais discussed *Miss Lonelyhearts* with several more producers and directors willing to share the rights with Goldwyn or buy them, and on each occasion they were met with the same enthusiasm, followed by conditions that caused them to back out. Motion pictures, they were advised, need to fill movie houses to make money, and to do that they had to make the picture-goer feel a little better about things, rather than leave the theatre contemplating existential trauma.

Malaquais remembers that there were a great number of meetings with film-makers who wanted the rights to *The Naked and the Dead*; at least fifty, he thinks. The war had ended only five years earlier, and novels based on personal experience of it were appearing regularly – but there were no movies based on these books. Memorably, the new movie company founded by Burt Lancaster, with Harold Hecht as a partner, was committed to the project. John Garfield, who had received an Oscar nomination in 1939, was keen to play Sergeant Croft, while Lancaster himself wanted the part of Cummings with a little less sadism and no hints at homosexuality. The venture flopped mainly because projected costs of re-creating open-air action scenes from the Pacific islands were becoming exorbitant.

6

THE DEER PARK

Mailer, Bea and Susan drove back to New York, via Chicago, at the end of May 1949. They stayed briefly in Brooklyn to introduce the Mailers to their grandchild and travelled to Boston to see Bea's parents for the same reason. From there they took the ferry to Provincetown and rented a large nineteenth-century house, near the beach. Once more, Mailer felt that the relaxed atmosphere of New England provided a perfect environment for the cultivation of ideas, this time on political extremism and its crazed outcomes, the themes of his second novel, *Barbary Shore*.

Shortly before he left California, he wrote to Gwaltney that Hollywood had been a 'sad mistake', and he did not mean that he was disappointed by his encounters with film-makers. 'Hollywood stinks,' he added, because Bea had become 'the Mother' and little more: 'Never sleeps at night, pushes me around. I just carry a fucking guilt complex all the time.' (Lennon, p126) His guilt ranged beyond his failure to help out as a father. As Shelley Winters reported, the birth of Susan caused him to relax his resistance to the fame-hungry girls who were drawn to him.

As they drove across America and performed as joyful parents for their respective families they were lying to most people they knew, but both were resigned to the fact that their marriage would soon be over.

On 15 August 1950 Mailer completed the first draft of *Barbary Shore*, and two weeks after that they travelled to Putney, Vermont, to look at a 150-year-old farmhouse. In October they bought it for $9,000, the cash equivalent today of about $120,000, but given the relationship between property prices and the cost of living closer to three quarters of a million.

It had twelve rooms, a wealth of what the realty agent called 'character', some outbuildings and about two acres of land. Mailer later reflected on the irony of the move. It was, he later claimed, their final attempt to reignite something of the early years of their relationship. They'd have a spacious place that was for the first time their own, far beyond the city, with enough rooms to provide generous accommodation to guests. They now saw little of Malaquais, but he had left an imprint on both of them as a mischievous Svengali, confident that neither really understood far-left ideology but were addicted to its social vogueishness. Mailer later described *Barbary Shore* in *Advertisements for Myself* as an 'insane insight into the psychic mysteries of Stalinists, secret policemen, narcissists, children, Lesbians, hysterics, revolutionaries ...' (p. 94). One review judged it to be a piece of 'lumpy and graceless prose ... strewn with quasi-intellectual chatter and stiff with echoes of radical jargon [and] "progressive journalism"'. (Irving Howe, *The Nation*, 16 June 1951). It is too chaotic to be treated as an allegory, but it does seem to give the thumbs up to Trotskyism over Stalinism, has no time at all for the 'fascist-consumerism' of America, and one has to feel slightly amused that shortly after he finished it its author joined the New England squirearchy.

Once more Bea tried to write a book, though nothing she later stated indicates whether it was a piece of fiction or something else. Mailer, kindly enough, claimed it would have prefigured feminist writings of the 1960s. They had visits from people they knew in the New York metropolis, but by the end of 1950 Mailer had become the equivalent of commuter between Putney village and the city. Ostensibly he met up with editors from Rinehart and other writers with whom he'd discuss new projects. In truth he wanted to get away from the stifling atmosphere of the farmhouse. Bea was aware that he was still a magnet for young women and that his time away was an excuse for one-night stands, but neither of them seemed able to address such things explicitly.

Mailer had first met Dan Wolf when the latter was a student of Malaquais' at the New School for Social Research, and Wolf now arranged for him to borrow an apartment in East 64th Street to use for his regular visits to the city. It was during one of these, when the two men were sharing a bottle of bourbon in a bar, that the conversation drifted towards what Wolf reported to Lennon as 'Norman ... making one of his big moves', but we will never know if he was referring to his decision to end his marriage or his wish to find a woman for another of his then habitual affairs. Wolf told him of a Spanish-Peruvian woman called Adele Morales, a painter with whom he had had a brief relationship two years earlier shortly before she moved in with Wolf's friend, war veteran and football player Ed Fancher. She had, barely a week before Wolf mentioned her to Mailer, ended her affair with a man who was making news among the more progressive circles in the city. His first novel had just been published, carrying the recommendation of the equally radical newcomer Allen Ginsberg. Publicity was boosted by gossip surrounding his arrest six years before as a material witness in the murder of David Kammerer. He was called Jack Kerouac.

Wolf phoned Adele and asked her to join them in Norman's borrowed apartment. She arrived by cab, excited by the prospect of meeting the famous novelist, and the two of them had sex several times that night.

Adele's description of how she felt is certainly vivid.

> I was feeling a real contact with him, as if someone had turned on a switch releasing the current between us. I'd never known anyone with such charisma, even Kerouac ... My heart beating, I leaned forward and kissed him. A kiss into closeness and sweet lust. A roller coaster going up and up and then the breathless, down and down. We held on, like it would never be again, and then a last kiss, sweet with the taste of each other ... (*The Last Party*, pp. 67–8)

Vivid, and generous, given that it was written long after their marriage ended following his attempt to murder her.

Adele was born in New York in 1925, her mother Spanish and her father native Peruvian. She majored in art at the Washington Irving High School and then studied at the Hans Hofmann School of Fine Arts; by the time she met Mailer she was impressing gallery owners with her own Expressionist paintings. Income from sales was supplemented by designer work for department store windows. Her striking dark good looks were set off by a taste for colourful gypsy-like outfits. She had no time for the opinion that free-spirited women should enjoy their freedom only with caution, frequenting as she did the bars of the city favoured by writers, artists and gangsters, but never feeling the need for a friend or chaperone. 'She,' said Mailer, 'was a strong woman. She profoundly resented the female role ... She was ... if anything, stronger than me.' (Dearborn, p81) Quite so, but he was here describing Bea. The women were very similar temperamentally, and both were attractive, but what drew him more to Adele was her status as a cultural fashion accessory. All of her partners had committed themselves to political or artistic indignation. One has to have doubts about Adele's recollection of their first night together as transformative, at least in that it marked the beginning of a special relationship. It might better be treated as the prelude to a prolonged bout of promiscuity and heedlessness, for both of them.

Irving Howe's review of *Barbary Shore* might seem abrasive, but it was one of the more generous. Of the twenty that appeared in national magazines and newspapers only two, Howe's included, offered it slight, begrudging praise. The rest dismissed it as variously as 'paceless, tasteless' (*Time*), a 'case of monolithic, flawless badness' (*The New Yorker*) and 'incomprehensible' (*The New York Times*). Many were stunned that a writer who had begun his career with a universally acclaimed bestseller could produce something so terrible. Some of them even questioned the legitimacy of Rinehart as a publisher of quality fiction: did Mailer's editors not read what they allowed to go into print?

The rooming house of the story is based on the rough brownstones in Brooklyn where Mailer had lived with Bea, particularly the less salubrious ones which the income from *The Naked and the Dead* eventually enabled them to avoid. But the setting is inconsequential because the characters themselves displace any proper sense of place and context. Lovett, the narrator, confesses to being stricken by a form of amnesia, unclear about the nature of his past and as a consequence confused by the present and what the future might involve. He is a shell-shocked aspiring writer and even questions his recollection of having served in the war, and his resemblance to his creator would have been self-evident to readers vaguely familiar with Mailer's publicity profiles. Mailer was not traumatised by front-line service, but this was a case of self-dramatisation. Lovett and his fellow roomers – Hollingsworth (a secret policeman, probably FBI), McLeod (veteran of the Bolshevik Revolution, now gone bad), McLeod's wife, the landlady Guinevere (probably embodying the US proletariat, if such exists), and Lannie Madison (who might well be a Trotskyite) – are almost laudable examples of how not to create fictional characters. None of them has anything resembling a personality. Rather, they are hammered into the book as avatars of ideological states of mind or creeds. Lovett is McLeod's political pupil, and the latter might be Malaquais or at least Mailer's misrepresentation of him.

In the closing quarter McLeod indulges in politically charged monologues, and it is implied that if McLeod could offer Lovett a secure template for his muddled, half-formed beliefs then the young man might suddenly acquire a sense of his role in the world.

An essay called 'The Meaning of Western Defense' appears in *Advertisements for Myself* in an edited form, largely to disguise its original date of composition and publication. It was originally called 'The Defense of the Compass' and appeared first in an obscure volume called *The Western Defences*, edited by J. G. Smyth and published in 1951. Look closely and the similarities between the essay and McLeod's ramblings in the later part of the novel are striking. Mailer first of all attempts to explain why the Stalinist economic system is performing less than perfectly and he comes up with 'Its chronic crisis has been the inability to increase production organically rather than the need to find a market for surplus profit.' (*AFM*, p. 204). I have no idea what this means and nor, I suspect, did Mailer, having probably borrowed it from somewhere else – possibly Malaquais – without attempting to digest it. He goes on to propose that if the productive capacities of Western Europe, 'specifically West Germany, France, England, and to lesser degree the Scandinavian countries and Italy ... could be diverted into the Soviet orbit ... The economic anemia could be solved.' (*AFM*, p. 205). He is vague about how this might occur, but proposes that while the United States would be dismayed by the outcome, World War Three could be avoided, and he foresees America eventually becoming attracted to joining the community of global socialism. It was the era of radical ideas, but even the most indulgent psychiatrist would have suspected a case of delusion here. In the novel Mailer, through Lovett, accuses his mentor, McLeod-Malaquais, of misleading him, rather as a distracted, shiftless student might hold his tutor responsible for his awful exam results.

One of the puzzling features of the novel is McLeod's concealment of the so-called 'little object', the nature or content of which remains undisclosed. It does, however, seem capable of providing a magical insight into the puzzles surrounding the roomers and their apocalyptic speculations; mainly what will and should happen to the world. The 'little object' remains a secret, just as Malaquais' disquisitions to Mailer endured for his pupil as gnomic and indecipherable. The novel is, in truth, about a novelist who is either unable or too lazy to come to a clear understanding of what he is writing about, and how he blames his puzzlement on the Buddha-like anti-hero, McLeod, or Malaquais.

While *Barbary Shore* was in production with Rinehart, Mailer began his third novel. He would base it on his experiences in Los Angeles and in June decided that it would be useful to revisit the place, to reinforce his sense of how it looked and, more importantly, the way people behaved. His friend Mickey Knox planned on driving to the West Coast to visit the actress Lois Andrews, who was already married to the actor Steve Brodie. Mailer had made arrangements to meet another Lois, Wilson, to restart their brief affair of 1949. Wilson would become the model for Dorothea O'Faye of *The Deer Park*, a not particularly flattering portrait given that Dorothea is presented as the louche degenerate host of parties at her home, 'The Hangover', where sexual inhibition is all but forbidden. Lois did introduce Mailer to two women who already knew him by reputation. Uncertain of which he found the most attractive he suggested that the three of them should go to bed, allowing each to compare his performance. Lois would act as impartial assessor. He reported his activities in a letter to Adele, assuming that this would be taken as a note of convivial intimacy – he was showing he could behave as she had done – but he misread the situation. She retaliated by having sex with a married couple, sending him a detailed account of the, almost, simultaneous sensations of heterosexuality and lesbianism. Eventually, he would hit back by recreating her in *The Deer Park* as Elena Esposito, a woman who relishes promiscuity in the same way that a chronic alcoholic enjoys drink.

During his time in California he, often with Knox, drifted between LA and Palm Springs. In the latter he took notes on the mansions built by stars and moguls which would become the basis for Desert D'Or of the novel. His letter to Adele was honest enough in that he told her of his fling with Lois, along with the threesome, but not of the three other young actresses with whom he'd indulged in the special brand of hypersexuality that seemed to come with the resort.

On his return to New York Mailer took a loft apartment in Monroe Street, or to be more accurate, two. One was for Adele, the other for him, and a shared bathroom linked them. It was, she later recalled, a declaration of their individuality. Following this they moved to two apartments on the same floor at 37 1st Avenue. Mailer rented them even though he had the money to purchase a far more comfortable property in a better area. While keeping things from the superintendent, he knocked down most of the adjoining wall, smuggling bricks and plaster down to the trash cans, which caused complaints from the collectors, who found themselves struggling with the weight of material that seemed to have come from a hidden building site. Despite having no experience as bricklayer, joiner or plumber, Mailer took it upon himself to give a unique character to these eccentric and spacious living areas; he installed a bath, shower and laundry in one of the bedrooms and removed even more walls to create, as Wolf later put it, 'a space for a salon'. The place resembled the kind of raw, undecorated interiors now fashionable in urban homes and restaurants. It became popular with writers and artists from downtown New York – Adele knew Mark Rothko, Franz Kline, Jackson Pollock and Willem de Kooning and invited them all.

The critic John Aldridge published *After the Lost Generation* (1951) shortly after Mailer and Adele met. In it he compared the post-war writers with their 1920s counterparts, naming the likes of Mailer, Vidal, Capote and Irwin Shaw as the successors to Hemingway, Fitzgerald and Dos Passos. He saw Mailer's 'salon' as the New York equivalent of Gertrude Stein's Paris apartment of a generation before. The 1st Avenue loft soon became the nexus for figures who would be associated variously with the Beat movement and New Journalism, but its main attraction was its reputation as a site for sexual licentiousness.

One evening Mailer held court on the subject of orgies and their benefits for all involved. Adele, apparently impatient, took off all of her clothes and suggested trial and error. Nothing ensued, at least in terms of sex, but Mailer apparently beamed in pride at his new partner's performance. Charlie Chaplin, Marlon Brando and Montgomery Clift visited when away from California and Mailer found them young female and sometimes male New Yorkers willing to service stars in his spare bedroom.

Malaquais remembers one evening. 'There were about fifty people there. Marlon Brando was sitting with a girl on his lap – he looked like a Buddha, like the man he'd impersonate in *Apocalypse Now*.' (Manso, p. 172). Word had reached people from outside the cultural establishment. Three or four punks crashed the party and asked for a girl, Mailer swore at them, told them to get out, and during the ensuing fight one of the invaders hit him on the head with a hammer. Despite blood pouring onto the floor, a medical student thought there was no evidence of a cracked skull. 'I don't know where Clift was throughout all this, probably off drunk somewhere, but he certainly didn't jump in to help,' Adele recalled. Thereafter, when Mailer left the building after dusk, he carried with him a small bag of nickels as a make-do knuckleduster. Everyone who knew him was aware that it was pointless to advise him to move. The loft had become part of a performance; people were attracted to it because of its cache as a place where political or cultural radicalism, along with other forms of intemperance, were conditions of entry. The setting – off-centre and faintly menacing – seemed enticing.

Ecey Gwaltney felt that his break with Bea and his relationship with Adele were part of his installation of himself as a key figure in a homegrown version of the Paris 'lost generation'.

Looking back, though, I don't think we realized what a traumatic time that was for Norman ... maybe Adele was a way of breaking with his family ... Adele was such a beautiful, exotic creature ... It was almost as if he was enjoying the rebellion – he'd rebelled and gone to this cold-water flat in a bad part of town. Living there, keeping Adele pacified, it was a balancing act, a show, a game ... It seemed to me it was the kind of tension that part of him found enjoyable. (Manso, p. 170)

Mailer might have caused the tensions that finally undid their marriage, but Bea wasted no time in creating a new life of her own. Dan Wolf had introduced Mailer to Adele, but within a few months of the beginning of their largely clandestine relationship he arranged for Bea to meet an athletic, charming Mexican man called Steve Sanchez, whom she would marry in 1952. Bea was happy enough in her new relationship, at first, but later referred to Wolf as a 'pimp'. The Vermont house was sold for little more than they'd paid for it and the money, along with everything else in their bank accounts, was divided equally between them. In an interview with Mills, Bea reflected on their year in Hollywood in 1949–50. 'I think he was so afraid of instincts in himself that would make him what he actually later became that he checked them abnormally.' If only she knew.

His novel on Hollywood, *The Deer Park*, was not published until 1955, and Bea's comments on their time in California are apposite. Hollywood, at least its most debauched aspects, did indeed cause him to acknowledge that he was much the same as everyone else who indulged their fantasises in a town dedicated to hedonism. But *The Deer Park* is not confessional, let alone remorseful. Instead, it reflects Mailer's private struggles between what he got up to in Hollywood and what he tried to cover up.

The first-person narrator is called Sergius O'Shaugnessy, who sounds like someone who has escaped from Joyce's *Finnegans Wake*, but as Sergius makes clear his name is a corrupt agglomeration of his myriad legacies, invented by unnamed officials after his adoption. At six feet two and with blonde hair and blue eyes he is unlikely to be mistaken for a Brooklyn Jew. For readers who knew Mailer, however, Sergius would have come across as Norman arriving at a party in ludicrous fancy dress, raised heels and a wig; a bizarre self-conscious failure to disguise himself.

He is an ex-serviceman – a fighter pilot in Korea rather than infantryman in the Second World War – who arrives in Desert D'Or, an undisguised version of Palm Springs, with $14,000 won at poker. Add to this the $20,000 paid to him by the head of Supreme Studios for the screenplay of his wartime experiences and this makes more than half of the amount offered to Mailer and Malaquais and shared between them. Sergius turns down several other acting and production deals which would be based on his life – a preposterous scenario since he has published nothing about it and his time in action was short-lived given that he was discharged for a vaguely described psychological condition. Secretly he wants to be a writer, and he is not prepared to prostitute his so far unrehearsed talents, along with his life story, for what he refers to as a 'slob movie'. The majority of people who bought *The Deer Park* would have been aware of Mailer's excursion to Hollywood at the close of the 1940s – it was very well publicised in interviews and articles – though they would not have had knowledge of what happened there and afterwards when he was writing it. In an interview with Lyle Stuart (*Exposé*, December 1955) shortly after the novel was published, Mailer came close admitting this:

> Stuart: Isn't *The Deer Park* really every young man's dream of paradise?
> Mailer: I'm beginning to wonder ...
> Stuart: Isn't this book really a love sonnet directed at the film industry?
> Mailer: Let's say a sonnet of love and hate.

The closing chapters of the book are absurd and revealing. Sergius gives up on everything Hollywood might have offered – fame, sex, money, literary prestige – and moves south to become a bullfighter in Mexico (anyone not living in a cave would have recognised the nod towards Hemingway). We say goodbye to him in his loft apartment in New York, where he might become a writer, but we are never clear on whether he realises his ambitions. It is a messy autobiographical novel in which Mailer can't seem to decide whether he wishes to apologise, perhaps to Bea, or to cover his tracks. It must be said that there are few other first-person narrators in fiction who merit comparison with Sergius. He records, often in vivid detail, the foulness of Desert D'Or and its inhabitants – sex in telephone booths, fellatio as a payment for a bit-part in a movie, etc. – but we never really learn of his opinion on all this, let alone his involvement in it. He comes across as being in the story but regretting his association with the sad and nasty individuals he observes. Herman Teppis is a combination of Samuel Goldwyn and his far more horrible associate, Louis B. Mayer, who was an alleged serial rapist. Harvey Weinstein would be their twenty-first-century heir apparent.

Sergius mutated in various drafts from a central character to one of numerous figures, whose thoughts and activities were described by a third-person narrator, to his eventual manifestation as the rather shifty, evasive presence who tells on everyone else but largely keeps himself to himself. It is evident from the manuscripts that Mailer was desperately attempting to hide from the world of Desert D'Or, or to be more accurate his memories of his involvement in it.

There are certainly aspects of Adele in the former flamenco dancer Elena Esposito, in that the two share stereotypically fiery Latin American temperaments, along with amoral dispositions. Elena has casual affairs with at least three of the significant male characters, a record not unlike Adele's when she met Mailer. There is, however, nothing between her and Sergius. He observes and reports on her from a distance, without explicit moral judgement but with a faint whiff of distaste. It should be noted that while Adele's apparent taste for promiscuity very much attracted her to Mailer when they met, he became uneasy about it as their relationship progressed. Essentially, he was a hypocrite hoping that his partner would subdue her dissolute sexual inclinations while he could indulge his.

Sergius has one affair, which lasts for most of the novel, with the outstandingly beautiful and sexy movie star Lulu Meyers. Some aspects of Adele are borrowed for her too, at least in the sense that she comes across as a nymphomaniac. She shows no inclination to have sex with anyone other than Sergius, but at the same time she seems unable, when in his company, to do anything else.

The amalgam of Elena, observed from a distance by Sergius and Lulu, is an accurate reflection of Mailer's confusions over Adele. Shortly after they met, he began to keep a private journal, the first parts of which record his dismay about his future as a writer, specifically the damning reviews and poor sales of *Barbary Shore*. By early 1952, when he had completed the first one hundred and forty pages of *The Deer Park*, Adele features very prominently.

Feb 22: Right now, today, the thing with Adele seems hopeless, with no future. I cannot conceive of myself as married to her. We drag upon each other so, we exhaust each other like leeches turned sucker to sucker. Without sex, I wonder if there would be anything at all in the relationship other than need. (Mailer's untitled 1952 Journal, quoted by Lennon, p. 142)

Read Sergius's account of his relationship with Lulu and the parallels and contrasts are striking. Lulu leaves him, and though he is not particularly pleased, he accepts her departure with sanguine resignation. In the journal, Mailer is torn between his dissatisfaction with what he and Adele have become and his fear of losing her. 'Yet a week ago, I felt very much in love with her ... I felt warm and close to Adele.' It is as though Mailer was using Sergius as his preferred, more durable fictional proxy.

Sergius is fascinated by his lover as a woman who has an insatiable appetite for sex, but he does not find this objectionable or a sign that she exists in an emotional vacuum. He is similar to her in that whatever affection there is between them is equalled by their addiction to physical pleasure, yet she presides over their relationship:

For odd hours, during those interludes she called at her caprice, things had come around a bit. To my idea of an interlude which must have left her exhausted, she coached me by degrees to something different. Which was all right with me. (*The Deer Park*, p. 136)

In an undated passage in the journal Mailer offers a vivid and less inhibited account of his sex life with Adele.

And yet she's beautiful as a Gauguin and all fuck. It is the adolescent hungers which never die, the idea that I am making love to a woman who is all fuck, who exists only to deploy herself sensually for me which furnishes such excitement ... She enjoys sex so much because it is dirty to her, because she is raped, ravished, taken, ground into nothing, and repaid with the sweetest kind of pleasure. It is probably the nature of women when all superstructure and complexity is cut away to be naturally, amoral whore and tender mother. (Mailer's untitled 1952 Journal, quoted by Lennon, p. 140)

Within a few short sentences Adele shifts between roles as sex maniac, decadent aficionado of pure filth and a woman who seems to take pleasure in being raped. In the novel, which is essentially Sergius's journal, he cleans up his account.

> Lulu's taste was for games, and if she lay like a cinder under the speed of my sprints, her spirits improved with a play. I was sure no two people ever had done such things nor even thought of them. We were great lovers I felt in my pride; I had pity for the hordes who could know none of this. Yes, Lulu was sweet. She would never allow comparison. This was the best. I was superb. She was superb. We were beyond all. (*The Deer Park*, p. 136)

In spring 1952 Mailer was invited to give one of the papers at a symposium plenary called 'Our Country and Our Culture', organised by the *Partisan Review*. The magazine had been founded in 1934 and was dedicated to radicalism in the arts and politics, committed resolutely to avant garde modernism and to various forms of radical left-wing ideas. Some were anxious about a repeat performance of his lecture at the Waldorf three years earlier where he had seemed to condemn both America and the Soviet Union as moving towards fascism. Others disapproved of a writer who had become famous by writing a novel, *The Naked and the Dead*, that was unashamedly conservative in the sense that the proletariat could read it; they favoured the kind of thing produced by Gertrude Stein or James Joyce.

He began: 'I think I ought to declare straightaway that I am in almost total disagreement with the assumptions of this symposium.' Everyone was stunned, because the symposium was not based on anything like a consensus of 'assumptions'. Mailer went on to condemn the expectation that a writer should 'accept the American reality, to integrate himself'. Instead, he advocated self-willed 'alienation', the exchange of 'participation in the rigors of American life' for 'silence, exile and cunning'. No one could make sense of what he meant, but there were murmurs of approval for something that sounded suitably unconventional and idiosyncratic. His vague, puzzling ruminations were prompted by his attempt to find a role for Sergius in the country and culture of his ongoing novel. Sergius would indeed become the individual who chooses 'exile and cunning' over being 'integrated into his society'. During the following two years, while he was completing, or rather perpetually rewriting, the novel, Mailer went for the opposite of his sermon on austerity – unrestrained hedonism.

He and Adele kept the Brooklyn apartment but spent almost as much time in Provincetown, where they had a twelve-month rental on a spacious timbered property, once more close to the beach. Adele began to associate with a large number of wealthy New York figures, mostly women, who had gone to art school and had enough money not to worry about how much their work fetched at galleries in the city. Norman and Adele had by 1953 become friends with the novelist and publisher William Styron and his wife, Rose, and with James Jones, whose novel *From Here to Eternity* was to become one of the most profitable and popular film adaptation of a Second World War novel. Styron flirted with Adele, as did Jones, and Mailer treated this as a compliment to his success in securing such a girlfriend. They regularly attended parties held on the coast and in the city where drinking became the equivalent of a competition, to the extent that by the beginning of 1953 Mailer was advised by his physician that unless he lessened his consumption of spirits, or preferably gave up completely, his already damaged liver might cease to function.

Adele and Mailer began to make regular visits to Mexico, where marijuana was easily available, and they also began to experiment with mescaline, a hallucinogenic drug made from locally grown cactus and consumed in the area thousands of years before the arrival of the Spanish. Both experienced the equivalent of derangement – sometimes lasting as long as two days – but treated the terrifying effects of the drug as a process of countercultural initiation.

Mailer's experimentation with such drugs played a part in his friendship with Robert Lindner, a prestigious psychoanalyst who became famous for his 1944 book *Rebel Without A Cause*, from which the title of Nicholas Ray's film was borrowed. The two men met at a party in New York shortly after Mailer had returned from one of his visits to Mexico and got on well from the beginning. Lindner saw Mailer as productive raw material for his research into the relationship between creativity and delinquency, and for Mailer the doctor was his sage on such questions as why his addiction to alcohol and drugs seemed a collateral effect of celebrity. Harold, the criminal psychopath of *Rebel Without a Cause*, popularised the book for non-specialist readers because he comes across as a character from fiction whose violent, sexually maniacal behaviour is offset by a very different, apparently cordial persona. Mailer was not interested in Lindner's patient as a model for his writing; rather he saw parallels between Harold and himself, a similarity that excited more than unsettled him.

Informally, Mailer and Lindner offered each other monologues similar to Harold's in which they allowed intimate disclosures that for others, their partners included, would have been either repressed or heavily edited. They exchanged private speculations on the extent to which social convention had caused them to deny homosexual inclinations, and Lindner assured his friend that a willingness to even admit to the possibility of being gay was a reasonable guarantee that he was not. He based this on his own experience of self-analysis, and as a consequence Mailer later in the 1950s confessed that his rampant homophobia – evident in his first two novels – was based on a fear that he might be what he despised.

Mailer also told Lindner about his divided feelings for Adele, that he was obsessed with her sexually yet had misgivings. Lindner's prognosis was that 'spiritually speaking she was a very expensive wife for me ... And Adele was no help socially to me. In fact, she was a drawback. She knew it and I knew it and there was a tension between us.' (Interview with Lennon, p. 165). Mailer was becoming a hypocrite, socially and emotionally, happy to indulge, indeed excited by, his wife's indiscreet behaviour while anxious that she might cast a shadow over his standing in the literary establishment. When we read the parts of *The Deer Park* in which Sergius describes his relationship with Lulu we come across a replica of Mailer's dilemma: limitless sensual pleasure with a woman who is relentlessly embarrassing and de trop at public events.

Much later Mailer reported to Lennon that 'Adele stood out like a sore thumb ... You know "You've brought the wrong person into the room", sort of ... It was awkward ... and Adele's fault was that when things got bad, they got worse ... if someone handed her a drink and she received it with the wrong hand or something ... it would be something of that sort ... Sure enough she'd drop the glass a minute later.' (Ibid.,

p. 168). Sergius, on Lulu: 'To eat a meal with her in a restaurant became the new torture ... I had to wonder what mathematical possibility there was for Lulu to eat a meal in sequence since she was always having bit of soup here and a piece of pastry there, joining me for breast of squab, and taking off to greet new arrivals ... There was no end, no beginning, no surety ...' (*The Deer Park*, p. 137).

It is not a coincidence that shortly after his most intensive sessions with Lindner Mailer decided finally that Sergius should be the sole narrator of the novel. Previously he had experimented with different voices and perspectives. Sergius would now share his confessional monologues with the reader while denying others in the novel any knowledge of how he perceived them. One has to wonder how they would have felt had he opened up to them, and this hypothesis becomes real when we consider what happened with Mailer and Adele. He tried to keep his journal to himself, but Adele saw some of it and immediately recognised parallels between his entries on her and Sergius's portraits of Lulu:

> ... it hurt her terribly, she felt it was the way I saw her, yet she accepted it, she loves the book. Part of it of course is her despised image of herself, but more important still is the terrific woman in her who accepts my work no matter how painful it is to her, who is even capable of wishing only the best for it. (Mailer's Journal, undated, quoted by Lennon, p. 188)

We have to take this on trust, since Adele did not comment even in her memoir on how she felt about becoming a martyr to high art. She did, however, tell of the deteriorating state of their relationship during the period when Mailer was completing the novel. 'Norman enjoyed provoking me by flirting outrageously at parties. One night, at Gloria Vanderbilt's, I saw him writing down a beautiful girl's phone number, not even bothering to be discreet.' At first she thought that this was his ritual declaration of sexual ascendency, 'as if to say "I know you're feeling insecure. Here's someone really gorgeous to rock your boat ..."' (*The Last Party*, p. 190).

But soon she began to find evidence that his conspicuous dalliances involved more than showmanship. 'I began finding names and telephone numbers on the inside of his matchbooks', and when she challenged him on them he stated, without a hint of remorse, that he met women for sex regularly. The electricity of their early relationship often resulted in rough-house verbal exchanges, but now she sensed something more unpleasant about him and, after an argument about his infidelities, 'Without warning, he backhanded me across the face. Dan [Wolf] was shocked, and I stood there speechless with shock and pain.' (Ibid., p. 204). This was, she adds, the beginning of his routine use of physical assault: 'Up to this point his abuse had been emotional, but now he was beginning to be more free with his hands.' (Ibid., p. 205). Mailer's presentation of Sergius's relationship with Lulu is his means of wiping the slate clean. Sergius is not perfect, but he is a chivalrous improvement on his creator: he never taunts Lulu by dallying with other women, certainly does not attempt to make her feel insecure or announce his infidelities sadistically – his desire for her is a tribute to her alluring uniqueness – and it is difficult to imagine that a man so coolly enigmatic could sink so low as to hit her.

Sergius's bizarre excursion to Mexico to follow his new career as a bullfighter was inserted into one of the revised drafts of the novel in late 1954. That year Mailer had purchased a Studebaker Commander, the most stylish, sporty and fastest car on the US market. Mailer and Adele drove south, calling at the Gwaltney ranch in Arkansas and then once more to Mexico, staying for a while with his sister Barbara and her husband Larry in Mexico City and then spending time with Bea and Susan. Bea was still distressed by the break-up but following her move to Mexico with her lover Steve Sanchez she agreed to that they should present their post-divorce relationship as friendly and harmonious Next, Mailer and Adele moved into a 300-year-old villa close to one that had been taken by Vance and Tina Bourjaily, writers they'd met in New York.

It was Bourjaily who introduced Mailer to the Mexican version of bullfighting, which is less polished than its Spanish counterpart. The matador is expected to despatch the defeated animal rapidly with a well-aimed plunge of the sword to a point between the bull's shoulders, but more often he missed and the beast died slowly and painfully. Mailer attended some fights and became a rather queasy Hemingway devotee, later confessing that while 'I got religion', he felt relieved at being denied what Papa enjoyed most of all, cruelty disguised as macho exhibitionism. Bourjaily and associates tried to arrange training for him as a matador but nothing came of it, and all we have is the fantasy of Sergius's new vocation.

Rinehart rejected Mailer's draft on the grounds that the censor would treat it as pornographic and forbid publication. This was ludicrous in that only one short passage could be treated as a representation of a sexual act, and even then, only by nuance. *Barbary Shore* had lost Rinehart money, so they consulted legal advisors on how they might use the threat of censorship as an escape clause from the contract even before he delivered the new book. They were less concerned with the sexual content of *The Deer Park* than its potential as another financial failure. Word spread within the East Coast publishing circuit, and it was turned down by seven more companies before Putnam offered Mailer a contract. The potentially lurid content of the book had already been aired by press commentators before the novel eventually went into print in 1955, which proved to be just as effective as the ability of Putnam to promote it, as within three weeks it had sold 50,000 copies. Substantial royalties would come to Mailer later in the year, and at the end of 1954 he had received $110,000 for the film rights to *The Naked and the Dead*. The RKO production of 1958 was a catastrophe, receiving unanimously bad reviews and attracting poor audience figures. Today, the adaptation of *From Here to Eternity* features regularly on terrestrial and satellite channels, but those seeking the film version of Mailer's book must trawl through pay-network databases. The movie contract boosted Mailer's already comfortable wealth immensely, and caused, for those who thought of it, an even more farcical contrast between the figure who continued to endorse a vague notion of Anarcho-Trotskyism and the one who had seemingly limitless access to money.

Mailer and Adele married at City Hall in Manhattan on 19 April 1954. At the ceremony he gave her a $13 fake gold band, indicating their indifference to showy materialism, but a week later he replaced this with a $500 eighteen-karat ring. Barney and Fan were witnesses, and the reception was held in the Brooklyn apartment a week later. Guests included the Lindners, Lillian Hellman, the poet and playwright Harvey

Breit, Ed Fancher, James Jones, Dan Wolf, and others who regularly attended their city and Provincetown parties.

In *The Deer Park* Charles Eitel is Sergius's alter ego, a friend, a man of kindred sympathies and political affiliations, but weak and dissolute. He testifies to the House Un-American Activities Committee and makes use of his position as a director to seduce and exploit women. Eitel is the unedited version of Mailer, a writer who is a magnet for young women and who does not reject their advances. The friendship between the two characters, often their conversations, is the driving force for the novel, not that there is much of a story. Little happens in Desert D'Or, apart from a catalogue of nuanced debauchery, but the relationship between Sergius and Eitel adds interest to the book as a piece of perverse autobiographical fiction. Reviews were mixed, mainly because no one was certain of what it was about. *The New York Times* saw it as 'a dreary story about the noisome affairs of a group of degenerate characters', while *The New Yorker* declared that 'only a writer of the greatest and most reckless talent could have flung it between covers'. It was about Norman Mailer, specifically the two dimensions of himself that he could not quite reconcile and which emerge in Sergius and Eitel.

During their 1954 visit to Mexico Mailer and Adele invited a couple round for cocktails on the understanding that the evening would conclude with them swapping partners. According to Adele in her memoir (pp. 170–71), the effects of drink and drugs meant that full sexual intercourse was not possible, but for both couples fellatio took place in the same room. It is interesting to compare Adele's description – albeit forty years later – with the passage in *The Deer Park* which caused Rinehart to reject it, when the disgusting Herman Teppis, head of Supreme Studios, promises a hopeless actress, Bobby, a career in return for a blow job.

In the novel insinuation replaces minute description, but only a naïve or innocent reader would fail to recognise what happens. More significantly, Teppis's pleasuring by the actress is described by Sergius, despite the fact that he is not there. Several critics remarked on Mailer's paradoxical use of Sergius as an omniscient first-person narrator – able to tell you what happens without witnessing the occurrences or being privy to what others are thinking – and indulged this as another contribution to experimental fiction, but more striking are the parallels between Sergius's description of Teppis's liaison with Bobby and Adele's account of what happened to her in Mexico. She tells of her distaste for 'Boris', who seems to treat her as his possession, much as Teppis does with Bobby, but there is an eerie impression that while she knows that Mailer is watching, he seems invisible. 'I looked around the bedroom, feeling like a frightened little girl in a place I didn't know, far away from home, with someone I knew once, a stranger now, who didn't love me, who had thrown me to the dogs like a piece of meat.' (Ibid., p. 172). These words might have been uttered by Bobby, her humiliation witnessed by a man she knows but who is, seemingly, somewhere else. In truth Sergius was another element of Mailer, a control freak who wanted to know what those closest to him were up to while keeping his own activities to himself. In Adele's memoir her husband insults her, mocks her for her sexual acts with 'Boris' while exempting himself from any notion of guilt or complicity; he is simply an observer.

Shortly before they married Adele discovered in Mailer's journal a series of phone numbers and remarks that indicated further evidence of infidelity, this time more specific. Frequently he referred to Lois Wilson, the actress he'd first met when he went to Hollywood with Bea and whom he visited again in California after he began his relationship with Adele.

Only a month after the wedding reception Mailer received a letter from Lois stating that in three weeks she would be in New York and asking if he could find places for 'fancy indiscretions'. She added that 'when I think of quality I think of Norman'. (19 May 1954). He wrote back stating that compared with her 'there's not a decent piece of ass', and asks her to bring the Polaroid photographs of her, naked, from their previous encounter: 'as the years go by, I get dirtier and dirtier' wishing to 'put both my arms around your big white moon'. (29 May 1953). *The Deer Park* is littered with passages like this, often from Eitel and reported to the reader by Sergius. The arrangement between the two of them, with Eitel unapologetically promiscuous and Sergius the uneasy witness, represents Mailer's struggle with two aspects of his personality. As his journal testifies, he was able to step outside his unconstrained, visceral preoccupation with sex and write about it as if he were watching someone else, but at the same time he knew he would never rid himself of it. Sergius's exchange of the debauchery of Desert D'Or for a new vocation as bullfighting instructor with literary ambitions is ludicrous, and though few if any readers would recognise it as such, it is a moment of candour by Mailer, if not contrition. Sergius does something too absurd to be true, excusing himself from what his author will live with for the foreseeable future.

The writer and critic Alfred Kazin told an amusing story of how Mailer had invited him to lunch in the Oak Room at the Plaza Hotel in New York. They were talking, mainly about books, and Kazin noted that his host was becoming more and more involved in their exchange, though not because either of them found it interesting: 'There was a fashion show going on, but he was so intent on the conversation that he ignored the models sweeping up and down before us. I thought it was very funny ... a typical Jewish attitude to sex ... there's always anxiety, fear involved.' (Manso, pp. 217–8).

7

NORMAN MAILER: THE DEATH OF THE NOVEL

Mailer would not publish another novel for ten years following the completion of *The Deer Park*, but his life during this period might have inspired one, at least one that appealed to fans of farcical surrealism.

In autumn 1954 Mailer and Adele rented a two-storey duplex apartment on East 55th Street. It was unfurnished, but Adele was offered limitless funds by Mailer to restyle the place. She hired men to replace the wallpaper with white paint on plaster and bricks and to strip the carpets to polished timber floors. She purchased minimalist, largely Danish, furniture, and guests found themselves gazing around at interiors they'd not previously encountered. Such design trends did not become fashionable until the late 1960s. They had, it seemed, gone noticeably upmarket in terms of locality and decor, but the downward spiral of their behaviour continued.

On average Mailer would empty a bottle of bourbon during a night out at parties or literary events. He would take one with him, swigging from it as the taxi paused at lights on the way and keeping the remainder close by as an emergency supply while accepting whatever wines, cocktails and spirits his hosts could offer. During the day he smoked marijuana continuously, which resulted in him veering between states of trepidation and rage. He ruled that since he remained addicted to promiscuity – *The Deer Park* had not purged him of this – Adele should be encouraged to behave accordingly. She didn't want to, but since she'd reluctantly kept him company in his misuse of drink and drugs, she tried her best with sex. She refers to them as 'the mad general and me, his aide-de-camp ... one lovely memory was of a bombed Monty Clift

and an equally bombed Adele necking on the white-carpeted stairs ...'
(*The Last Party,* p. 218). She later commented that they went on to the
bedroom; in her view Clift was bisexual rather than exclusively gay.

After moving into the apartment Mailer began to mix with members
of the more radical group of journalists and writers that had energised
the cultural infrastructure of the city since the end of the 1940s, notably
Dan Wolf and Ed Fancher. Sometime in 1955 they set up a competing
paper *The Village Voice*, though who invented the new title remains open
to dispute, but its echo of the nearby *Villager*, a liberal-mainstream
magazine established in the early 1930s, indicated that they wanted to
reflect grass-roots, anti-establishment opinions. Mailer was certainly
involved, mainly because he matched Fancher's $5,000 investment in
the expansion of the magazine with five thousand of his own. Wolf put up
an equal amount and the three men divided ninety per cent of the stock
hold equally between them. Fancher would be the publisher, controlling
the practicalities of producing it, and Wolf the editor. The remaining ten
per cent was owned by Charles Rembar, the lawyer who had arranged
the establishment of *The Village Voice* as a corporate entity, and Mailer's
role was unspecified. It was, however, accepted that the magazine would
be his means of becoming something completely unprecedented. As he
declared to his co-editors, novelists could not alter society. Aggressive
oracles, such as Norman Mailer, must speak directly to readers; offend,
and provoke, rather than hide behind fictional proxies.

He began this exercise with a letter to his long-term hero, Ernest
Hemingway, which he published and despatched hard-copy to Havana.
Along with an inscribed copy of *The Deer Park* he enclosed a brief missive
in verse form:

TO ERNEST HEMINGWAY

  — because finally after all these
years I am deeply curious to know
what you think of this.

  — but if you do not answer, or if you
answer with the kind of crap you

use to answer unprofessional writers,
sycophants, brown-nosers, etc., then
fuck you, and I will never attempt
to communicate with you again.

– and since I suspect that you're even
more vain than I am, I might as well
warn you that there is a reference to you on page 353 which you may
or may not like.

NORMAN MAILER

The novel and the poem came back from Cuba a week later, marked
'Return to Sender' in Spanish.

Mailer produced sixteen articles for *The Village Voice* over twelve
months between 1955 and 1956. In each he oversteps the boundaries
between decency and profanity, the rational and the deranged, the
lucid and the incomprehensible. Prior to his first column he bought
a page to promote *The Deer Park*, opening with the announcement
that his novel is 'getting nothing but RAVES' and following this
with quotations from only the worst reviews, memorably: 'Moronic
mindlessness' (*New York Herald Tribune*); 'The year's worst smoke pit
in fiction' (*Cleveland News*); 'Sordid and crummy' (*Chicago Sun-Times*).
This was not a demonstration of masochism, let alone an admission
of failure. It was a prelude to a piece that would be published a week
later called 'Quickly: A Column for Slow Readers' in which he treats
with loathing everyone who feels that they are capable of assessing the
quality of a literary work. He reserves particular contempt for the
cultural in-crowd, reviewers included, notably those who read *The
Village Voice* as a badge of metropolitan affinity.

Greenwich Village is one of the bitter provinces – it abounds in snobs
and critics. That many of you are frustrated in your ambitions, and
undernourished in your pleasures, only makes you more venomous.
Quite rightly. If I found myself in your position, I would not be
charitable either. Nevertheless, given your general animus to those

more talented than yourselves, the only way I see myself becoming one of the more cherished traditions of the Village is to be actively disliked each week.

In his third column, he picked out for caricature some of America's most esteemed critics and literary journalists. Max Lerner became 'Wax Burner', Hedda Hopper of the *Daily News* was 'Cheddar Chopper of the NY *Daily Nose*', and Dorothy Kilgallen, who wrote for the *New York Journal-American*, emerged as 'Dorothy Kill-Talent of the *NY Churlish-American*'. None of them complained because the parodies were so poorly executed, coming across as pieces by an embittered adolescent. In 'Wax Burner', for example, Mailer expands on his recent lecture tour of American universities and reflects with confidence on what he finds of the coming generation. 'They show an informed interest in getting married. They are frank in their lack of fear of sex. One the other hand they are not not-afraid of sex. They realise it can be abused.' And so on for seven hundred words. As a satirist he is embarrassing, as are his attempts to blend surrealism and philosophical insight.

> Like when you see someone on the subway with a shoe on his ear. You think: 'How strange, the shoestrings aren't tied.' You tell the stranger and he ties the shoestrings. Your original thought spurred the stranger to action. This can be called communication. (Column Eight)

Jerry Tallmer, then a freelancer who did theatre reviews for the *Voice* but would later become theatre critic at *The New York Post*, told Mills that in the office Mailer used his position as major shareholder to bully his partners and other contributors. On one occasion he announced that the texture of the paper and the typesetting were far too conventional, that if the paper was to appeal to those who routinely took drugs and behaved badly it should itself look dishevelled. Tallmer: 'He prided himself on knowing something about art ... In fact he once told me that he knew about art because he was married to a painter.' (Mills, p. 170). Mailer went into the backroom and created a new typeface made up of letters cut randomly from various newspapers, magazines and the telephone directory. Tallmer recalls that his sample front page resembled letters from blackmailers that featured in B-movies. 'We all looked at it and there was a long, profound silence. Finally, I said, "Well, it's okay, Norman, but I think it's a little high school."That tore it.' He did not speak to his fellow editors and contributors for two days.

Aside from writing for the *Voice* Tallmer was responsible for the practical task of putting together and checking copy and delivering drafts to the typesetter. Before Mailer's campaign to redesign the typeface there was an even more hilarious incident. Mailer was notorious for delivering copy either minutes before the deadline or shortly afterwards, with the result that Tallmer and Fancher had to edit his contributions minutes before they were typeset for printing. Inevitably quite a number of typos were missed and, as Fancher put it, 'Norman got very paranoid and thought that Jerry was doing it or the printers were doing it too or somebody was doing it to destroy him.' (Mills, p170) A solution of sorts was found when the printers agreed to deal with the *Voice* copy as their final job, allowing Tallmer, Fancher and Dan Wolf an extra two hours to do a final copy-edit, which also meant that they worked until after 2.00 am. Mailer replaced his previous paranoia with anger after reading his newly 'clean' columns. The misprints were, he now claimed, his 'radical signature' that others had removed to further undermine his radicalism.

Part of his fantasy that he was the voice of a revolutionary paper involved him volunteering for several months as distribution manager. In truth he and editorial assistant Florence Ettenberg made up the entire distribution department and spent all Wednesday mornings from 4.00 am onwards driving around the Village and lower Manhattan leaving stacks at agreed drop-off points and even persuading old Jewish ladies on food and newsstands to take and sell copies. It remains open to question as to how many of these stall-holders' customers were drugged hipsters, Mailer's target audience. His own daily routine still involved marijuana, two packets of cigarettes, a bottle of whiskey, plus a mixture of tranquillisers, Seconal and Benzedrine.

Tallmer said to Manso that 'Norman's column ... was basically turgid and unreadable ... at the time he was under the stress of drugs, there was *The Deer Park* crisis, and whatever was going on in his marriage'. (Manso, p. 226). Is 'unreadable' a little harsh? Judge for yourself:

> On those occasions when we do not know if it is God or the Devil we must fear, do we not have insomnia with *Angst*, does not madness insinuate itself? There is a suggestion to go out on the street and look for the adventure One or the Other is demanding. Most of us stay home. All right then, so we die of cancer, goes the sigh in the wind of our small depleted courage.

Mailer also employed his friend Mickey Knox and paid him from the *Village Voice* budget.

> He hired me to make the rounds of bookshops in New York, posing as a buyer, a guy coming in off the streets, in order to find out what salespeople felt about the book [*The Deer Park*]. Sort of market research. I took notes. He was desperate to know why the fuck it wasn't selling better. (Manso, p. 220)

We should be cautious about interpreting this preoccupation with book sales as evidence of sanity. At the same time that he took on Knox as a market researcher Mailer decided to adopt what was not so much a pseudonym – in print he made it clear who he really was – as another burst of arbitrary nonconformity. He began to announce himself in the *Voice* and in the office as 'General Marijuana', and alongside this he slipped, seemingly at random, between accents that no one who knew him had previously heard him use, even when he was attempting to tell jokes. Recollections vary on their range and number but five were memorable: a Texas brogue that would blend into the kind of Southern gentleman almost as bad as found in *Gone with the Wind*; the speech habits of an English aristocrat, again seemingly borrowed from the Hollywood brand of British gentry; rough-house Irish, which he might have come across during his youth in Brooklyn; an imitation of a threatening New York gangster; and what appeared to most to be impersonations of black jazz players, at least those who had been interviewed on the wireless or on screen. He never explained why he did this and no one thought it necessary to ask; it was, in its way, consistent with everything else. Often, in his columns, he used the third person, even substituting 'Mailer' for 'he'. In novels this might be taken as an acceptable option, but friends found peculiar his increasing habits of adapting this in speech. At editorial meetings he might state that 'he is not happy with this contribution ...' or even 'Mailer is not happy ...' and soon afterwards revert to the 'I'. Sometimes, at meetings, he requested that he should be addressed by all present as the 'Village Villain'.

Robert Lindner died of a heart condition in February 1956, and Mailer devoted two columns to him, quoting verbatim from many of his books while affirming that although psychoanalysts were endemically flawed, Lindner was the miraculous exception. He emphasised the precept of *Rebel Without a Cause* that unfocused vitriol was a key element of creativity. In short, Mailer was not mourning his friend as an individual; rather he was regretting the departure of a figure who had evolved an excuse for Norman Mailer at his worst. At the funeral his tearful, uninvited eulogy touched the same note and caused distress to all present, not least because he was clearly drunk.

Shortly before the Democrats nominated a candidate for the presidency in 1956, Mailer announced that he would propose the most suitable runner in his forthcoming column, Number Twelve. In the office bets were placed on who he would back. Adlai Stevenson was the frontrunner in polls, but the more liberal, left-leaning Estes Kefauver was close behind, and the prosperous old-family businessman W. Averell Harriman was gaining support. The shortest odds were on Mailer choosing Kefauver, yet no one ruled out that he'd go for no-hopers such as Farrell Dobbs of the Trotskyist Socialist Workers Party, who would eventually receive 7,800 votes. His column went to the printers in a sealed envelope, and when it appeared all bets were voided. Mailer championed Ernest Hemingway, even though Papa had not, as yet, announced his candidacy.

> Finally, Hemingway's lack of a previous political life is an asset, I would argue, rather than a vice ... The glimmer of hope on all our murky horizons is that civilization may be coming to the point where we will return to voting for individual men (or individual women) rather than

for political ideas, those political ideas which eventually are cemented into the social network of life as a betrayal of the individual desires which gave birth to them ... (*AFM*, pp. 316–7)

Compared with his other pieces the prose is coherent, and his colleagues assumed that he'd adopted the relatively sane persona to conceal the wry smile forming behind the article. No, he declared, he genuinely believed that Hemingway was the political messiah, and that he, Mailer, could persuade him to stand for the presidency.

His sixteenth column was called 'The Hip and the Square':

To a Square, a rapist is a rapist. Punish the rapist, imprison him, be horrified by him and/or disinterested [sic] in him, and that is the end of the matter. But a hipster knows that the act of rape is a part of life too, and that even in the most brutal and unforgivable rape, there is artistry or the lack of it, real desire or cold compulsion, and so no two rapists nor two rapes are ever the same. (*AFM*, p. 319)

This passage is rarely quoted directly these days but not because of some collective act of forgiveness. It, along with many other seemingly outrageous comments, is accepted as part of the radical discourse of 'Hip'. Mailer explains elsewhere that the 'hipster' is the American existentialist; Sartre shipped across the Atlantic. Hipsters live in 'the undercurrents and underworlds of American life ... the defeated, the isolated, the violent, the tortured and the warped' (*AFM*, p. 293), and by their nature they reject the conformity of America, which seems to mean that hipsters are by their nature unfixed regarding vocations, but Mailer persistently argues that brutal nonconformity cultivates artistic inspiration. So perhaps he conceives rape as a nuanced gesture, not so much a particular attack on a given woman as a symbolic, albeit male, assault on comfortable habits or morality and thinking. Possibly, but his much more frequently quoted comment of ten years later that 'A little bit of rape is good for a man's soul' is what? A joke?

If he had proposed that the lynching of African Americans rather than rape involves 'artistry or the lack of it, real desire or cold compulsion', his comments would probably not have survived the test of liberal tolerance. Literary artists who advocate and practise bad behaviour towards women seem to have a special licence, generally denied to unapologetic racists. Later, in *The Prisoner of Sex*, he wrote that women are 'low, sloppy beasts: they should be kept in cages'. In 1956 even throwbacks to the Confederacy would have been reluctant to voice this opinion if it were in regard to African Americans, at least in public. There is no evidence from Adele that he ever forced her to have sex by an actual or implied threat of physical violence, but throughout her memoir insinuated coercion is an ever-present feature of their physical relationship: consent was mutually agreed but he was in charge of the agreement. Once, when they visited his parents' empty apartment, he demanded that they must have sex on the living room floor, and then in Fan and Barney's bed. She was appalled but he insisted it would be fun, as he did when a man at a party asked if he would 'lend' Adele to him. Once more she found the prospect repulsive, having never even spoken to the debauchee before, but she went along with it because it 'was part of being with Norman.' If we extend this phrase to the way that sexual assault in today's legislature is defined as 'manipulating someone to witness or participate in any sexual acts', 'being with Norman' in the 1950s was the equivalent of now living with a sexual abuser. Hipsterdom was, for some, a lazy hedonistic version of anarchism, but for Mailer it comes across more as a smokescreen for vileness.

There is no consensus on what precisely caused Mailer to leave the *Voice*, but his determination to make it the vehicle for his obsessions played a part. He came close to ruining it financially. Fancher:

> Norman, as time went on, said the *Voice* should be very radical, full of sex and drugs. Dan and I pointed out that we were working seven days a week, twelve hours a day, trying to put the paper out. We had no money, we were losing a thousand dollars a week ... (Mills, p. 166)

A friend of Fancher, Howard Bennett, joined the magazine as the fourth shareholder in February 1956 and invested $15,000, but even this influx could not prevent the haemorrhaging of funds caused by Mailer's determination to alienate readers. The *Voice* achieved a special level of notoriety in New York, and those who bought it took masochistic pleasure in being appalled by what its chief columnist had to say. But there was not a sufficient number of morbid voyeurs to enable sales to exceed costs. Wolf later recalled that 'What he [Mailer] wanted at the time was a big explosion that would make the scene. He felt that if you just pressed the right button, all these people would come up from the underground.' (Mills, pp. 166–7). Mailer's hope for a potential readership involving thousands as deranged as him did not come about.

In his goodbye column he laid blame for his departure on his 'Editor and Sub-Editor', who he alleged had conspired against him and devised 'errors' in his pieces to persistently and maliciously distort his representation of the joys of hipsterdom. In the light of his permanently drunken and drug-addled state this earnest statement of betrayal is almost comic. Almost, because it hardly merits comparison with an episode that occurred in September 1956. After he and Adele returned from a dinner party Mailer took their two poodles, Tibo and Zsa Zsa, for a walk, and according to Adele he arrived back with 'His raincoat … torn and filthy, one eye was swollen shut, and he had some bloody cuts on his face and head. "Look at your face, dammit, who did this?" I wailed.' Mailer explained:

> 'Well, I was walking by these guys, and one of them pointed to Tibo and said, "Mister, your dog is queer." I wasn't going to take that so I asked the other guy to hold the dogs, and I went for the bastard who made the crack. Tibo, the coward, never came to my defence and neither did Zsa Zsa.' (*The Last Party* p219)

The two 'guys' were sailors, and according to Adele the one who fought with Norman was an 'eye gouger'. To comment on the episode would ruin its absurdity but one should note Adele's codicil, which she offered without the slightest hint of irony.

> Poor beautiful Tibo, how did he know that his crazy master was getting beaten up for defending him? After all, he was just a pampered pompom-tailed fancy dog, not a police dog. (ibid.)

Mailer's final review column for the *Voice* is almost as farcical as the incident with the dogs and the sailors. On 2 May he dismissed completely

Beckett's *Waiting for Godot*, which had recently opened on Broadway, admitting that he had neither seen it performed nor read it. Persuaded by Adele that this was a little impetuous the couple bought tickets for it the night he submitted copy. The following day he delivered a lengthy piece that began with an apology for his groundless attack on the work. His essay on Beckett appeared on 9 May and he makes it clear that while the play has gained his respect, virtually everyone else who has celebrated it – professional critics included – are 'people who don't have the faintest idea of what he [Beckett] is talking about ... [who] scream, gurgle and expire with a kind of militant exacerbated snobbery ... the worst sort of literary type, invariably more interested in being part of some intellectual elite than in the creative act itself.' (*AFM*, pp. 326–7). Such pretentious overreachers cannot do justice to, let alone explain, the importance of Beckett's work. This task can only be undertaken by the playwright's aesthetic equal, Norman Mailer, and he spends around three thousand words explicating and solemnising *Godot* in a manner that endures as unique.

Picking up on the term 'impotence' used by Beckett in a recent newspaper interview, Mailer homes in on sex – sexuality, sexual acts, sexual impropriety, the inability to have sex – as the play's predominant theme. He then veers away from this and treats Beckett's visionary insights as almost identical to his own. 'I know that for myself, after years of the most intense pessimism, I feel the hints, the clues, the whispers of a new time coming.' From the fear in the 'White South' of the 'growing power of the Negro' to the 'ebbing' strengths of the 'two colossal super-states of the Cold War' and most of all the 'creative nihilism of the Hip' with all its 'violence, its confusion, its ugliness and horror', 'change' is imminent. There is no evidence that Beckett read the article, but if he did he would probably have been surprised to find that his play was so astonishingly wide-ranging in its impetus, that it was essentially about everything.

Waiting for Godot has over the years generated vast amounts of jargon-laden drivel, especially from academics, but Mailer's piece on it is special in that it almost matches the play in its incomprehensibility.

There is no obvious reason for the Mailers' decision to visit Paris shortly after he left the *Voice*, but it is likely he thought a break in his routine would enable him to relax his equally habitual dependency on drugs and drink, especially Seconal and Benzedrine, both of which caused him confusion and anxiety when taken with alcohol. They boarded the SS *United States* on 15 May 1956. During the voyage Mailer reduced his intake of addictive substances, and their previously fraught marital relationship began to improve. They stayed at the Hotel Palais Royal on the quai Voltaire, a stylish and pricey establishment, and the fact that they booked a room indefinitely indicated that they were not ruling out taking an apartment.

Jean and Galy Malaquais had moved back to Paris two years earlier, and the Mailers regularly went to their flat. It was at a Malaquais drinks party that Norman was introduced to James Baldwin, the internationally acclaimed African-American writer. His *Go Tell It on the Mountain* (1953) is a quasi-autobiographical story of black experience in America and is treated as one of the major novels of the twentieth century. Baldwin emigrated to Paris in 1948 in an attempt to escape several forms of prejudice. Racism was the most strident, but Baldwin was also openly homosexual, and he felt that even if he earned recognition as a writer in America it would be an inverse form of success; he would be seen as a curiosity, a beguiling exception to the predominant social prejudice that saw black people as inferior and gay people as abnormal.

Malaquais arranged the introduction because he assumed that the two men had much in common; both were, though for different reasons, at war with the establishment. However, the factors that made Baldwin who he was and that lay behind his feelings of alienation were also those that caused him to feel sometimes aghast at Mailer.

One was a US magazine dedicated to the gay community. It began publishing in 1953 and commissioned Mailer as an early contributor, on the assumption that his widely advertised left-wing, radical ideals would guarantee his sympathy towards gay rights. The article he delivered, however, was both candid and unsettling. 'The Homosexual Villain' is a peculiar piece, and the editors of *One* should be given credit for publishing it. Certainly, Mailer confesses to his past prejudices, mainly his creation of fictional homosexual characters in a manner that reflected his own innate bigotry, his suspicion that being gay was coterminous with being evil. But he goes on to reveal that his prejudices were based on his fear that he too might be gay. Once he was secure in his heterosexuality, he could stop feeling that homosexuals are unpleasant, without conceding that they are 'normal'. Disturbingly, it is evident that he treats homosexuality as something that is optional. In the closing paragraph he declares that 'many homosexuals go to the direction of assuming there is something intrinsically superior about homosexuality', by which he means that gay people, like Christians, communists or vegetarians, assume that the intellectual or moral underpinnings of their chosen mien are superior to those taken up by others.

During their evening at the Malaquais' and on several other occasions in Paris Mailer and Baldwin got on well, at least according to others present, but Baldwin's 1961 article for *Esquire* called 'The Black Boy Looks at the White Boy' tells a different story.

When they met Baldwin was just completing *Giovanni's Room*. It was published later, in 1956, and proved immensely controversial, with its narrator David, an American in Paris, finding that his bisexuality leads to catastrophe for himself and others. His affair with the eponymous barman has nothing to do with the latter's murder of the bar owner, Guillaume, and his execution for the crime, but there is a horrible implication that a malign form of natural justice awaits those who 'deviate from the norm', in this case in terms of their sexuality. Baldwin had recently ended an affair with a Swiss man who was the model for Giovanni, and although metropolitan France was relatively relaxed about homosexuality, he was cautious about talking with anyone about his various feelings of guilt and despair. Instead, he channelled these into the novel and spent most evenings drinking heavily in gay bars and jazz clubs. In this respect his depressive, unfocused lifestyle mirrored Mailer's, though the latter was troubled largely by his growing sense that his marriage to Adele was destined for failure; his reliance on drugs and drink had returned, despite the false optimism of the Atlantic voyage. Like his new acquaintance Mailer sometimes stayed out much of the night. As he put it in an untitled poem he wrote during the visit, 'I would come back/ after combing the vistas of the Seine/ for glints of light to bank in the/ corroded vaults of my ambitious and/ yellow jaundiced soul ...'

Each man detected signals of despair and torment in the other, but their apparent similarities were the cause of what would become, on

Baldwin's part, feelings about Mailer that came close to anger. Mailer, he realised, wanted to talk about race and sexuality not because, as a white, heterosexual liberal, he felt the need to understand and sympathise, which was patronising but no more than could be expected at the time. Rather, he treated Baldwin as would a soulless anthropologist studying a new sub-species of humanity, in Mailer's case for his forthcoming work 'The White Negro'.

In the *Esquire* article Baldwin wrote that 'it is still true, alas, that to be an American Negro male is also to be a kind of walking phallic symbol: which means that one pays, in one's own personality, for the sexual insecurity of others'. Baldwin felt that whatever Mailer had intended to do in 'The White Negro', its general effect would be to reinforce the racist stereotype of black people as ill-disciplined sex maniacs. Aside from the parts of it he found offensive Baldwin commented that on the whole the essay was 'impenetrable'.

8

'THE WHITE NEGRO'

When the Mailers returned to New York in August 1956 Adele was pregnant, and Danielle was born in March 1957. In the interim they decided to move from the city to rural New England, a repeat of the exercise of six years earlier when Bea and Mailer, with their child, had relocated to an old farmhouse in Vermont. Once more the official explanation – this time that the countryside was better suited to the rearing of young children – was a cover for their true motive: a radical change in circumstances and local mores might in some way help them to save their marriage.

The poem Mailer composed in Paris on his night-time roamings through the 'vistas of the Seine' continues with:

> ... and there back
> in bed, nada, you lying in bed in hate
> of me, the waves of unspoken flesh
> radiating detestation into me because
> I have been brave a little but not nearly
> brave enough for you, greedy bitch,
> Spanish lady, with your murderous
> Indian blood and your crazy purity
> hung on courage in men as if it were
> your queen's own royal balls ...

And so on, in a free verse ode drenched in loathing which he alleges is felt by Adele for him. In truth it was the other way around.

They bought a timber farmhouse near Bridgewater, Connecticut, with a barn and fifty acres of pasture. The building was tastefully preserved, and Adele was angry that Mailer had no interest in fitting it out with appropriately vintage furniture and antiques. Instead, he hired a removal company to bring to it their modernist fittings from the city flat, which looked ludicrously out of place.

He made use of his self-taught DIY skills to convert parts of the attic into a studio where Adele could paint. After buying himself joinery tools Mailer turned one of the barns into a workshop. He began with basic items of furniture and some ornaments, notably large eggs, of the size estimated to have been laid by dinosaurs, wrought from solid trunks of elm. More adventurously he put together a large, open wheel in which an average-sized person could be strapped and rolled down a hill. No one was asked to endanger their lives in this thing, but Mailer himself used it and claimed that he had constructed it in accordance with the theories of energy and sexuality developed by the Austrian psychoanalyst Wilhelm Reich. More specifically he built his own version of Reich's legendary, and some would say ridiculous, orgone box, a sealed wooden container in which the patient, removed from the distractions of the outside world, would acquire formidable strength, self-healing capabilities and, famously, the ability to experience explosively powerful orgasms. This last was what attracted Mailer to the home-made box, though there is no record of whether Reich's invention fulfilled its promises, for its builder or his guests. The locality was well settled with people the Mailers had met and known before. William and Rose Styron lived close by, as did John Aldridge and his wife, Leslie, the film producer Lewis Allen and his screenwriter wife, Jay, and, for a short period after the Mailers moved in, Arthur Miller and Marilyn Monroe occupied the house later taken by the Aldridges.

On the surface the situation appeared idyllic. Susan, Danielle's half-sister, visited regularly, and Adele was a frequent guest of their neighbour Julian Levy, who kept a gallery in New York and entertained a steady stream of visitors from the metropolis connected with the visual arts. Levy agreed to exhibit some of Adele's paintings. Her abstract work is often quite impressive, with touches of Mondrian and Pollack.

Having given up smoking on the advice of his physician – he had developed severe breathing problems – Mailer compensated by drinking even more bourbon than ever before, sometimes two bottles a day, along with a gargantuan intake of steak and French fries. He was slightly under five feet eight, and by spring 1957 he weighed close to 190 pounds; to lose weight he built himself a gym. Its centre point was a punch bag which he assaulted rabidly for at least an hour and a half a day, and he supplemented this by using dumbbells and heavier weights. The bag made him lose half a stone, and the weights enabled him to turn himself into a rather short but well-muscled light heavyweight. Mailer insisted on being present at the birth of Danielle, common practice these days but unusual in 1957 and sometimes forbidden by midwives. His rationale was that since he had created the child, he had the right to witness its emergence from Adele's vagina. Also, he forbade the midwife from shaving Adele's pubic hair, a standard procedure at the time, believed to help reduce infection. Mailer insisted that a 'natural' birth would be tainted by the removal of anything apart from clothes.

He later admitted that in 1956 he felt unable, even disinclined, to write anything. In *Advertisements for Myself* he wondered if being without cigarettes played some part in this but then confronted the more depressing possibility that 'I had burned out my talent'. Lyle Stuart was a publisher and investigative reporter whose single mantra seemed to be the causing of shock or offence. In 1953 he had published *The Secret Life of Walter Winchell*, exposing the columnist as a liar and a sadist. It prompted Winchell to take Stuart to court, though Winchell's objections were ruled to be unfounded. Mailer had met Stuart several times and invited him for a long weekend in Bridgewater, hoping that he would find a media outlet for his increasingly controversial and often outrageous conjectures. Stuart was running a small independent newspaper called the *Independent* through which he attempted to test the boundaries of current notions of free speech, and during their time together he issued a challenge to Mailer: write an article that the national monthlies and weeklies would never dare publish, and the *Independent* would run it. For the first time since he had left the *Voice* Mailer was determined to write something explosive, and the night after Stuart left he prepared a 1,000-word piece that he thought would be rejected by all mainstream newspapers. It was, ostensibly, about the issue of school integration in the South, which at the time was no more than a matter for debate in the ex-Confederate states, at least for those few figures willing to give it consideration. Its implementation seemed as likely as a manned space flight to Mars.

Mailer ignored matters such as equality and civil liberty and focused exclusively on why white people in the North as well as the South felt uneasy about their children having to associate with black people: '... the white loathes the idea of the Negro attaining equality in the classroom because the white feels the Negro already enjoys sensual superiority.' He goes on to contend that 'Negroes' 'hate whites' because the latter have possessed black women since the beginning of slavery, though he does not explain the relevance of this to integrated schooling. The article is brief, and apart from its initial mention of school policies in the South it focuses obsessively on sexuality as the cause of tension between black people and white people.

In the end Stuart chose not to publish it, but not because it riled his principles or sensibilities. The *Independent* made money by running scandalous or outrageously controversial pieces that would be bought by other news services. Mailer's content did not worry him, but he was unsure if other outlets would take it seriously. They might, he suspected, wonder if the wild man of the *Voice* was role-playing, caricaturing a sex-obsessed Southern Evangelist.

But Stuart first decided to test the waters of response by seeking opinions from, among others, William Faulkner, Eleanor Roosevelt, W. E. B. Du Bois and Murray Kempton. All had heard of Mailer, but they agreed that the piece carrying his name was a disingenuous parody of ludicrous beliefs. Faulkner, for example, recalled similar fears advanced by God-fearing middle-aged women of the small-town Midwest, most of whom had never met a black person and who, in Faulkner's view, would benefit from the attention of a psychiatrist. Mrs Roosevelt judged the piece to be 'horrible and unnecessary'. All of this confirmed Stuart's fear that no other paper would buy it because each would regard it as a joke.

The article served, astonishingly, as the keynote for a much longer piece that would alter Mailer's future as a writer and become one of the most intensely debated theses of the mid-twentieth century.

Mailer completed the 9,000-word-plus 'The White Negro' during the three months following Stuart's decision not to publish his piece in the *Independent*; or to be more accurate, he cobbled together first drafts

of material from his columns for the *Voice*, rewrote key passages to shock
and appal and added a few anecdotes and scenarios involving violence,
race, sex and mass murder.

He sent it to Irving Howe, one of the editors of the fashionably radical
Dissent magazine. Howe had savagely reviewed *Barbary Shore* but found
something extraordinary in Mailer's polemic and decided that it would
appear in a special edition in late summer 1957.

Ordinary readers largely ignored it, but within the intelligentsia
there were expressions of horror and exaltation, sometimes in the
same response. The consensus seemed to be that (a) its incoherence
guaranteed its value as an example of the ideological avant garde, and (b)
if it enraged those members of the establishment who bothered to read
it, it must be exquisite. William Phillips, editor of the *Partisan Review* and
later Professor at Rutgers and Boston universities, summed things up.

> The mood was different then, and while one may have felt he'd gone
> too far, one accepted it. There was a feeling in the air that fiction
> writers are allowed anything, so while 'The White Negro' was
> considered intellectually non-acceptable, it was still acceptable for
> purposes of fictional exploration. (Manso, p. 296)

Phillips does not suggest that 'The White Negro' is a work of fiction,
where anything can be said, but, he implies, it is written by a novelist
who is exempted from the responsibilities to which the rest of us are
answerable. Later, Mailer's biographers seemed to agree. Dearborn
concedes that it 'is a difficult piece and is not marked by the clarity of its
writing. Yet it demands close, careful reading.' (p. 127). She sounds like
an uncompromising professor insisting to her disgruntled students that
the magical resource of 'close reading' will enable them to make sense
of, even appreciate, anything. Lennon is even worse:

> ... one cannot help but feel the seductive energy of the essay – energy,
> in fact, is its pith and marrow. 'The White Negro' is a dithyrambic
> hymn to energy which pulses in a universe that is not a fact, but 'a
> changing reality whose laws are remade each instant by everything
> living ...' (p. 220)

And so on for about five hundred words. For most of his biography Lennon maintains an accessible, common-sense manner, but 'The White Negro' brings the gibberish of academia to the surface, and Mills and Rollyson follow the same distressing route.

With each, one feels the need to interrupt them and ask: but what does it mean? The passages of Mailer's essay that do make sense are uniformly ghastly. It is worth quoting the opening sentence in full. 'Probably, we will never be able to determine the psychic havoc of the concentration camps and the atom bomb upon the unconscious mind of almost everyone alive in these years.' This seems sound enough, given that nothing quite like Hiroshima and Nagasaki and the Holocaust has been so at odds with our aspirations to civilised existence, at least in recent history. The expectation, therefore, is that Mailer will look at whether the human race can learn something from what it had shown itself capable of doing. But no. Over the next twenty-three pages he takes us in all manner of directions, with the only relatively consistent element of these excursions being his celebration of bad behaviour. The figure who epitomises these seemingly limitless transgressions against what most would treat as the norms of decency and order is the 'Hipster'. The Hipster, usually male, takes a little from the philosophy of Sartre's existentialism, but more significantly he borrows from a quintessentially racist model of 'Negro' behaviour. For the purposes of his thesis Mailer treats African Americans as rootless, alienated, conditioned to the worst that life can offer – notably deprivation, imprisonment and discrimination – and consequently:

> The Negro has the simplest of alternatives: live a life of constant humility or ever-threatening danger. In such a pass where paranoia is as vital to survival as blood, the Negro had stayed alive and begun to grow by following the need of his body where he could. (*AFM*, p. 347)

The need of his body included drink, criminality and, predominantly, sex. Even jazz, an offshoot of black culture, is essentially an expression of sex, bordering on sexual violence.

... in his music he gave voice to the character and quality of his existence, to his rage and the infinite variations of joy, lust, languor, growl, cramp, pinch, scream and despair of his orgasm. For jazz is orgasm ...(ibid.)

'Orgasm' is, along with the Negro and the Hip, one of the three prevailing shibboleths of the essay, though 'psychopath' comes a very close fourth. But his quartet of watchwords does not involve a random or equitable mix. Throughout, it is the visceral inclinations and behaviour of the 'Negro' that predominate. Subject this to the kind of 'close, careful reading' recommended by Dearborn and we come upon a thesis that licenses, for white men, the kind of sexual activity that is aggressively male and equates the pleasure of orgasm as something like the successful completion of rape. According to Rollyson,

Mailer wants to abolish moral categories not because he is against morality but because he rejects categorised thinking of the type exemplified by the social worker ... [which] devour[s] and deaden[s] the world by categorising it. (Rollyson, '2',p. 112)

Dearborn (1999), Lennon (2013) and Rollyson (2008) look back at 'The White Negro' from a period when racism in America is recognised by most people as an abhorrent and endemic element of an earlier generation, at least by people like them — educated liberals. How then can they not see the essay for what it is, an intellectualised foreshadowing of white supremacy that flourished during Trump's Presidency? The 'Negro', who informs virtually every sentence, serves persistently as a justification for nasty behaviour by white people. The entire argument of the piece is grounded upon the model of the African-American male as an animalistic sub-species of humanity, a state that the clever, artistic white male can borrow for his own purposes, principally to qualify as a 'hipster'.

So, there was a new breed of adventurers, urban adventurers who drifted out at night looking for action with a black man's code to fit their facts. The hipster had absorbed the existentialist synapses of the Negro, and for practical purposes could be considered a white Negro. (*AFM*, p. 347)

In the most appalling passage Mailer ponders degrees of heroism and cowardice that underpin the activities of the average psychopath. He considers the case of two eighteen-year-old hoodlums who 'beat in the brains of a candy-store keeper'. Are they 'hip' by simply breaking the law, or does their victim disqualify them from this honour by virtue of being a 'weak fifty-year-old man'? He concludes that since they had 'entered a dangerous conflict with the police' and 'violated private property', they deserve respect as apprentice hipsters, despite having battered the property owner to death.

'The White Negro' is still seen as the most radical contribution to the post-war American counterculture pioneered by the likes of Ginsberg, Burroughs and Kerouac. Ginsberg's performance poem *Howl* went into print less than a year before Mailer's piece came out and Kerouac's *On the Road* a few months after its publication. The title of Norman Podhoretz's 'The Know-Nothing Bohemians' (1958) indicates the mood of the early begrudgers: Podhoretz feels that Mailer's, Ginsberg's and Kerouac's recommendations of anarchistic style and behaviour are based on intellectual laziness rather than principle. Through the late 1960s Mailer was attacked by feminists, notably Kate Millett (in *Sexual Politics*, 1970), who, quite rightly, read 'The White Negro' as an endorsement of male authority up to and including rape as a permissible creative gesture. When cultural studies sidelined mainstream literary criticism and common sense, the work began to be treated as an example of the erosion of boundaries between purist notions of literature and other types of 'discourse'. Joseph Wenke (in *Mailer's America*, 1987), for example, claimed that it is a work of fiction, though not because it in any way resembles a novelette. It is fictional because its speaking presence is allowed to transgress the standard regulations of, say, journalism or political writing, in which rarely is murder recommended.

Overall, a consensus formed around the essay. A few, such as Millett, found it objectionable, but even she conceded that it is a major contribution to the cutting-edge, avant garde intermeshing of literature, culture and political radicalism. Podhoretz, who first condemned it as 'morally gruesome', had by 1959 begun to change his mind. 'Bored with my own sensibly moderate liberal ideas ... I saw in Mailer the possibility of a new kind of radicalism – a radicalism that did not depend on Marx

...' (Mills, p. 187). As we've seen, each of Mailer's biographers see it as important not despite but because of its moral and stylistic infractions. The fact that everyday readers might not understand it or, if they do, might feel unsettled by it, confers a sacramental status on the work; it carries, they imply, an almost magical quality that would be ruined by such crude and vulgar notions as making sense of it, let alone daring to judge it.

Let us return to the murder of the candy-store keeper: 'One murders not only a weak fifty-year-old man but an institution as well, one violates private properly, one enters into a new relation with the police and introduces a dangerous element into one's life.' The use of 'one' unites Mailer and his readers in this act of anti-establishmentism, but what if the victim had been a librarian, a museum curator, a physician, nurse or poet? The 'weak' middle-aged shopkeeper is expendable because he is a junior element of the 'institution', not, one assumes, too clever, cultured, or part of the circles in which Mailer and his intellectual fellow travellers mixed.

One can take the indulgent route and assume that Mailer was, when writing it, too drunk and drug-addled to realise that he was casting African Americans as an animalistic sub-species. That, however, is too generous. All that prevailed when he put together this horrible accident of prose writing was his ego. He wanted fame and he was determined to shock.

The Pew Research Center Website is the source of fascinating details gathered by mass polling on what might be termed the state of mind of the American public over the past six decades. When surveys began in 1958, 80 per cent of the electorate, irrespective of party allegiance, declared that they trusted the people in the federal government, in the Senate, Congress and the presidency, with their lives and their future; 67 per cent were 'satisfied with the state of the nation'; 65 per cent believed that government was 'run for the benefit of the people'; and only 28 per cent suspected that it was 'run by big interests', principally industrial and financial institutions. The findings are not surprising given that the post-war economic boom reached its peak at the end of the 1950s, with unemployment at a record low and the depression the nightmare of a previous generation. Home and car ownership were commonplaces, irrespective of class, and consumer goods such as refrigerators and televisions were things that the vast majority of households could take for granted. There is, it seems, a causal relationship between the experience of a pleasurable lifestyle within the population and their feelings of contentment with the people who ran America and the country as a whole.

Eighteen months after 'The White Negro' appeared, Mailer published another essay in *Dissent*, 'From Surplus Value to Mass-Media', an attempt to graft modified Marxist theory onto the media-driven consumerist culture of 1959 America. His argument is that the proletariat were no longer exploited as they were during the Industrial Revolution, when those who controlled industry treated them as assets. Now ordinary people had an abundance of leisure time and material resources, and because of this they were subjected, unheedingly, to brainwashing and control by the capitalist oligarchy. In short, revolution would not come about while the oppressed were too busy enjoying themselves.

I mention this because it raises questions about Mailer's projected audience when he began 'The White Negro'. It seems unlikely that the ordinary American reader would be attracted to a manifesto for anarchic misbehaviour – life was too good for that – but as Podhoretz indicated there was still a belief within the American intellectual aristocracy that the entrepreneurialist/materialist culture of their homeland should be exchanged for something else. Marx was no longer fashionable, so Mailer's hymn to irresponsible anarchy was a beguiling alternative. It didn't matter that it was ludicrous. It was unconventional and therefore his route to the top. Malaquais describes things shrewdly.

I wondered why Norman was jumping into all this hipster nonsense ... it was *à la mode*, and Norman jumped into it. Aside from the erotic myth – that Negroes are good fuckers – there seems to be a thread running through Norman's life that drives him to be on the first rung, the center of attention. Suppose spinsters go down the street and start singing lewd songs – Norman will be there with a theory. He'll try to blow up the occasion into some momentous event. Why? Because, lacking a proper philosophical background, he aims at building a system of his own. To pick things out of the air and mark them with his own stamp is an especial talent of his. (Manso, p. 255)

A few months after 'The White Negro' came out, Mailer produced a short story called 'The Time of Her Time'. It is the only surviving part of his plan for a full-length sequel to *The Deer Park*, and once more its narrator is Sergius O'Shaugnessy, now a full-time teacher of bullfighting in New York with numerous instruments of his art distributed through his apartment. The most memorable passage involves his description of sex with a New York University student, an exercise in verbal pornography that is by equal degrees hyperbolic and embarrassing. It is almost that Sergius's feelings of rage and disappointment while he is 'pronging her' with his 'avenger' come from his having used his author's recent essay as an instruction manual on sexual encounters. Sample a passage.

> I lunged up over the hill with my heart pounding past all pleasure, and I came, but with hatred, tight, electric, and empty, the spasms powerful but centered in my heart and not from the hip, the avenger taking its punishment even at the end, jolted clear to the seat of my semen by the succession of rhythmic blows which my heart drummed back to my feet. (*AFM*, p. 510)

This goes on for around three pages, and Sergius peppers his description with frequent references to 'hip', 'Negro' and 'orgasm'.

He does not forcefully have sex with the unfortunate young woman, but throughout the episode violence and sexual satisfaction, his at least, are coterminous. His 'avenger', for example, is also referred to as 'the killing machine', with which, a page earlier, he plans to 'prong her then and there ... grind it into her ... eager to ram into all her nasty little tensions'.

In August 1958 the Mailers put the Connecticut house up for sale and leased an apartment at 73 Perry Street in Greenwich Village, a spacious ground-floor unit with a terrace garden which they paid almost a thousand dollars to a landscape artist to pave and turf as an outdoor space for their drinks and dinner parties. Kerouac and Ginsberg were regular visitors, along with other lesser-known Beat writers such as Michael McClure. McClure was uneasy about Mailer mainly because the Beat movement, which in any event was a formation of vague ideas from the late 1940s, was now united in its acceptance of pacifism as the only appropriate response to the political and cultural establishment. Mailer and his alter-ego the hipster seemed addicted to the actual and symbolic nature of violence. Ginsberg: 'Kerouac thought that Norman was being an intellectual fool … Norman's notion of the hipster as being cool and psychopathic and cutting his way through society with jujitsu was a kind of macho folly that we giggled at.' (Manso, p. 258) The Beat writers knew that while he presented himself to them and the media as a maniacal nonconformist, he sought the attention of the literary establishment.

The literary critic Diana Trilling offers a hilarious account of an evening hosted by the Howes, Diana and her husband the academic Lionel. She was on Mailer's left at the dinner table, and on his right was Constance Askew, wife of the millionaire art dealer Kirk Askew; an East Coast dowager, with an ear trumpet, who might have been invented by Henry James. Mailer was 'so mannerly. He gave her his full attention … Norman wasn't only correct by traditional social standards, he was even courtly.' Once he'd paid his respects to Mrs Askew he 'turned to his left' to Diana 'and said. "Now, what about you, smart cunt?"' (Manso, p. 262). Diana Trilling and many others saw him as a chameleon, slipping easily between the radical, potentially violent hipster persona and a figure who enjoyed the company of the social and cultural hierarchy. Irving Howe recalls that he was unsettled by Mailer's tendency towards 'mild schizophrenia', particularly his ability to conform while shortly after treating conformity of any kind as a justification for something genuinely unpleasant. He would 'present his Howe face, his Trilling face', often with '… suit, tie, vest, the whole stylized deal straight from Oxford', but he felt that beneath this gentrified surface something quite different was going on. 'It was clear to me the distance between where I was and where he was going … simply the deification of self, the celebrator of self … The energy, the adventure.' Howe sensed that the monsters Mailer had exalted in 'The White Negro' had become part of his psyche. 'From simulated shock you have to go to real shock, and there was a sense that this could only lead to some kind of explosion, the particular nature of which we couldn't say.' (Manso, p. 268).

Aside from what he had written about 'hip', Mailer appeared to be experimenting with various forms of physical antagonism. At parties he challenged women to staring matches, on the unspoken assumption that his bodily superiority would guarantee victory. There was, however, something about his aggressive posture and facial expression that meant few of his female opponents would accept his invitation as an act of fun; most declined to take part, and those who took him on soon gave in, feeling distressed, often frightened. In her memoir Adele tells of how during the summer before they left Connecticut, she and Mailer had taken one of their regular drives to New York to attend a party and returned with him at the wheel, drunk, pushing his beloved Triumph TR3 sports car to speeds of over 90mph. As usual, they argued, mostly about their flirtations with others in New York, and when they reached the Connecticut house the exchange became violent with Mailer punching her in the eye and her right cheek. Her face remained black and swollen for more than a week. Adele's mother was staying over, looking after Danielle, and though she urged her to consider leaving him, her daughter dismissed the suggestion. Mailer did not acknowledge the wound to either woman, let alone apologise. Outside their close family no one knew that Mailer's version of the hipster involved domestic bullying and violence, and there was other evidence that he divided up aspects of his temperament and persona as he saw fit.

The Howes, Trillings and Podhoretzes were part of the Mailers' high-culture network, and he also became a regular invitee to events hosted by the younger, flashier coterie of literary celebrities. Bruce Jay Friedman and Philip Roth were being celebrated as the new generation of literary radicals, and Mailer was treated by many as their appropriate mentor. Editors who worked for newspapers and publishers, notably Jason Epstein and Bob Silvers, all younger than Mailer, gravitated to him as the figure who would electrify book launches and literary parties simply by being there. He got on well with George Plimpton, who had edited The Paris Review in France and had recently returned to New York to begin his glittering career as journalist, sportswriter and media celebrity. Like Mailer he enjoyed participating in what he wrote about. He played non-league baseball and ice hockey and sparred with some major professional boxers, including Sugar Ray Robinson. Along with this he came from a wealthy WASP family, was strikingly good looking, and his parties at his East River apartment would always be well attended by beautiful models. Mailer was a regular guest.

Those who'd known Mailer from his time at the *Voice*, Wolf and Fancher particularly, no longer met him regularly, but both later commented that within less than four years he seemed to have become a living parody of 'the Hip and the Square', the socialite who mixed with members of the intellectual elite and the affluent while still declaring his commitment to insurrection as a state of mind and a political strategy.

Perhaps to remedy this evident anomaly he exchanged the staring matches, usually involving women, for men-only contests. Thumb-wrestling might have seemed less combative than the arm-and-elbow version, but because the thumb is a more delicate appendage damage was sometimes serious, with combatants unable to use knives and forks or pens the following morning, and sometimes there were dislocations requiring hospital treatment. Mailer practised at home by having Adele press her heel down against his raised thumb with his forearm flat on the floor. More bizarre was the contest invented by Mailer where he challenged male guests at parties to high-speed head-butting. Hands would be placed behind backs and the two contestants would bend forward and charge towards each other across the room, probably over a distance of about six feet. There would be a horribly loud clash of skulls and at best dizziness resulted, but in some cases men were taken concussed to bedrooms or sofas.

Mailer persuaded himself that he could imitate Plimpton as a serious sportsman, and his choice was boxing. He had trained before, mostly with a bag, but now he went looking for professionals who would take him seriously as a sparring partner or even as a man they would train to their own level. His old friend Mickey Knox introduced him to Bill Walker, who had been a professional welterweight and now worked as a bodyguard for actor friends of Knox and as a nightclub bouncer. Through him Mailer got to know Roger Donoghue, who ran a training camp in New Jersey, and Ralph 'Tiger' Jones. Donoghue was now a coach, but after he had turned pro in 1948 he came close to contending for the world middleweight title. None of them read too many books, but they knew of Mailer's reputation as a celebrity and agreed, for a fee, to teach him some skills despite his being in his late thirties and still slightly overweight. They got beyond sparring and convinced Mailer that he was holding his own in eight-round fights. In truth, as Knox later disclosed, they were experienced enough to make him believe he had survived the pulled-punches they delivered, and his largely hopeless blows had been only moderately effective.

In September 1959 Mailer published *Advertisements for Myself*. As a literary work it was unprecedented, at least for living authors, given that it resembles the collection of works and manuscripts put together by respectful editors who saw it as their duty to curate the legacy of a late great writer. In this case Mailer was his own memorialist, including passages from his longer pieces of fiction, full-length short stories and non-literary essays, and bringing these together with self-composed preludes and reflections. It was, he implied, a collection of his finest writing, which deserved an honest, confessional commentary by the author himself. It was a cross between a self-regarding autobiography and a set of respectful commentaries by a ghost editor invented by Mailer. He did not tell lies in these pieces, but he left so much out that the truth as he presented it was laughably questionable. He said nothing about his encounters with, even his feelings for, women while subjecting the reader to limitlessly fraught revelations on the private traumas that accompanied his particular writings. He included extracts from critics, notably on 'The White Negro', but edited them carefully and refused to tackle any accusations directly. It was the equivalent of allowing people to question him on stage, refusing to respond and leaving the dais with a wry smile.

Having sold the Connecticut house, he and Adele took a lease on a large property in Provincetown, his old haunt, now even more densely populated by artists and writers from the New York metropolis. Styron was there, but they had not spoken since 1958, and Mailer made a point of pretending to not notice him if they were on the same street. Baldwin sometimes stayed there as a guest of other writers, the Mailers included, one of the few African Americans in town who was not there for domestic work. Other black people would be seen on the streets or in stores but spent much of their time in the servants' quarters of white residents. Mailer, like other white intellectuals in the area, chose not to discuss this with Baldwin, and for the latter this reinforced his suspicion that they lived in different worlds. Neither of them spoke of 'The White Negro.'

Mailer enjoyed trying out his new-found boxing skills on men at parties in the town, and one night, disappointed in his failure to provoke some kind of Cape Cod hipster violence, he was walking back to the house with Adele when she sensed he had become agitated. He crossed the road and began stopping others in their path. 'What was it he hoped would happen? ... Another fistfight? ... What demons of the evening were riding him?' (*The Last Party*, p. 189). Eventually, a police car appeared, slowed and then passed them. Mailer ran after it, shouting 'taxi, taxi!'. It stopped, and he explained to the two officers that he thought the sign on the roof advertised a car for hire. They were not amused, and they put him into the back seat. After a night in the cells Adele bought him out of custody with $50, finding that he needed fifteen stitches in his head after a beating with a nightstick. There are different versions of what went on after he was arrested, and the truth remains entirely a matter for speculation. He was charged with being drunk and disorderly, and at the trial he pleaded insanity. The judge, exasperated, let him go without a penalty on the understanding that any similar behaviour in the future would be dealt with less leniently. He wore his stitches and later his scar as a badge of honour.

His alienation from William Styron and James Jones began at one of the Provincetown gatherings. As usual, Mailer had tried to turn exchanges of opinion into fistfights, and one of these involved Styron, who later recalled that he decided to remove himself only when he sensed that Mailer's comments were becoming deliberately provocative. He was therefore surprised to receive a letter from Mailer a few days later in which he accused him of 'passing a few atrocious remarks about Adele', specifically her sex life, and went on to promise that 'I will invite you to a fight in which I expect to stomp out of you a fat amount of your yellow and treacherous shit' (12 March 1958). Styron was shocked not because Mailer had threatened violence – that was a commonplace – but because while he and his wife had rarely got on with Adele, he had not mentioned her on the night in question, let alone made 'atrocious' remarks about her sex life.

Styron spoke to Jones and his wife, Gloria, genuinely puzzled and distressed at what had caused their mutual friend to write to him in such a way. They were more familiar with Mailer's psychological make-up and advised him that while his hatred was sincere it had been prompted by something other than the alleged remark about Adele; principally that, as a fellow writer, Styron was now one of many receiving the wrath of a man who thought himself better than the rest. Two weeks before, Mailer had written to Jones about his recent novel, *The Pistol*, calling it 'very frankly, a slipshod presentation' (25 February 1958). After returning from a brief visit to Florida Mailer found a belated reply from Styron stating that his letter was 'so mean and contemptible ... so utterly false, that it does not deserve even this much of a reply' (17 April 1958). Mailer wrote first to Jones, as if he took for granted that the two men had discussed the feud, and the letter veers between the malicious and the deranged. 'I wouldn't get into a fight with you unless I were ready to kill you, and I always instinctively assumed that was true for you.' (20 April 1958). Next, for Styron, 'So I invite you to get together with me face to face and repeat that my letter is mean, contemptible, and false – if you feel up to it. If you don't, recognise your reply for what it is – a crock of shit.' (27 April 1958).

In an interview with Lennon (p. 230) on his fallings out with the two writers, Mailer states that there were during this time 'a lot of orgies' which involved Adele being 'lent out'. 'But I couldn't stand it, I couldn't stand a man making love to her', which seems a little contradictory given that he was happy enough to act as the equivalent of her pimp. It is possible that his moral ambivalence regarding her sex life – involving a combination of permissive and possessive moods – might have had something to do with his untruthful allegations against Styron. His next admission is even more fascinating.

Very selfish from my point of view; those were the years I was having two women and that gave me a feeling of great superiority. I'd feel, "Oh well, these other literary lights, they had their social superiority, but I had my sexual superiority", and that was what was feeding me.

The notion of sexual excess as a route to literary 'superiority' carries a dissonant echo of 'The White Negro', and quite soon Mailer would produce what amounts to an appendix for his unhinged manifesto.

Within a month of his quarrels with Styron and Jones he began an essay which was written exclusively for inclusion in *Advertisements for Myself*. 'Evaluations – Quick and Expensive Comments on the Talent in the Room' is a statement of purpose, his estimation of the qualities of his literary contemporaries, and his further declaration of 'superiority'. In ten pages he deals with thirty American writers who had established themselves over the previous fifteen years – in short, the entire ongoing generation of the 'talent'. He opens by declaring his 'love' for Jones and commenting that while *From Here to Eternity* 'has been the best American novel since the war', it is also 'ridden with faults, ignorances, and a smudge of the sentimental', and that after his debut Jones had 'sold out badly', persistently failing to realise his early potential and writing but 'I would never write him off, not even if it seemed medically evident he had pickled his brain in the gin' – something of a backhanded compliment. Styron is treated with much less mercy – 'his mind was uncorrupted by a new idea' – and Mailer lines up Truman Capote ('tart as a grand aunt'), Kerouac ('lacks discipline, intelligence, honesty'), Saul Bellow ('I cannot take him seriously as a major novelist'), Salinger ('no more than the greatest mind ever to stay in prep school') and Gore Vidal ('imprisoned in the recessive nuances of narcissistic explorations') for the same treatment. As for women writers of the past two decades: 'I have nothing to say about any of the talented women who write today … I do not seem able to read them. Indeed I doubt if there will be a really exciting woman writer until the first whore becomes a call girl and tells her tale.'

He, Jones and Styron had certainly discussed each other's work, but it is clear enough that Mailer's other evaluations are arbitrary, in that while he hurls insults at authors randomly, as if from a thesaurus of abuse – 'insignificant', 'vain', 'without life', 'miserable', 'hopeless', 'weakness' and so on – there is no evidence that he has read their books. He writes like the unhinged despot of a literary cosmos certain that everyone else must be reminded of their inferiority, while by implication he is greatness personified.

According to Dearborn 'the storm center was the Paris home of Jim and Gloria Jones', where they read condemnation of them 'in a kind of drunken, masochistic fashion'; Baldwin and Styron responded similarly.

Jones and others were disturbed because while they were used to diatribes by Mailer at parties, usually when he was drunk, a similar level of abuse in print caused enduring pain: spoken words are ephemeral but condemnation on the page would stay there. While Mailer intended *Advertisements for Myself* and this essay in particular as his personal manifesto, most level-headed members of the literary establishment saw it as a combination of delusion and self-regard. *The Saturday Review of Literature*, *Atlantic* and *The New York Times* thought it verged on the insane, with *Time* judging it the 'record of an artistic crackup'.

Gore Vidal, one of Mailer's victims, reviewed *Advertisements for Myself* in *The Nation* (2 January 1960), observing that 'Mailer is forever shouting at us that he is about to tell us something we must know or has just told us something revelatory ... So each time he speaks he must become more bold, more loud, put on brighter motley and shake more foolish bells.' Vidal demonstrates Mailer's foolishness without going in for outright condemnation. Instead, he invites us by implication to compare his own beautifully nuanced prose with Mailer's jagged hyperbole. 'Yet of all my contemporaries I retain the greatest affection for Mailer as a force and an artist. He is a man whose faults, though many, add to rather than subtract from the sum of his natural achievements.' The first sentence sounds like the kind of eulogy that might be offered to a slightly unsound relative and the second almost as a compliment, until one reads it closely: his faults are the sum of his achievements, and one can imagine the patrician pleasure Vidal took in writing this.

Throughout the volume Mailer is intent on blurring the boundaries between literary and political writing and between writing per se and political action. He opens the introduction with 'Like many another vain, empty and bullying body of our time, I have been running for President these last ten years in the privacy of my mind ...' The tone seems self-mocking, but given Mailer's record of grandstanding we begin to suspect that it is closer to the truth than he would like to admit, with the notion of the 'Presidency' cropping up again and again in his reflections on writing, culture, the radical delights of Hip, orgasms, the fulfilling power of violent sexuality, etc. And one is reminded of his essay for the *Voice* in which he insisted that only Hemingway, through force of his violent idiosyncratic personality, was the exemplary candidate; and unlike the other contenders he possessed the magical status of being a writer. Mailer was convinced that only writers had the quasi-mystical wisdom to navigate the potentially catastrophic future of global politics. He had made it clear in 'Evaluations' that his peers weren't up to it – and it was evident enough that the only person who could do so was the one he had not mentioned.

9

HOW NOT TO MURDER YOUR WIFE

Mailer had been writing for *Esquire* for three years, a magazine that was split between soft-core verbal pornography and photographs and an affiliation to radical causes, notably the Beats and hipsterdom. It began to serialise *Advertisements for Myself* immediately before publication in 1959. A few months later its features editor, Clay Felker, visited the Five Spot Café in New York, and the head waiter, assuming that he had come to meet Mailer, who was already there having drinks with Adele, her sister, Joanne, and Mickey Knox, guided him to their table. They had hardly spoken before, but Felker had read extracts from *Advertisements for Myself*, and he asked Mailer how he intended to cover the 1960 presidential election: a series of articles? a book? Disingenuously Mailer stated he hadn't thought about it, and Felker suggested that he should go to Los Angeles to write about the 1960 Democratic National Convention.

He flew there with Felker, and the latter recalled that his companion's first encounter with John Kennedy marked an 'epiphany', which Mailer later described for Manso: 'He was in the back seat of an open car, his face suntanned, and there was a crowd of gays on the other side of Pershing Park, all applauding, going crazy, while the convention itself was filled with the whole corrupt trade-union Mafia Democratic machine. And I could feel these two worlds come together.' (Manso, p. 305). Or, as he had put it in 'From Surplus Value to Mass-Media', 'If there is a future for the radical spirit, which often enough one can doubt, it can come only from a new revolutionary vision of society, its sicknesses, its strengths, its conflicts, contradictions and radiations ...' Felker asked him to write a leading article on Kennedy, which would eventually be called 'Superman Comes to the Supermarket'. In Mailer's view, Kennedy's campaign and, he hoped, victory would be a crossroads in the history of twentieth-century politics and culture. One passage is particularly striking:

> Since the First World War Americans have been leading a double life, and our history has moved on two rivers, one visible, the other underground; there has been the history of politics which is concrete, factual, practical and unbelievably dull ... and there is a subterranean river of untapped, ferocious, lonely and romantic desires, that concentration of ecstasy and violence which is the dream life of the nation. (*The Presidential Papers*, p. 38)

This opens with what appears to be a straightforward observation, if couched in rather opaque language. By 'double life' he seems to refer to a division between those who had survived the depression largely unscathed and others who remain horribly damaged in its aftermath. He does not refer to any statistics let alone economic assessments of America three decades after the recession. Rather the 'underground' of US society is a projection of the hyperbole of 'The White Negro'. Who, one wonders, will be able to channel the 'subterranean river of untapped, ferocious, lonely and romantic desires' into the body politic? Who would become 'the fleshing of the romantic prescription'? Supposedly, this figure is John F. Kennedy, but the 'double life' Mailer refers to is an accurate though inadvertent portrayal of his own shifts between ambition and self-delusion. Quite soon he would attempt to make up for Kennedy's failings as the political messiah.

Mailer worked on the article in Provincetown during July and August 1960. Felker decided that it had the potential to increase the esteem of *Esquire* nationwide and allowed him at least 13,000 words, most of a single issue. This was the run-up to an election in which one candidate was seen as the most liberal and left-leaning since Henry A Wallace, founder of the Progressive Party, and this profile of him by his equal, at least in the intelligentsia, was seen as something that would influence undecided centrist voters. There was already gossip and speculation among those in the media and the press, and this led to exchanges between Felker and two of Kennedy's advisors, Peter Maas and Pierre Salinger, on the possibility of a meeting.

The Kennedy family home in Hyannis Port is about an hour by car from Provincetown, and Mailer was informed by Felker that Kennedy had agreed to do an interview, including the preferred date and time at less than a day ahead. He had almost completed the article, but this one-to-one would make it unique. He arrived in a suit and tie 'sweating like a goat' and was greeted by Maas, whom he'd met once or twice in New York, Salinger and Prince Radziwill, husband of Jacqueline Kennedy's sister, Caroline, all of whom were casually dressed in open shirts and cotton trousers, as was Kennedy when Mailer sat down in his office, 'tense at the pit of my stomach'. If Mailer made notes none survive, but it was later disclosed that Kennedy, originally reluctant to do the interview, was briefed in advance by Salinger and Maas on Mailer's reputation as an ideological wildcard. They advised him that any misgivings Mailer might have about Kennedy would be sidelined if he was convinced that Kennedy admired his books. Kennedy was told to first express his enthusiasm for *The Deer Park*, which some critics had treated as pornographic, rather than the safe option of *The Naked and the Dead*. There is no evidence that Kennedy had read either novel, but Maas had cleverly picked out features of both that would persuade Mailer that he had. Mailer left the Kennedy compound exhilarated by the idea that the potential future president liked his work. On the way out the likely First Lady introduced herself and invited him to drive back the following day so that she and her husband could talk again, adding that she would like to meet his wife.

One moment that Mailer recalls from the interview involved them talking of an election poster he'd brought with him. In part it was a reproduction of one put together by the Democrat campaign team featuring a picture of Nixon looking swarthy and devious, with a speech bubble: 'Would you buy a used car from this man?' The new version was a retaliation from the Republicans, and included a photograph of Kennedy – handsome, smiling with his beautiful wife – with the caption: 'However, if you bought the car from Jack Kennedy, you would trust him and you would buy the car, and then after you'd bought the car, he'd drop by to pay a visit and see how it was working, and then he'd seduce your wife.' At the time Kennedy's taste for infidelity, often with actresses supplied by the so-called 'rat pack' media clique and sometimes by mobsters, was a reasonably well-kept secret among his political closed circle, but the Republican's piece aroused suspicions within the Kennedy set that stories were circulating among the press.

In truth, this was the principal reason that Mailer had been invited to talk with Kennedy. The campaign team were aware that Mailer was on good terms with both conservative and radical media outlets; they wanted to know what he knew and if necessary to enlist him as an infiltrator. Kennedy asked Mailer, 'I don't really know what that means, do you?' (Dearborn, p151). Kennedy did his best to sound genuinely puzzled, but beneath his calmness he was anxious, and it was at this moment that he excused himself, left Mailer with the clipping, and next door asked his wife to interrupt Mailer when he left and invite him back. Kennedy assumed that if Mailer and Adele felt they had become honorary members of the elect they would be very willing to share information on rumours circulating in the media. Mailer swore he knew nothing and commented only that, compared with the shifty-looking Nixon, Kennedy was photogenic and had a taste for smart suits. Clearly, he was unaware of any Kennedy family secrets, but it was too late for John to ask Jacqueline not to issue the invitation.

Adele, in a state of shock, spent the evening and early morning thinking about what to wear. Mailer dressed down in accordance with his hosts and found himself racing towards the Kennedy house not knowing how Adele would be received or what had prompted this precipitous second meeting. This time Jacqueline had been briefed, and she stunned Adele by telling her that, apparently, she had seen her work in New York galleries. She showed Adele some of her own paintings and gave the impression that, by comparison, she was but an amateur.

'Superman Comes to the Supermarket' sent sales of *Esquire* beyond 10,000; a reprint of the issue was done because of the impact of the piece. Mailer made it clear that Kennedy would be America's saviour: 'one [Nixon] was sober, the apotheosis of opportunistic lead, all radium spent, the other [Kennedy] handsome as a prince in the unstated aristocracy of the American dream.' (*MoO*, p. 143). What Mailer does not make clear is how exactly this man would rescue America from its various ills. Instead, he creates for him a personality cult, assembled from fragments of biography, mostly verifiable but sometimes exaggerated. A war hero whose courage and tenacity touches upon the suicidal, a man whose life seems to have been clogged by catastrophe – an almost disabling back problem when at college, suspected leukaemia and a severe gastrointestinal illness, among other ailments – but who drove himself forward through service for his country and a career in politics, as if sensing that a colossal destiny awaited him. And, in Mailer's portrait, he looked the part – 'handsome as a prince'.

> … only a hero can capture the secret imagination of a people, and so be good for the vitality of his nation; a hero embodies the fantasy and so allows each private mind the liberty to consider its fantasy and find a way to grow. Each mind can become more conscious of its desire and waste less strength in hiding from itself. (*MoO*, p. 125)

This kind of conjectural hyperbole was the keynote of Mailer's writing for a decade, involving no practical solutions to the problems facing the world's most powerful nation. Nonetheless, he ventures a few examples of the figures which embody his complex notion of the political hero: Roosevelt, Churchill, Lenin, de Gaulle and Hitler all feature. The latter is, he concedes, 'odious', yet he 'gave outlet to the energies of the Germans'. Amusingly, when he and Felker were discussing the piece, Mailer confessed that he was apprehensive about doing an article on realpolitik – 'the only political writing I know anything about is Marx' – and his understanding of Marxism was questionable, to say the least. He confessed to being flattered by Kennedy's admiration for his novels and stated that even if, as rumoured, 'Kennedy was briefed … (which is most doubtful), it still speaks well for the striking instincts of his advisers' (*MoO*, p. 130). Here he implies that their brief encounters would be the beginning of something like a partnership.

Peter Hamill of *The New York Post* commented that 'It ['Superman Comes to the Supermarket'] went through journalism like a wave … Norman took political journalism beyond what the best guys – Mencken, Teddy White, Richard Rovere – had done.' He meant that it was a transformational moment during the pioneering years of New

Journalism, important because its visionary speculations came from a person who had actually spoken with Kennedy.

Its influence on the way people would write, let alone vote, was slight compared with its effect on its author. Mailer believed that he had found 'the one ingredient' that made Kennedy electable, that he had, through the essay, convinced Adlai Stevenson's team to give the Kennedy campaign their belated support. He 'had a feeling that if there were a power which made presidents' then he personally had harnessed it, 'that is what I thought ... [and] I still do' (*The Presidential Papers*, pp. 60, 89). Following Kennedy's election, by the narrowest of margins, Mailer remained convinced that he would soon be contacted by the White House and invited to become an advisor or consultant for the administration. No such invitation arrived, but he persuaded himself that his new role as a man who could influence politics by writing about it would enable him to become a version of Kennedy.

Shortly after the election Mailer met H. L. 'Doc' Humes, chairman of the Citizens' Emergency Committee, a group set up to contest criminal cases against political subversives and black people in New York. The city had enabled its law enforcers to constrain selected theatre performances, cabarets and jazz events by requiring those involved to carry licences and identity cards. Otherwise, the events could be closed down and performers could be faced with arrest. A large number of those detained were black musicians or people involved in Beat culture and related leftist causes. This crackdown was a spin-off from the McCarthy anti-communist neuroses of the early 1950s, flavoured by fears of left-wing involvement in the civil rights movement in the Southern states and most of all from the sense of anxiety felt in America by a communist revolution taking place only a hundred miles off the coast of Florida. Humes's *The Underground City* (1958) is a sprawling experimental novel that makes Mailer's fictional and non-fictional explorations of creative psychopathy seem conservative. The two men got on well, and while Humes admired Mailer's presentation of Kennedy, he also convinced him that the new president would, despite his best intentions, remain an instrument of the political and economic establishment. What was needed, he argued, was a figure who would stand out as the president's junior revolutionary consort; part rival, part ally.

The Citizens' Emergency Committee was also vocal in its support for Castro's attempts to overthrow Batista in Cuba. Even before his election, in the months between summer and autumn 1959, Kennedy had spoken publicly about sending a 'relief force' to Cuba. At the time the Soviet Union had hardly heard of the place, but the American political establishment feared that it would soon become a Caribbean version of the Soviet bloc, a communist outpost adjacent to US democracy. Mailer was appalled by Kennedy's stance and wrote to his advisor Arthur Schlesinger instructing him that if the candidate pursued a politically aggressive policy, following his hoped-for electoral victory, the consequences would be 'tragic', involving 'some yet undefined Marine corps lumpen proletariat for the invasion of Cuba ... a chilling [but] perhaps forgivable mistake due to the excesses of campaigning' (Mailer to Schlesinger, 28 October 1960). That he expected Schlesinger, and Kennedy, to take him seriously testifies to his delusional condition. As late as 1999 he commented that 'I wanted to be an advisor ... I felt that, you know, I might have a certain talent for it.' (Lennon, p. 274).

Within two days of his letter to Schlesinger, Mailer decided to use Cuba as a central issue in his decision to stand in the New York City mayoral election of 1961. He discussed his candidacy with Irving Howe and several on the editorial team of *Dissent*, who were tolerant enough until he announced his intention 'to establish New York as the West Berlin of the world'. The Berlin Wall had yet to go up, and Mailer idealised the western part of the city as quasi-autonomous and politically unaffiliated, his model for New York City. He followed this by reading them his 'Open Letter to Fidel Castro', which requested that the revolutionary leader form an alliance with him in an 'existential campaign' so that voters would sense the potential for New York City as, along with Cuba, 'a force in the world'. He added that he had recently despatched a signed version to 'Comrade Fidel'. Howe, rather stunned, advised him as diplomatically as possible that this policy might not win over too many middle-class voters, who were principally concerned with local taxation.

Nonetheless, Mailer continued to refer to the letter throughout his campaign, despite having received no reply from Cuba. He praised Castro 'for sending the wind of new rebellion to our lungs'. Most significantly, he compares the tyranny of Batista with the ongoing authoritarian politics of America. 'In Cuba, hatred runs over into the love of blood; in America all too few blows are struck into flesh.' But he promises that he will inspire his fellow repressed citizens into acts of physical violence. He does not give a particularly clear account of who would suffer these attacks or to what end, but the rambling verbosity of the piece – threats of brutality strung together with jargon from Marx, existentialism, etc. – was more or less consistent with the material he had produced over the previous five years. The difference this time, however, was that he promised to implement them as leader of America's most powerful metropolis. In the parts that were relatively coherent he laid out the nature of his active constituency, those he would inspire as his agents of savagery: the disenfranchised in general, and in particular, prostitutes, runaways, the homeless, drug addicts, recreational junkies, 'Negroes', criminals of every hue, and of course hipsters. While most treated his journalism as both entertaining and the harmless rants of a publicity-hungry novelist, he was now putting himself forward as the political incarnation of mass, cure-all barbarity.

During the few weeks between the publication of *Advertisements for Myself* and the beginning of his campaign, Mailer sent letters to, among others, Stephen Spender, John Brosnan, John Cheever, T. S. Eliot and Jackie Kennedy. His topics were various but each was underpinned by his assumption of his great potency and, more absurdly, that his correspondents would take him seriously. The ostensible subject of his letter to Eliot was the refusal of André Deutsch, the British publisher of *Advertisements for Myself*, to include 'The Time of Her Time' in their edition. They were reluctant to do so because of its vivid emphasis on sex. Eliot was not directly involved with Deutsch, but Mailer assumed that they would listen to one of the most eminent figures in London publishing, who would address them on behalf of the mayor-elect of America's greatest city. He introduced himself to Eliot as 'Prince Mailer the Norman of Principath to T. S. Lord King of Eliot, Impervious to Compassion, Blind by Pride, Royal as a Royal Roach who has Earned his Place which is High ... do challenge your inflexible taste by presenting the fruits of my orchard and the war of my castle' (October 1960). He closes with 'Do answer. No answer is war, and one would detest that.' But there is no record of a reply from T. S. Lord King of Eliot.

In his letter to Jackie Kennedy, posted five days before her husband's victory, Mailer becomes an omniscient 'Superman', capable of understanding history and seeing the present from the past in a quasi-mystical manner. Throughout, he comes across as her friend and, potentially, seducer, suggesting that he should visit her in Hyannis Port to discuss, specifically, the life and work of the Marquis de Sade. He assumes that they share an interest in him and states that he intends to write a biography of de Sade. 'I might be able to throw a hint or two on the odd strong honor of the man,' he writes, declaring that surely Jackie would love to compare notes on de Sade as 'a fair climax to the Age of Reason' (3 November 1960). The soon-to-be First Lady thought it best not to respond to her suitor. Norman Podhoretz recalled that after her husband's assassination, Jackie would ask him to invite writers he knew to parties at her New York apartment, but 'told me I was not to include Norman Mailer' (Ex-Friends, p. 208).

The first formal meeting of supporters for Mailer's mayoral campaign took place on 15 November at Downey's Steakhouse in Manhattan. Allen Ginsberg was present, along with Doc Humes and Mailer's friends Noel Parmental Jr, who had come up with the tagline on Nixon versus Kennedy as competing car salesmen, and Seymour Krim. After the meeting Mailer returned to 250 West 94th Street with Humes, who had secured an apartment there for him and who lived on the floor below with his wife, Anna Lou; they had decided that the building would become campaign headquarters.

The following day, Mailer's sister Barbara arrived at the apartment to deliver material she had typed and copied as fliers for the campaign. He was unhappy with what he read but not because Barbara was responsible for any typographical errors. He accused her of altering the original and hit her across the side of her face, causing a bruise and breaking her glasses. She was appalled, but he followed up the assault by accusing her and the rest of the family of conspiring against him – unlike the Kennedys, he added, who were united in their support for John. Ten years later he recalled the event and stated, without a hint of remorse: 'I had something to do in the world.' (Lennon, p 278).

On the 17th, the day after the incident with Barbara, Mailer gave a lecture at Brown University, Providence. The students and academics had been promised a talk on the modern novel and were rather surprised when Mailer opened with 'I come to bring you the existential word', followed by a rambling, improvised version of his election manifesto. Some, such as Professor John Hawkes, attempted to give the performance shape by posing questions about his fiction, which he ignored. One student asked if he would read them the passage when the repulsive Cummings watches the 'chow line' of private soldiers queuing for food in *The Naked and the Dead*, and this time Mailer did respond, by pointing at his groin and inviting the student to 'Eat this!' Eventually he began to hurl invective and threats of violence at the audience for refusing to listen to his political message. Most left, but the few who remained thought that they had witnessed a piece of exorbitant performance prose – a tribute to Ginsberg, plus verbal abuse.

During Friday 18 November he made plans for the formal announcement of his campaign via newspapers, the radio and, he hoped, television, which would take place on the following Tuesday, the 22nd. Saturday was the birthday of his boxer friend Roger Donoghue, and Mailer promised to host a party for him at the 94th Street apartment. Unknown to Donoghue, however, Mailer had also plotted to turn the party into a prologue to the politicking of the following week, mostly by inviting as many influential people as possible. He enlisted the assistance of George Plimpton, who telephoned David Rockefeller of Chase Manhattan Bank, Stephen Kennedy, the police commissioner, Sadruddin Aga Khan, the publisher of *The Paris Review*, and the bandleader Peter Duchin. One must assume that Plimpton felt that he was participating in some kind of noir farce, albeit unintended, given that Mailer had already explained to him how he intended to empower and arm the city's constituency of criminals, drug addicts, etc., in order to depose the establishment; specifically, those who were guests at the party. But the alchemical host and candidate had kept from Plimpton his 'surprise': that along with his invitations to authority figures, he had asked Doc Humes and his associates in the Citizens' Emergency Committee to seek out recently released offenders, delinquents, streetwise thugs and vagrants and to invite them to come along.

Mailer was planning an enactment of the thesis advances in his manifesto, but instead of posing hypothetical questions about the wondrous power of the dispossessed, he wanted to let them loose, literally, on those who governed and suppressed them. Sometimes Mailer comes across as an unfocused nonconformist, but look back to his first piece of non-fiction, 'A Credo for the Living' (1948), and we find the seeds of his political philosophy that would evolve over the subsequent twelve years. In 1948 he was wrong in his prediction that Western Europe would accommodate and improve Soviet socialism and that this revolutionary tide would sweep away the 'moral wilderness', the enfeebled capitalist ethos of America. At its core one finds an ominous prediction of his 1960 model of Cuba as the model for a riotously transformed New York City.

Plimpton did not seriously believe that his correspondents would attend or even respond. The invitations were issued at very short notice to people who had had other things to do, and he would probably not have made the phone calls at all had he known what Mailer had in mind.

Nonetheless, there was still an impressive cohort of well-established people. Ginsberg was there, as was Norman Podhoretz, the editor Jason Epstein, C. Wright Mills, a well-known sociologist, the poet and critic Delmore Schwartz, the actor Anthony Franciosa, *New York Post* columnist Leonard Lyons, Plimpton and many others of Mailer's acquaintances from the publishing and media industry along with friends and family. Those who remember the event estimate that at least 150 guests were present, perhaps 200. By mid-evening, around 8.00 pm, those who were known to each other personally or by reputation began to note that another event seemed to be taking place. Attendees to this were dressed in updated 1930s zoot suits with very thin ties and fedoras, others wore leather or bomber jackets with denims, and an equal number appeared to have attired themselves with whatever they could find in rubbish bins. In terms of race there was an impressive diversity, with as many black people and Latinos as white people. All were men.

There is no record of who these individuals were, in the sense that Humes, following Mailer's instruction, had picked them out as embodiments of the suppressed, the marginalised and the maniacal without bothering to ask their names. And nor is there any evidence that they were responsible for causing fights, which was Mailer's intention, yet through the evening individual confrontations did begin to take place, usually between men who were temperamentally pacific. Podhoretz and Ginsberg, for example, began by shouting at other and followed this with light blows to chests, seemingly careful to avoid inflicting harm or pain. They appeared to be reluctantly drawn into a danse macabre, led by Mailer. The mild-mannered and slight editor Jason Epstein was greeted at the door by the host with an invitation to box. Epstein, who had never thrown a punch in his life, remembers that 'I just held out my hand as if to make him go away. I didn't touch him, and he fell over.' (Lennon, p281).

Twice Mailer attempted to start a fight with Plimpton, most memorably when the latter went downstairs to check on the reported 'mayhem' on the pavement. 'Mailer', he remembers, 'was on the street fighting people who came out of the apartment house.' Most escaped without injury because the host was too drunk to do anyone serious damage and because Donoghue, a boxing professional, had laid him out after he had demanded a 'proper contest'. Epstein, also about to leave, tells of Mailer 'chasing George Plimpton up the street, kicking George in the leg like a little dog chasing a pony'. (Mills, p221).

The journalist and reviewer Richard Gilman later told Mills that 'fights [had] quickly broken out in corners, sexual stalkings and contretemps, envies and jealousies staging themselves as group therapy' (Mills, p. 221). Most others thought that the violence was unfocused and without motive, with the only exception being Mailer's apparent determination to stir unrest.

Lewis and Jay Allen, fearing for their safety, bade Mailer goodbye, though he insisted on accompanying them in the elevator. Two floors down they were joined by a stranger, unconnected with the party, whom none of them knew. Without warning Mailer hit him in the stomach and the man, still unknown, followed by flooring Mailer with an uppercut to the chin.

Podhoretz, by equal degrees horrified and fascinated, had gone back to the apartment and watched as Mailer returned with his colourful bullfighter's shirt drenched with blood. 'It was a very ugly night. There was a lot of bad feeling in the air, most of it emanating from Mailer.' (Mills, p223). Plimpton offers the most pertinent comment on the bizarre event. 'The whole evening was predicated on this sociopolitical thing that failed.' (ibid). The envisaged confrontation between the political and social elite and the proletariat had gone wrong; the most prominent figures from the establishment had not turned up, and in any case the desperados of the streets and back alleys didn't understand why they were present. They enjoyed the prodigious amounts of free drink, and a few made half-hearted attempts to take part in what looked like a curiously polite, bourgeois brawl. Others were suspicious that some of the men in smart suits were plain-clothes police, kept a low profile and left as soon as they could.

There is evidence that Mailer's own manic desire to start fights was prompted by disappointment. What Plimpton refers to as his 'sociopolitical thing', his attempt to transform his ludicrous ideological thesis into an actual revolutionary body politic, had clearly gone amiss. It hardly seems necessary to point out that the evening was an attempt to bring the bizarre thesis of 'The White Negro' to life. Something comparable might have occurred had Jonathan Swift tried to do the same with his 'A Modest Proposal'.

Plimpton stated to Dearborn that shortly before he tried to assault him on the pavement Mailer had hit him over the head with a rolled-up newspaper and demanded an explanation for why he had failed to round up the 'power structure' for the event.

Just as the atmosphere became ugly in the apartment, Adele approached Harriet Sohmers, a friend from Provincetown, and asked her if they could lock themselves into the bathroom and talk. All Sohmers remembers is an apology: 'I want to tell you that Norman made me do that thing in Provincetown ... It was all his idea, and I felt terrible about it.' (Mills, p. 222). The 'thing' had occurred about a year before, when Adele, following Mailer's instructions, had accused Sohmers of spreading rumours about his sexual orientation. Both women were half naked – it was at the close of a beach party – and the men, led by Mailer, cheered loudly as they wrestled with each other on the sand. Adele had started the fight, again prompted by her husband, and her gesture of remorse towards a woman she hardly knew might well have been triggered by her fear that something more dreadful was now brewing in Mailer's agitated mind. Three days earlier, after Mailer had struck Barbara, she had said to Adele, 'Has he gone mad? I've never seen him like this', and Adele replied with grim resignation that worse was to come; 'I have.' The night before the party Mailer had taken Tibo for a walk, returning with a bloody nose. He told to Adele that after the dog slipped its lead and ran into the park he had decided to get into a fight with a 'prep school type', without explaining why Tibo's behaviour had prompted him to attack the young man. There seemed no reason for the confrontation, but Adele seemed to take it as a prelude to something worse. Tibo was uscathed.

By 2.30 am most people had gone home and the twenty or so who remained assumed that the madness of the previous hours had burned itself out, but Mailer suddenly returned from an escapade on the street and ordered all the remaining guests to stand and arrange themselves into opposing groups: those who supported him and those who were against him. No one seemed willing to take part in this, so he forcibly divided them into teams seemingly at random, except that he declared that their maid, Nettie Biddle, was the only person who was genuinely his ally. Prior to this he had hardly spoken to her, but as a black Caribbean she probably appealed to his drink-fuelled notion of the oppressed versus the oppressors.

Shortly after 3.00 am Mailer became bored and left for the Podhoretz apartment a block away, attempting to call him out for another confrontation. Podhoretz and his wife were asleep and heard nothing. On his way back he came across Donoghue and another man and, pitiably, attempted a second fistfight. Donoghue, himself a little drunk, pushed him over onto the sidewalk, and by the time Mailer left the elevator for his own apartment it was around 4.30 am.

He walked directly from the hall to where his wife was standing in the dining room and stabbed Adele twice, once in the back and once upwardly beneath her lower ribs. The second incision was almost fatal, penetrating the pericardium, the conical sac that envelops the heart and contains most of the veins and arteries closest to it.

Accounts differ on how many others were still present, probably because those who later testified either for the authorities or the media closed ranks around Mailer and omitted to name others who might have witnessed the event. The report that Adele provoked him by mocking his heterosexual masculinity and his sexual prowess (...'come on you little faggot, where's your cojones, did your ugly little mistress cut them of...?) is part of an often repeated, false mythology. The implication is that others heard this but in truth the only report was by Adele herself in her memoir written decades later (*The Last Party,* p351). The general consensus is that there were four witnesses, but only two, the Humes, said anything of what happened, and Doc and Anna Lou had no choice since they carried Adele down to their apartment and had her lie still upon a mattress, which probably saved her life. Their insistence that she must not move lessened the amount of blood that she was losing from the arteries severed by the attack. The blade had come within less than a quarter of an inch of her heart.

Every account of the incident quotes Mailer as barking at those attempting to help her: 'Don't touch her. Let the bitch die.' The statement features in numerous accounts of the night, in a film dramatization of Mailer's life, in social media sites, and within months of the event it had become part of the common currency of gossip. To this day, however, there is no authentic source for it. The Humes did not corroborate it and nor has anyone else.

Doc and Anna Lou effectively coordinated subsequent events. First, they phoned their private practitioner, Conrad Rosenberg, who lived close by. He arrived within minutes, did a preliminary examination of the wounds and then organised an ambulance to take Adele to University Hospital on 20th Street and 8th Avenue where she was received by the surgeon Dr Macklin. He decided that an operation was immediately necessary to stem internal bleeding, and Adele was not allowed back onto a ward until midday on the day after the party.

Following his phone call to Rosenberg, Humes contacted a psychiatrist, Dr Emmanuel Ghent, calculating that a diagnosis that Mailer was mentally unstable at the time of the stabbing would provide an initial defence against police charges of assault or attempted murder. Humes later recalled that after he returned to the Mailer apartment following the removal of Adele, Norman seemed to him to be in a 'zombielike state'. Before the ambulance arrived Humes also persuaded Adele to tell anyone who asked that she had fallen onto a broken bottle. This would not have been convincing, given the nature of the wounds, but it might delay the progress of an investigation.

Next Humes telephoned Fan, Barbara and her husband, Larry, who between them arranged for Betsy and Danielle, the Mailers' children, to be taken care of, and, most importantly, arranged a conference at the Mailer apartment while Adele was in hospital. The Podhoretzes and Mickey Knox made plans for dealing with inevitable media enquiries. Fan, Barney and Barbara discussed how they would contact members of the immediate family with a view to creating a wall of silence. The Donoghues prepared a narrative of events that omitted a clear account of what exactly had happened, made a list of those still present during the early hours, and began phoning them to see if they would be willing to do the same. One person who had not attended the party was a friend of Humes, a lawyer, who gave advice on the manner of criminal investigations to all involved and most importantly on strategies of evasion. The only person absent from this defensive colloquium was Mailer himself.

Within a few minutes of Adele's removal from the apartment Mailer began a diary dedicated exclusively to the stabbing. The first passage veers between the present and past tense, as though he can't quite decide on which events are recent or ongoing. The most interesting sentence is 'Adele mocks me (fag crack) – I rush the door, others try to push me out, I flail, fight, succeed in getting in, Adele looks away in scorn, I hit her, then order others out' (Harry Ransom Center Archive, quoted by Lennon, p. 282). Nowhere does he state that he did anything more than 'hit' Adele, though he writes of '… Humes – glass tale … he drops bottle behind him on floor …' In its own right this makes no sense except that it corresponds with Humes's attempt to create a cover story by persuading Adele to state that she had fallen onto a broken bottle. Humes was, it seems, diligent in the preparation of circumstantial detail.

The events of the thirty-six hours following the party are so bizarre as to defy plausibility. Members of Mailer's and Adele's families and some close friends waited at the hospital until mid-afternoon, after the completion of the operation. Dr Macklin had informed them that while the surgery had gone well, the wound was so severe that she would not be allowed visitors for at least four hours.

During this period Mailer was driven around the city by Knox; boredom, his friend hoped, might have a calming influence. Mailer insisted on being delivered to the Donoghue apartment, where he was met by Roger and a retired police detective. Who had arranged this liaison remains a mystery, but the fact that Mailer knew when to arrive suggests he had been informed of it in advance, probably during the conference held by his friends and family. The ex-policeman had clearly been told of what had happened because he advised Mailer that without witnesses who would testify to exactly what had occurred officers would only have circumstantial evidence, potentially conflicting. Therefore, he urged him to leave the city as soon as possible, check in to a hotel under an assumed name and return, suitably shocked, in a few days when the case would probably have been shelved. Mailer nodded in agreement but added that he would feel more content in Cuba and asked if either could arrange transport. He had already asked Knox to ensure that his open letter to Castro was publicised, almost as though the previous twenty-four hours amounted to the apotheosis of his predictions on violence, revolution and self-realisation. Donoghue and the detective maintained a respectful silence and escorted him to Knox, who was waiting in his car. By the time Mailer reached the hospital Adele was receiving visitors. She asked nurses to keep him away from her, but he shouldered them aside and said to her, 'Do you know that I watched you being wheeled into the operating room, and I'd never seen you look so beautiful.' He continued. 'Do you understand why I did it? I love you and I had to save you from cancer.' (Lennon, p285). 'Cancer' as a synonym for moral or political degradation features persistently in Mailer's prose, and Adele recalls in her memoir that he had once used the word against her when they were having sex. He had realised she was using a diaphragm, hit her, pulled it out and accused her of infecting the pure sexuality of their relationship with a 'cancer'.

Prior to the party Mailer had arranged an exchange with the TV interviewer Mike Wallace on his mayoral campaign, and following his brief meeting with Adele he went to WNTA-TV to record it for the following day. Wallace knew nothing of what had happened at the party, and Mailer proceeded to elaborate on his election manifesto. He began by describing his 'existentialist ticket', spiced with something like the revolutionary programme currently being implemented by Castro. He then referred specifically to the symbolism of the knife. For various types of criminal and for juvenile delinquents 'the knife is very meaningful ... You see, it's his sword – his manhood.' During their drive around the city Knox tried several times to persuade Mailer to give him the penknife hidden in his coat pocket, but he refused, insisting that he needed it 'for personal reasons'. On the Wallace show he expressed doubts that criminality could be eradicated by attempting to disarm those who carried knives. Indeed, an attempt to do so would diminish the rebellious energy that made this constituency a key feature of Mailer's mayoral vision. Instead, he suggested that these figures should participate in 'gangland tournaments', comparable with the gladiatorial games of ancient Rome. But this would not be a spectator sport for the social elite; rather, a transitional ceremony whereby the violent proletarians would turn their urgent masculinity into a force for change. The parallels between this and Mailer's own recent attempt to turn his party into a mass brawl are clear enough. What is fascinating is that Mailer seemed confident that his candidacy would continue to be taken seriously, irrespective of what he had done two nights before. Wallace asked about his black eye and swollen cheekbone. Mailer laughed and answered, 'Yes, I got into quite a scrape Saturday night.'

On his return to the hospital Mailer was met by Dr Rosenberg, who spoke to him briefly and prepared a report in the expectation that it would be cited during a subsequent investigation. 'In my opinion Norman Mailer is having an acute paranoid breakdown with delusional thinking and is both homicidal and suicidal' – a description that is at odds with the quintessentially exuberant and ambitious Mailer of the TV interview taped barely an hour earlier.

Shortly afterwards, Mailer was arrested by three policemen, who searched him and removed the penknife. Detective Francis J. Burns told him that Adele had informed them that he had stabbed her. He was handcuffed and taken to West 100th Street police station, where he stated that he would refuse to respond to any questions put to him. He was detained and taken the next morning to the felony court at Centre Street in Lower Manhattan, where Rosenberg's account of his mental condition was read out. Mailer responded:

Naturally I have been a little upset, but I have never been out of my mental faculties. I only saw Dr Rosenberg for thirty seconds or a minute. It's important for me not to be sent to a mental hospital, because my work in the future will be considered that of a disordered mind. My pride is that I can explore areas of experience that other men are afraid of. I insist I am sane. (Lennon, p 286)

This is terrifyingly convincing, particularly his private redefinition of sanity as exploring 'areas of experience' that others are 'afraid of'. Presumably this included his assumption that attempted murder was within his authorial gift.

The magistrate, Reuben Levy, stated that 'Your recent history indicates that you cannot distinguish fiction from reality'. Levy, we must assume, was referring only to recent events, but if we take into account Mailer's continuous attempts over the previous decade to turn what others saw as reality into his own vision of a utopia of orgasmic violence, then his comment is crisply apt. Mailer spent the subsequent seventeen days in Bellevue Hospital, under detention along with other suspected criminals. While there he made notes on, among other things, his conversations with 'Fred W', who had cut the throat of his lover with a broken beer bottle and confessed in detail to the police in return for a pack of cigarettes and a pint of sherry. Mailer probably thought he was mixing with those who would prosper in his mayoral nirvana. He remained confident that he would continue with his campaign following his release from Bellevue.

In his absence Adele refused to make a complaint against him to the police, despite having stated that he had stabbed her, and when Mailer faced a grand jury on 30 January 1961 she again refused to sign a letter corroborating potential charges. Instead, she declared that she and her husband were 'perfectly happy together'. On 9 March, after several inconclusive court procedures, Mailer pleaded guilty to felonious assault and was placed on probation. On 13 November he received a three-year suspended sentence. Ironically, the sentencing took place a week after the mayoral election. Mailer had dropped out shortly before pleading guilty in March.

In 1961 the recommended sentence for attempted murder was fifteen years minimum, extending to twenty-five years at the discretion of the court. Mailer was treated generously, partly because those who witnessed or were aware of the events of the 19th of November offered vague or conflicting accounts of what occurred. His guilty plea, and the irrefutable fact that his victim was almost fatally injured, seemed, in the eyes of the sentencing judge, to merit a penalty roughly equal to that routinely issued to first-offence burglars. Exemption by literary entitlement perhaps.

During the early months of 1961 the Mailers tried to repair their marriage. He was grateful to Adele for refusing to press charges, and she stated later that the trauma suffered by their daughters from the press coverage could be healed by them being reunited as a family. Also, she was convinced that stabbing was a reasonable price to pay for being the wife of a genius, as she would later make clear in *The Last Party*.

In early 1961, between the numerous court appearances, Gore Vidal invited the couple to Edgewater, his estate on the Hudson River, along with Saul Bellow, Ralph Ellison, Mary McCarthy, Richard Rovere and others from the cultural hierarchy. Ostensibly this was a show of solidarity, but in truth Vidal had arranged the party as an exercise in schadenfreude. Mailer was being put on display like a creature on loan from the zoo.

During the five months following the stabbing Mailer wrote nothing but poetry, which was published in *Deaths for the Ladies* (1962). There were few reviews, but May Swenson in *Poetry* sums up the general opinion. 'He longs to be a true primitive, a child making figurines out of his excrement, but ... the result is apt to be simply a desperate exhibitionism.' Swenson is showing some mercy, given that it is difficult to find a collection in print as execrable as this. Mailer largely adopts the style pioneered by the Imagists E. E. Cummings and Ezra Pound, but with none of their poise. Redistributing prose on the page more or less at random smacks of juvenility, but consider what happens when the unpoetical sentence is itself embarrassingly vacuous.

One
 of the
 things
  I loathe
 about
 polite
  society
  is that
 one
 cannot
 discuss
 the nuances
 of cannibalism.

One piece is quoted frequently but rarely commented on, for obvious reasons.

So long
 as
 you
 use
 a knife,
there's
 some
 love
  left.

This and other poems were recited by Mailer to a packed audience at 92nd Street Y, a Jewish cultural centre in Manhattan, on 6 February, approximately a month before he pleaded guilty and while he was still facing several court appearances. The reading had been arranged during the previous summer, and it was assumed that most of the audience would be young poetry enthusiasts, predominantly Jewish, but when the event took place, any unbooked seats were occupied by journalists. After Mailer had read the poem about the knife, the centre's educational director, Dr William Kolodney, asked his assistant to lower the curtain, and it came down during the next piece with the two closing lines just audible.

> Dear Kike
> I wish you were a dyke.

Some saw this as cause to question his sanity, which was exactly as he intended. Mailer was ruthlessly calculating. He knew that everyone in the audience was aware of what had happened three months earlier, and that most had followed the story of his court appearances and related speculations on whether his state of mind would be regarded as evidence. For all involved, perceptions of Mailer after the stabbing were becoming as enthralling as hard facts, beginning with the broadcast of the Wallace interview, which occurred at the same time that the press were publishing conflicting reports on what he had, allegedly, done and on Adele's condition. Over late 1960 and early 1961 the news-hungry reader encountered what seemed like a short story, a bundle of psychological clues and motives that would add something special to the mystery of why a mayoral candidate had become the embodiment of his radical ideas on catharsis and violence.

Similarly, Mailer's theatrical statement to the felony court on how Rosenberg's diagnosis of mental instability was flawed, that he was 'sane' and capable of exploring 'areas of experience that other men are afraid of', would whet the appetite of spectators wondering what would happen next and cause them to treat the crime as part of a drama rather than a real attempt by a man to kill his wife. In his 1963 collection of writings *The Presidential Papers* there is a prose passage that echoes the poem about the knife. 'One got out of Bellevue, one did a little work again. The marriage broke up. The man wasn't good enough. The woman wasn't good enough. A set of psychic stabbings took place.' (p. 64). The third-person manner indicates that he has removed himself from the story, abdicated responsibility, leaving us with the portrait of a man and woman equally not 'good enough', equally at fault. And the actual stabbing had been replaced by assaults mounted by each upon each, none of them real, but 'psychic'. The crude but irrefutable message is that 'she got what she deserved'.

The Mailers filed for divorce at the end of March 1961. According to friends of Adele, along with her two daughters, she never fully recovered from the psychological trauma of the attack. Her bewilderment at being almost killed by a man who regularly proclaimed his love for her endured. For decades she appeared addicted to attending events hosted by Mailer, as if by being there she might gain some insight into what had previously eluded her, and her dubious, uncorroborated claim to have provoked the attack seems the more perplexing in the light of this. Perhaps she was desperate to make sense of it.

TIME FOR SOMETHING DIFFERENT?

In mid-March 1961, when Mailer and Adele were still, on the face
of things, attempting to rebuild their marriage, they were invited to
a party at Gore Vidal's New York apartment. Once more Vidal was
exhibiting his maniacal friend to those on his social circuit. Adele was
feeling unwell and Mailer went alone. He was talking with the lawyer
and politician Jacob Javits and his wife, Marion, who introduced him
to a woman standing nearby, Jeanne Campbell, or as she added wryly,
'Lady Jeanne Campbell'. She was five years younger than Mailer
and almost attractive in a way that combined debauchery with horsy
reliability. He knew nothing of her past, but as they talked she disclosed
a background that fascinated him. They then had sex in one of Vidal's
spare bedrooms.

Jeanne's maternal grandfather was Max Aitken, Lord Beaverbrook,
the millionaire newspaper proprietor, and her father was the 11th
Duke of Argyll. Marital problems of various sorts resulted in her
being raised mainly by Beaverbrook, who sent her to the best boarding
schools and thereafter allowed her to live in whatever way she wished,
with generous provisions of money from both sides of the family. She
boasted of having had affairs with John F. Kennedy, Randolph Churchill
(Winston's son; she had, she confessed, set her sights on Churchill
himself, but age was a problem), Ian Fleming, Nikita Khrushchev,
Fidel Castro, Oswald Mosley and, most recently, Henry Luce II of
Time magazine. Some questioned her claims, but there is convincing
evidence that she had slept with at least four of the eight. She was
honest in her pursuit of sexual diversity, political and otherwise; when
Vidal asked her later, once she and Mailer had become a couple, why

she had become involved with him, she answered, 'Because I never slept with a Jew before.'

We do not know who informed Adele of the liaison, but the fact that Mailer had tried to keep it secret confirmed her suspicion that he was still the mendacious, unfaithful figure she had barely managed to tolerate before he tried to kill her.

Mailer and Jeanne were married in April 1962, following her discovery the previous Christmas that she was pregnant. The marriage lasted only eighteen months and the relationship as a whole just over two years. It is wrong to treat it as a transitional period, except that he exchanged one woman for another. This was habitual. He was a serial fornicator, but throughout his adult life he never spent more than a couple of months without being attached to a particular woman. Commonly one relationship would begin sometime before the previous marriage had ended, formally at least. Jeanne replaced Adele in much the same way that the latter took over from Bea. There were always overlaps, but what would not change was the perverse singularity of Norman Mailer. One might have expected that he would decrease the obsessions that preceded the attack on Adele, but quite the opposite occurred. He became even more bizarre.

Barely a month after he met Jeanne, he published an open letter to Kennedy in *The Village Voice*, addressing him as 'Dear Jack' and reprimanding him for the recent failed attempt by exiles to invade Cuba. The Bay of Pigs was a disaster, but Mailer was unconcerned with military tactics; rather he held 'Jack' to account for following the advice of the CIA when his old friend Norman Mailer would have provided more judicious counsel. He reminded the president of the piece he had written in November 1960 when he assumed that his mayoral campaign would earn him an advisory role at the White House, and he reiterated his point that Kennedy and Castro had much in common as political radicals and would be able to find common ground, with the assistance of Norman Mailer.

Neither 'Jack' nor any of his representatives responded to Mailer's letter, so he contacted the publisher Lyle Stuart, who had visited Cuba and spoken to Castro on several occasions. He asked Stuart if he could arrange a meeting with Castro. He would, he informed Stuart, become the mediator between the White House and Havana and from this become a conciliator between NATO and the Soviet bloc, and bring the Cold War to a close.

Later that year, in autumn, Jeanne was sent by her employer, the London *Evening Standard*, to cover the meeting in Bermuda between the British prime minister, Harold Macmillan, and Kennedy. They were discussing a joint policy on the recent creation of the Berlin Wall, which effectively imprisoned the Allied part of the city within Communist East Germany. All across Europe countries now part of the Stalinist superstate were ensuring that their citizens would not have the opportunity to cross borders to the democratic West. The *Evening Standard*, owned by Jeanne's grandfather Lord Beaverbrook, was the bastion of British conservatism. It regarded the Soviet Union as an enemy just as threatening as Fascist Germany. Jeanne was a pragmatist, fully convinced that the Soviet Union and the West were involved in an undeclared worldwide conflict and that the notion of the Eastern bloc as a socialist nirvana was delusional. She reported on the meeting between Macmillan and Kennedy with cool impartiality, extrapolating from it a balanced account of two global empires set against each other. She and Mailer seemed to exist in separate universes.

Jeanne later recollected that they fought continually: 'We could clear a room in minutes.' Throughout the first eight months of their relationship, before Jeanne discovered her pregnancy, they performed as a couple mainly to attract the attention of the media, contemplating such headlines as 'British Aristocrat Dates Mailer While He Awaits Sentencing' – and there were quite a few. Mailer later commented that 'I was screwing everybody I could', but that the attraction of Jeanne was about something other than sex. 'There I am, from a middle-class Jewish family ... I'm a well-known author, in a certain sense I'm part of the establishment. But I'm a criminal, a felon on parole. There she is, Lady Jeanne, her father is a duke.' (Interview, Lennon, p. 296). They were ludicrously ill-matched in terms of background, upbringing and politics, and Mailer was enthralled by this because it was like the plot from a novel that defied credulity. More and more he fixated upon crossing the line between invention and reality. Jeanne had both amused and repulsed him with her stories of what she had done before they met. In Moscow when working for the *Evening Standard* her fling with Khrushchev was the stuff of gossip column legend, but she also disclosed to Mailer that she had slept with Yuri Gagarin, the first man in space. She claimed that in 1959, while covering his failed bid for an anti-immigration Parliamentary seat, to have gone to bed with Oswald Mosley – lifelong admirer of Hitler, outspoken supporter of racial segregation and Holocaust denier – to see what evil was like in the flesh.

Mailer did not know whether or not to believe her, but the incredulity was as exciting as the lurid detail. He too had blurred the line between sexual fantasy and self-regarding ambition, notably with Jackie Kennedy. If Mao Zedong had been available for interview, Jeanne would probably have added him to her list of the great, the good and the bad. Mailer later disclosed that he had, in part, been thinking of Jeanne when he created Deborah, the estranged wife of Rojack, in *An American Dream* (1965). In the opening pages Rojack strangles her and throws her over the balcony.

In July 1961 Jeanne went with Mailer to Mexico to meet his first daughter, Susan. All seemed to go well until news reached them that Hemingway had shot himself, after which Mailer entered a period of histrionic mourning. Aside from obituaries the American press was swamped with articles by major writers and politicians on the departure of a man acknowledged as the nation's greatest writer. Kennedy praised him in *The New York Times*. Mailer was appalled that no newspaper had asked him to contribute to the exercise in national commemoration, 'sick in that miasmal and not quite discoverable region between the liver and the soul' (*Of a Fire on the Moon*, p. 3). He even approached a number of magazines to which he had regularly contributed, only to be informed that they had already commissioned pieces. In desperation he persuaded Jeanne to have her grandfather accept something for his *Daily Express* in London. It never went to press and Mailer published it later in one of his essay collections. He praised Hemingway's passionate singularity, comparing him with the then undefeated newcomer to professional boxing, Cassius Clay; his raging narcissism reminded him of Henry Miller, yet his moral vision equalled that of St Thomas Aquinas. 'Hemingway's style affected whole generations of us, the way a roomful of men is affected when a beautiful woman walks through

...' The first part is heartfelt if sometimes overwritten, but after that it becomes profoundly ghoulish. He imagines the preparation, the loading of the shotgun, Hemingway moving its barrel to his head and testing the pressure of his finger against the trigger. Then he verbalises his idol's mental state during the last few seconds of his life:

> ... God bless, umbriago, hose down the deck, do it clean, no sweat, no sweat in the palm, let's do it clean, gung ho, a little more, let's go in a little gung ho more ho. No! Oh no! Goddamn it to Hell. (*The Presidential Papers*, pp. 104–5)

Not long after composing the tribute, Mailer decided to return to fiction-writing after a seven-year hiatus. First he began to extrapolate from the notes he had made during detention at Bellevue, treating criminality and criminal derangement in particular as the best means of exploring the repressed potency of America.

This and other stimuli proved unproductive, and he spent the next two years, roughly the duration of his relationship with Jeanne, testing his ideas for the novel by provoking as many people as possible in interviews and articles.

In the June 1962 issue of *Playboy*, he claimed that America had been weakened by 'womanization'. Feminism in the United States was still in its infancy as a political and ideological movement, but Mailer was infuriated by the ability of women to 'unman' males by taking control of sexual relationships. Contraception was becoming far more available to married and single women, and in his view their ability to choose whether or not to become pregnant was unnatural and onanistic. In an interview in *The Realist* later that year he proclaimed that contraception and masturbation are one and the same and that 'the ultimate direction of masturbation always has to be insanity'. Elsewhere in magazines such as *Voice* and *Esquire* he railed against the bland characterless nature of American architecture, without suggesting an alternative; television was part of a conspiracy, an attempt to deaden the intellect of the nation; fluoridation of water and the use of antibiotics had become cowardly means of enabling men (women were not mentioned) to avoid fighting disease face to face. Education of all types, from early-school to university, smothered radical ideas, particularly those which endorsed violence. The word 'cancer' surfaces again and again. Apparently it held the state in its deathly grip, but not once does he stray into its meaning as a literal disease. For Mailer, 'tumours', 'sarcomas', 'lymphomas', 'malignancies', etc., are only ever referred to as part of his thesaurus of weakness, degeneration and ruin, in everything from the Cold War to the dire consequences of 'self-abuse'.

Many of these articles and interviews are often addressed directly to the president – 'Dear Jack'. Mailer created a sufficient amount of controversy to draw sponsorship for public performances. In September 1961 he and Jeanne had gone to England to promote the British edition of *Advertisements for Myself*. They loved the publicity, and Mailer was interviewed several times on his writing and his private life, the most memorable being with the philosopher Richard Wollheim, who asked him questions about his obsession with violence as a cathartic experience. Mailer picked up on the recent trial of Adolf Eichmann, one of the major organisers of the Holocaust, and reflected on the nature of morality and justice. In his opinion, 'life always advances far ahead of morality. Morality is the quartermaster corps bringing up supplies to starving soldiers.' His thesis was based on a Sartrean notion of existential immediacy, with his own misconception of Hemingway thrown in. Individual acts of violence were different from the collective 'miasma' of moral judgement and punitive retribution that followed. Had Eichmann 'killed 500,000 victims with his bare hands, he would have been a monster ... worn the scar of his own moral wound ... [and gained] our unconscious respect'. (Lennon, p303). His argument was riddled with self-contradictions, but he wasn't thinking about Eichmann. He was still awaiting sentencing for his own act of violence committed with 'bare hands' less than a year before. Some in the British press picked up on the allusion, but his use of one of the organisers of the Holocaust as his out-of-court defence outraged many Jews, members of his family included.

In August 1962, sponsored by *Esquire*, Mailer flew to Chicago to cover the Sonny Liston–Floyd Patterson fight. The *National Review* had in advance invited him to take part in a verbal bout with its editor, William F. Buckley Jr. The exchange, which was to take place at the

Medinah Temple, originally designed as an auditorium was promoted as the intellectual prelude to the boxing match, and 3,600 people bought tickets for it. The topic was 'What is the real nature of the right in America?', designed to place Mailer in the invidious position of defending seemingly irreconcilable standpoints. In his recent essays he had veered between hard-line social illiberalism – his opinions on gender equality resembled conservative views on race in the South – and his long-term sympathy for an ill-defined international socialism. Buckley and the *Review* were more conventionally conservative, defenders of the East Coast social and political establishment and in favour of the expansion of the US nuclear arsenal as a deterrent against communist incursions into ex-colonial territories, especially in Asia.

Buckley opened with an attack on the pro-Soviet, pro-Castro left's blindness to the authoritarian nature of both regimes and accused Mailer, pointing his finger, of his 'swinishness' as a thinker and an individual, implying that the same moral incomprehension caused both a fondness for dictatorships and domestic violence. The audience seemed to appreciate Buckley's sharp innuendo, and Mailer tried to divert their attention by reciting his familiar catalogue of the false antidotes to the general ills of humanity (antibiotics, vitamins, tranquillisers, contraception, etc.), condemning them as shrinking the soul of the American, particularly the American male. His solution to the growing tension between two global superpowers was 'to end the Cold War', though he did not explain who would initiate this or how it might be achieved. He added, 'Let Communism come to those countries it will come to.' 'Whether they like it or not' was his nascent sub-clause.

At the other fight Patterson, the title holder, was the favourite, partly because he was the good Catholic small-town boy who epitomised boxing as an honourable sport. Liston, on the other hand, had a prison record for violence, was believed to be backed by the Mafia and was portrayed by the media as a thug. Mailer backed Patterson but when Liston knocked him out in just over two minutes he was conflicted. He claimed to fellow reporters that Liston had given his opponent the 'evil eye'; 'Liston was Faust.' He had done a deal with the devil in a dark, metaphysical sense and not just because of his association with the mob. 'He was the hero of every man who would war with destiny

... the cigarette smoker, the lush, the junkie ... the fixer, the bitch, the faggot, the switchblade, the gun ...' (*The Presidential Papers*, p. 242). He found himself recognising that the victor was the kind of individual he had idolised in his writings of the previous fifteen years, while Patterson was 'a churchgoer ... a liberal's liberal'. The next morning Mailer was ejected from the post-fight press conference. He had stayed up all night drinking, hurling abuse at anyone who tolerated his presence, and had urinated in a corner of the room.

Next, Mailer flew to London and took the train to Edinburgh to appear at a literary adjunct to the annual festival, called 'The Novel Today', and continued where he had left off in Chicago. On stage with Mary McCarthy he contended that the figures who controlled the United States imposed moral imperatives because they thought that too much sexual freedom would make young Americans weaker than their Russian adversaries. Again he was concerned only with the fate of men. The moralists were wrong, pronounced Mailer. 'One had to enter this terrible borderland of sex, sadism, obscenity, horror, and anything else because somehow the conscience of Western man has become altogether muddy in refusing to enter it ... we have got to get into it' (Ted Morgan, *Literary Outlaw*, p. 339). In this respect he recommended the work of William Burroughs, who was also on the panel, praising him as an individual who personified Mailer's own subversive aesthetic. Eleven years earlier Burroughs had shot his wife dead in Mexico but fled before conviction, ultimately receiving a two-year suspended sentence for homicide *in absentia*.

The nature of Mailer's thinking and writing during the early 1960s resurfaces in his 1966 collection *Cannibals and Christians*. Much of this is made up of interviews where he reflects persistently on matters that most would choose to avoid, notably a hypothetical 'dramatic encounter with death', which, fear not, might 'give room to easier and more sinuous desires'. Hemingway, never far from his thoughts, was apparently made up of 'a quick lithe animal' but also 'shackled to a stunted ape, a cripple, a particularly wild dirty little dwarf ...' In Mailer's assessment, 'he was not brave enough, and the dwarf finally won' (p. 271). His unhinged assertions are familiar enough, but the intriguing feature of the interviews is that they involve only one person. The interviewer exists on the page but he is Mailer's invention, serving as a link between his monologues, frequently offering verbal nods of agreement or appreciative comments. It would be too simple to write this off as a calculated exercise in narcissism, because in many ways the imaginary interviewer was an extension of Mailer's perverse relationship with the real world. He was sufficiently obsessed with his own intimations to feel secure in pretending that the ideas of others either did not exist or would soon come to reflect his own.

For example, at the time of the Patterson–Liston fight, civil rights conflicts in the South had come to a head when James Meredith became the first black person to be admitted to the University of Mississippi, once the sole preserve of the Confederate gentry and their successors. Riots ensued, and shortly after his return to New York from Chicago Mailer sent a telegram to the attorney general, Robert Kennedy, demanding that he 'Go to Oxford, Mississippi'. Kennedy should also 'arrange for me to go down' by some form of government transport. The two of them, Mailer promised, would bring calm to the situation: 'I can talk to those students.' Mailer's belief that Kennedy would act on the telegram mirrors his relationship with the invented interviewers.

Shortly after he met Jeanne, Mailer bought a spacious three-storey brownstone on Columbia Heights. It boasted views of the Statue of Liberty, the Manhattan skyline and the Brooklyn Bridge. Over more than six months he employed joiners, bricklayers, plumbers and decorators to utterly redesign the interior of the building, creating a mezzanine office for himself in the roof and rebuilding several floors as almost independent apartments where guests could stay and then circulate in communal areas such as sitting and dining rooms. Aside from his habitual excursions to the country it would thereafter become his permanent residence. He owned it and used it for the rest of his life, but during his first two years there it was a battleground. For every visitor the prevailing memory is of Mailer and Jeanne entering into differences of opinion on anything from her cooking – which he hated – to her class and his ambitions. Whatever the topic the result would be rage and the hurling at each other of derision, abuse and sometimes objects. Mailer said that 'I like to marry women whom I can beat once in a while, and who fight back' (*Writer's Digest*, December 1969). Apart from throwing objects, which she undertook as enthusiastically as Mailer, he never actually hit Jeanne because she frightened him. 'She's the toughest babe I've ever known', he later wrote to Mickey Knox (13 June 1963), adding that 'most of her friends I find intolerable and sickening … upper-class types.' This was something of an understatement.

The things that first attracted him to her at Vidal's party would ensure that their relationship was doomed from the start. During their first visit to England, he and Jeanne went to a ball, preceded by a gymkhana, at the Somerset country house of Janet Kidd, her mother. In a letter to his friend Ann Fleming, a fellow guest, Evelyn Waugh, described the event: 'Two bands, one of niggers and one of buggers, a cabaret, an oyster bar in the harness room, much to the distress of the horses…' He reports that one of the horses 'bit an American pornographer who tried to give it vodka'.

> I had never before met Lady Jeanne Campbell and was fascinated. She came to us next day bringing the bitten pornographer … a swarthy gangster straight out of a madhouse where he had been sent after his attempt to cut his wife's throat. (23 September 1961)

Jeanne might well have walked out a novel by Waugh, and her marriage to a character from one of Hemingway's was implausible and hilarious.

Mailer's first encounter with Jeanne's family occurred shortly after her pregnancy, when they visited first her grandfather in his luxurious villa on the French Riviera and then her father's seat in Scotland, Inveraray Castle, a medieval fort turned in the eighteenth century into a Gothic Revival pile. Beaverbrook spoke to him once and for the rest of the evening ignored him. Argyll outdid this by talking exclusively to his daughter throughout dinner in the memorial hall. He did not greet Mailer and made a point of refusing to acknowledge either his presence at drinks or meals or his departure from the castle two days later.

Mailer met Beverly Bentley on 10 March 1963. She was an actress, blonde and good-looking, and had privately stalked Mailer for several months. She was particularly impressed by his interview following a boxing match in which Emile Griffith had landed so many head blows on the Cuban Benny Paret that the latter had gone into a coma and died ten days later. Mailer had launched into his standard celebration of violence, death, sexuality and race – both men were black – as liberating forces for conformist America, to the extent that some of his expletives were bleeped out. Beverly loved it and started to make contact with people she knew in boxing and the media to engineer a 'chance' encounter.

Mailer had become a regular at P. J. Clarke's bar in midtown Manhattan, frequented by celebrities such as Dean Martin and Frank Sinatra, boxers, other professional sportsmen and the occasional gangster. Founded in 1884 it prided itself on its rough-house charm. On the 10th of March Mailer went there for drinks with Donoghue, who exchanged a wave with Jake LaMotta, now retired but a living legend for his bouts as world middleweight champion. He had also been accused of throwing a fight for a bribe from the Mafia and had served six months on a Florida chain gang for procuring underage girls for other men. Mailer delighted in the company of such characters, and when one of the women at LaMotta's table shouted 'Hey, Norman Motherfuck Mailer, come on over!', he and Donoghue joined LaMotta's party immediately. Mailer was particularly interested in the woman who had not called him over. They introduced themselves and started to chat, until LaMotta stood up and growled 'Hey, get lost!' Mailer replied that 'I'll leave when the lady tells me to', causing LaMotta to go face to face with him. LaMotta was notorious for making use of his brutally destructive skills outside the ring, but Mailer was saved by the woman who had prompted their exchange. 'No, Jake, Mr Mailer is my date for tonight,' she said, and LaMotta left the bar. They continued to talk, and while Mailer had nothing to tell her about himself that she didn't already know, he was fascinated by her history, which he might have invented. Indeed, aspects of Beverly would resurface in *An American Dream* (1965), the novel he began shortly after they met, though she shared the fictional stage with other women he had known.

She had grown up in Florida as Beverly Rentz but had adopted her anglicised surname on the advice of her agent/boyfriend when she moved to New York. When she met Mailer, she was thirty-three, and classically pretty in the manner of Cybill Shepherd. She had appeared in two films before 1963, notably *A Face in the Crowd*, and between theatre and the movies had been a hostess on TV game shows such as *Beat the Clock* and *The Price is Right* along with working as a model. Mailer was most impressed by her account of Hemingway's sixtieth birthday party at a millionaire's villa in Malaga in 1959. Everyone present, she reported, seemed intent on drinking and having sex for three days without pause. She did not explain how she had been invited or for what purpose, but Mailer hazarded a guess. The thought of her as one of Papa's birthday presents exhilarated him. Equally thrilling was her disclosure that she was presently having an affair with Miles Davis.

It had become Mailer's habit not to waste time for a second date, and as Beverly later reported, 'He walked me to my apartment. That night he was wonderful in bed.' (Lennon, p 328). At this point his marriage to Jeanne was turbulent, to say the least. He resented the recent humiliations at the hands of the British gentry and she loathed the rituals expected of the Brooklyn Jewry, notably weekend dinners with Mailer's parents involving kosher hotpots or gefilte fish such as poached carp.

Jeanne had moved to a Manhattan apartment roughly two weeks before Mailer met Beverly, but the separation was experimental. Five months earlier on 18th October, 1962, she had given birth to their daughter Kate, who she took with her; Mailer visited his wife and child roughly twice a week. When Beverly moved into 142 Columbia Heights in May many of Jeanne's things, clothing included, remained in the first-floor apartment which she had occupied separately as a testament to her independence. Little more than a month after that Jeanne received news that her husband's latest liaison was something other than one of his habitual one-night stands, and she began divorce proceedings which were finalised in December 1963. He and Beverly married in December 1964.

During the summer of 1963 Mailer and Beverly set off on a tour of the United States which took in regions that were virtually a map of his personal history. They visited the Gwaltneys in Arkansas, as he had done shortly after meeting Adele, and went to Los Angeles to look up some of the people he had known in the period before *The Deer Park*. Finally, they drove south in his Triumph sports car to meet Beverly's family, and things seemed to go well. He described her father to Gwaltney as 'an ex-Southern master sergeant ... one of the boys. He's like so many guys we used to know [in the army]'. (10 September 1963).

They also went to Las Vegas so that Mailer could cover the Patterson–Liston rematch. Once more Mailer predicted that Patterson, as the thoughtful tactician, would prevail over the 'thug', but this time Liston disposed of his opponent even more rapidly; he was counted out at 2.10 of the first round. The fight lasted only four seconds longer than the previous one. Mailer had met up with promoter Harold Conrad and a few other reporters the day before the bout, got drunk and started several fistfights. All were inconclusive, given that the protagonists were too intoxicated to inflict harm on each other.

Beverly had stayed in their hotel because, she claimed, she would feel out of place. Given her associations with boxers and boxing, LaMotta in particular, this seemed a questionable excuse. Her real reason was that she was waiting for a telegram from Arkansas where, without informing Mailer, she had seen a doctor. It arrived shortly before he returned to their room, hungover. She was pregnant. As usual Mailer had held to his mantra that contraception diminished manliness and the orgasmic purity of sex. On hearing Beverly's news, he went slightly mad and raged at her, but after they drove out into the desert he accepted that he would hold himself to account for insisting that they did not use a condom or any other form of protection. Kate, his daughter with Jeanne, was less than a year old.

Following their return to New York, Mailer continued to work on various drafts of a novel which would eventually become *An American Dream* (1965). He had written two short stories after his release from Bellevue. One, 'The Killer: A Story' (*Evergreen Review*, 1964), is autobiographical; a prisoner reflects on his moral character and the benefits, or otherwise, of being on parole. 'Truth and Being, Nothing and Time: A Broken Fragment from a Long Novel' (*Evergreen Review*, 1962) is a rather desperate attempt to bury the consequences of the stabbing in a blend of fiction and philosophy. It is narrated by Dr Joyce, with a nod to one of the high priests of modernism, who in this case becomes the 'archbishop of the New Royal Scatological Society'. Joyce is dying of cancer, which enables Mailer to once more turn the condition into a protracted metaphor for the decay of civilisation. For

Joyce, the anus and the expulsion of faeces involve the only means by which we can 'pour [out] the riches' of Satan. The anus is the 'final executor of that will within us to assign value to all which passes through ... expel the exquisite in time with the despised'. Throughout the story the figurative and literal wrestle for supremacy, or to be more accurate Mailer can't decide what exactly he is writing about. He is known to have been disgusted by the largely open-air lavatory facilities at Bellevue, seeing them as another level of humiliation and punishment. As with 'The Killer' the story is partly autobiographical, but in this case he attempts to smother his memories of the months following the stabbing with a chaotic mixture of coprophilia and Manichean gibberish.

Evidently Mailer sensed that the energy for his novel would come from his private traumas of the previous three years, but he knew also that if he turned 'The Killer' into a full-length piece of fiction it would be the equivalent of a statement from the prisoner from the dock, lasting most of the day and involving either lies or admissions of guilt. Two hundred plus pages of an expanded version of 'Truth and Being' would not find a publisher, let alone an appreciative audience of reviewers and readers.

The assassination of John Kennedy on 22 November 1963 affected Mailer as much as Hemingway's suicide, at least if we compare the enormous amount that he wrote during his later life about the departure of both men. What is intriguing is the impact it had on the progress of his novel. He wrote to Mickey Knox on 17 December, on how New York was united in a state of despair. 'Women were crying in the streets (mainly good-looking women), a lot of middle-aged Negroes looked sad and very worried ...' For Mailer it was one of three events 'having something profoundly in common':

Pearl Harbor day and the death of Roosevelt being the other two ... The main loss I think was a cultural one. Whether he wanted to or not Kennedy was giving a great boost to the arts, not because Jackie Kennedy was inviting Richard Wilbur to the White House, but somehow the lid was off ...(Mailer to Knox, 17th December, 1963)

He continues, 'The book of course falls by the side in all of this, one of the million minor casualties. With Kennedy alive it was a good book, but with him dead, it's just a curiosity, and somehow irritating in tone. I don't even mind the loss in a funny way.' In truth the said novel was already at a dead end. The shock of Kennedy's death caused him to compress the sprawling drafts of the original *American Dream* into a very different, shorter work that he would finish in less than a year. He made an arrangement with the editor of *Esquire* for the magazine to publish 10,000-word monthly instalments from January to August 1964. He did not offer *Esquire* a synopsis of this serialisation – in truth he did not know where it would go – but he provided himself with a sequence of deadlines. He was following an old-fashioned precedent, made famous by Dickens, where the reader would read a chapter over four weeks which would whet their appetite for the next. It was a form of highly disciplined improvisation. Nine months of pressurised deadlines would oblige Mailer to put together something engrossing and readable, he hoped, rather than the directionless ramblings of the previous two years. Dial Press brought out a hardback version of the *Esquire* instalments, with some minor revisions by Mailer, as *An American Dream* in 1965.

The story occurs over a period of roughly twenty-four hours, opening with the narrator, Stephen Rojack, visiting the home of his estranged wife, Deborah. There, after she belittles him, he strangles her to death. He then has sex with the maid, Ruta, who has no knowledge of what he has done, and when he returns to Deborah's room he throws her still warm body out of the window to make her death appear to be suicide. He is investigated by the police but manages by various means to escape justice. Notably his story to Lt Leznicki, the investigating detective, is that Deborah was suffering from cancer, implying that this caused her to kill herself. He had made this up, but her post-mortem examination does in fact disclose the presence of tumours.

The macabre similarity between this passage and Mailer's statement to Adele shortly before her operation is clear enough. 'I love you and I had to save you from cancer,' he'd said. Adele was not suffering from cancer and, as far as Rojack knew, nor was Deborah. Once more we come across Mailer's weird preoccupation with cancer as much as a state of existential malignancy as a disease. In the novel it becomes the engine for Rojack's destiny, and it re-emerges frequently. In the Epilogue, for example, Rojack's doctor friend has him witness the autopsy of an old man riddled with tumours, and with ham-fisted symbolism we are informed of how the indescribable smell from the incisions stays with him as he heads further west across America.

The novel's opening paragraph is embarrassingly revealing.

> I met Jack Kennedy in November, 1946. We were both war heroes, and both of us had just been elected to Congress. We went out one night on a double date and it turned out to be a fair evening for me. I seduced a girl who would have been bored by a diamond as big as the Ritz.

The girl was Deborah, whom he would marry, and whose millionaire family would help him in his various careers as politician, writer and academic. It is clear enough to Rojack that he owes much of his eminence and wealth to Deborah's blue-blood connections and that she deserves to die because of this. Read Mailer's political pieces, especially those following 'The White Negro', and you'll find the politics of this act explained, or at least laid out in quasi-ideological jargon. Rojack admits that Deborah 'was not capable of murdering him' herself, but she 'lay a curse' on him, a 'Great Bitch' who 'delivers extermination to any bucko brave enough to take carnal knowledge of her'. One can't help but recall Mailer's alleged declaration when friends attempted to help Adele as she lay on the floor bleeding: 'Don't touch her. Let the bitch die.'

He wanted to turn his recent past, which was in truth shameful and unsavoury, into an existential dilemma. It was as though he had borrowed the clothes of Dostoevsky as a disguise for drunken savagery. Minutes after Deborah's death Rojack describes having sex with Ruta, the maid. He finds her on her bed 'all five fingers fingering like a team of maggots at her open heat'. He joins her, and 'My bare foot came up from the carpet ... drawing up on the instant out of her a wet spicy wisdom ...' When they have sex, 'I felt for the first time in my life like a healthy alley cat, and I stroked at her with delicate hatred lacquered clean up to a small flame by the anticipation of my body.' (p 47).

Soon afterwards, 'I had a desire suddenly to skip the sea and mine the earth, a pure prong of desire to bugger.' She resists, 'Not there! *Verboten!*', but he continues – 'I could feel the pain in her ... and I was in, that quarter-inch more was gained and the rest was easy. What a subtle smell came up from her then ...' After a brief return to vaginal sex, when 'I could feel her begin to come', he returns to her anus; 'I jammed up her ass and came as if I'd been flung across the room. She let out a cry of rage. Her coming must have taken a ferocious twist.'

These are brief extracts from Rojack's description of sex with Ruta, which is about three thousand words in length and driven by ferocious enthusiasm, tinged with sadism. At one point he reflects on how 'There was a high private pleasure in plugging a Nazi ... I felt as if I were gliding in the clear air above Luther's jakes ...' Aside from Ruta's German origins she has no known political affiliations, having been an infant at the end of the war. But Rojack seems addicted to turning sex into something associated with evil. As late as 1999 Mailer wrote that Kennedy had disappointed him by failing to get America 'back to the instinctive life ... a return more to the pagan, to the sense of oneself as an animal who lived in a field of senses', (Lennon, p 274) or, as he put it more vividly in 'The White Negro', 'energy, life, sex, force ... the paradise of limitless energy and perception just beyond the next wave of the next orgasm'. Rojack has attained this state within minutes of, or more accurately because of, killing his wife. And Ruta is a mere appetiser for what awaits him during the rest of the novel. For Rojack, killing Deborah is cathartic. It does not pilot him into a state of hedonism in the conventional sense, and it certainly involves nothing relating to guilt, but he lives out the dynamism of sex and violence that Mailer preached as the cure for the deadening ordinariness of American society. For Mailer the attempted murder of his wife – for that is what it amounted to – extinguished his political ambitions but didn't change him as a man. Rojack kills Deborah and is rewarded with a life sentence of moral exhilaration.

Elizabeth Hardwick wrote in the *Partisan Review* of 'a fantasy of vengeful murder, callous copulations, and an assortment of dull cruelties. It is an intellectual and literary disaster, poorly written, morally foolish and intellectually empty.' This view was echoed in most of the established magazines and newspapers, though younger writers such as Joan Didion at *Vogue* praised its innovative 'openness'. The bad reviews caused the sales of the book to rocket during the first few weeks of publication. During the week after it came out 60,000 copies left the shelves, sending it close to number one in the bestseller list, his greatest success since *The Naked and the Dead* seventeen years earlier. Readers were enthused by the condemnations of it because the reviewers' descriptions of the activities of Rojack bore such a resemblance to the bizarre, widely reported true-life narrative starring Norman Mailer.

APOCALYPSE NOW

On 21 May 1965, little more than a month after *An American Dream* appeared, Mailer gave a talk at a protest organised by the Vietnam Day Committee against the ongoing war, in Berkeley, California. As per typical Mailer his speech was inversely related to its ostensible topic. Instead of rationally addressing the situation in South East Asia he ruminated on the, for him, disturbing features of American society that had become apparent since the death of Kennedy.

> Our country was fearful, half mad, inauthentic – it needed a war or it needed a purge. Bile was stirring in the pits of the national conscience … We took formal steps toward a great society … of computers and pills, of job aptitudes and bad architecture, of psychoanalysis, superhighways, astronauts … where censorship would disappear but every image would be manipulated from birth to death. Something in the buried animal of modern life grew bestial at the thought of this Great Society – the most advanced technological nation of the civilised world was the one now closest to blood, to shedding the blood and burning the flesh of Asian peasants it had never seen. (*Cannibals and Christians*, p. 74)

The passage is topped and tailed by allusions to Vietnam, but in between its topic is the long-term existential manifesto of Norman Mailer. His most ludicrous statement is that 'something in the buried animal of modern life grew bestial at the thought of this Great Society' and caused America to shed the blood and 'burn the flesh of Asian peasants'. For more than a decade his proselytising mandate was that growing 'bestial' and joining the savage underworld must be the true spirit of the new revolution. Now, however, these same impulses had turned Americans into murderous colonialists.

The piece is riddled with self-contradictions, mostly because Mailer was improvising, drawing randomly on his earlier political diagnoses and peppering them with catchphrases from the anti-war movement. It was also, however, an inchoate rehearsal for a novel he would begin less than a year later, *Why Are We in Vietnam?* (1967).

In September writers and intellectuals associated with the *Partisan Review* addressed an open letter to the president and the government expressing their doubts about 'the present or past policies of the United States' in South East Asia and stating that 'the time has come for some new thinking ... about what's happening in different parts of the world, regardless of what the United States does or fails to do'. It could hardly be more vague and non-committal, as if being a member of the intelligentsia obliged them to speak on profound issues while excusing them of saying anything in particular.

Mailer opted out of the collective letter and published his own in the same issue of the magazine, suggesting that instead of provoking wars in small third-world countries, the superpowers should purchase a large tract of land in South America to enable war games to take place for those so inclined, with live television coverage and phone-in audience participation. In response to the letter writers' failure to offer an alternative policy to the one presently being pursued, 'I offer [one]. It is to get out of Asia.' He obviously regarded as irrelevant Eisenhower's 'domino theory' – that when Chinese militarised communism took control of one country its neighbours would be swallowed up, until Korea, Vietnam, Laos, Cambodia, Thailand, Malaysia, Indonesia, Burma and even India became China's South East Asian version of the European Soviet bloc. He did not bother to even mention it, let alone dispute it. The style of the piece is an improvised scattergun of obscenities:

... all those bombed out civilian ovaries, Mr. J., Mr. L. B. J., Boss Man of Show Biz – I salute you in your White House Oval; I mean America will shoot all over the shithouse wall if this jazz goes on, Jim. (Dearborn, p 219).

Quite soon the idiom of the letter would be handed over to Randy D.J. Jethroe, the narrator and chief protagonist of *Why Are We in Vietnam?*

As was his habit with new marriages, Mailer began to divide family life between the city and New England. Beverly gave birth to their second son, Stephen, in March 1966, roughly twelve months after the arrival of Michael, their first. In late summer he bought the spacious nineteenth-century house at 565 Commercial Street, Provincetown, ostensibly as a gift to Beverly but also as somewhere large enough for him to receive his expanding brood of children, now six. Only Kate, daughter of Jeanne, was absent from the US for long periods but Mailer and her mother remained on good terms; Jeanne and Kate lived permanently in England but the latter's ongoing work as a journalist took her across the Atlantic at least twice a year and she made sure that Mailer saw his daughter as often as possible. Susan, his and Bea's only child, was now eighteen. She had spent much of her life in Mexico with her mother but was due to enrol at the prestigious Barnard College in New York in 1967. During her year of accustomising herself to the East Coast she made regular visits to her father in Provincetown. Adele was still traumatised by the stabbing but ensured that their two children, Danielle and Elizabeth, neither yet in their teens, spent periods during the summer in the resort.

They had been together for less than two years, but Beverly was beginning to see behind the literary star she had idolised from afar. At the start things seemed perfect. Charlie Brown, Beverly's half-brother, who helped her in her early career, went to stay with them in New York.

> My impression was that Beverly had gotten exactly what she wanted. She was running the household and being the queen bee, and there was also the amazing social scene ... I met some of their friends at their dinner parties ... Obviously, Norman was a major power on the social scene, and I started meeting all these people – political people, the hierarchy of the literary world, major writers. There were also some Kennedy people around ... My god, Norman knows so and so. He's a heavyweight – this joker could be President or something. (Manso, p. 398)

But it soon became apparent to Beverly that he was close to suffering from manic depression. On the one hand he was preoccupied with the proprieties of a decent home life, a legacy of his middle-class upbringing. When they were not hosting parties for establishment celebrities, he insisted that Beverly should cook meals for the family, and in New York she was initiated into the ritual of Friday night dinner with Barney and Fan. His mother regarded her as an improvement on Jeanne, a seemingly obedient, Gentile version of the ideal Jewish wife. Away from home Mailer turned into something very different from his various domestic personas. When he went out drinking with male friends, he would routinely return with bruises to his face and sometimes cuts that would require the attention of the local physician.

Beverly was particularly horrified when they were invited to Truman Capote's ball of 28 November 1966, at the Plaza Hotel. Men were asked to attend in black tie and dinner jackets, and although Mailer sported a dark bow tie, he accompanied it with a dirty gabardine raincoat and a shabby, unwashed suit. Some saw the event as vulgar and decadent given the political issues of the time, specifically Vietnam; ornate facemasks resonant of pre-Revolutionary France were also recommended. A few guests thought Mailer was protesting, but in truth he was aiming to provoke even a mildly disparaging comment which he could turn into a fight. He asked several men to 'step outside' to settle their differences; in the end, Lillian Hellman intervened and ordered him to leave. Beverly felt ashamed. It was as though the hierarchy she had joined as Mailer's wife had exposed him to her as a lout.

One occasion when the domesticated patriarch invited his off-the-leash alter ego home was witnessed by the boxer José Torres, who, along with his wife, stayed with the Mailers in Provincetown in March 1966, shortly before Beverly gave birth to their second child. Beverly and Mailer became involved in a bitter argument on household chores, or so Torres first thought. The exchange of indiscernible but clearly irate whispers had escalated to something something more than a dispute on who should clear the table. Their faces were inches apart until Mailer drew back and raised his voice. 'Wait a minute,' he said to her, 'I don't want any punches.' Beverly turned to Torres and explained that he was not begging her to spare him. Rather he was addressing himself. It had become his routine for him when he was angry and they were alone to punch her around the crotch, she reported to Torres. Mailer remained silent, but glared at her and promised, 'Beverly, I am going to get up and throw you out the window.' (Interview with Torres, Mills, p. 279). Torres walked him around the town to calm him down. Beverly gave birth to Stephen just over a week later, and Mailer celebrated with a night out in New York, most of it in bed with an air stewardess he had picked up in a bar. He confessed this to his wife as she was nursing their newborn.

Ecey Gwaltney remembers a party held by the Mailers in New York seven months before the Provincetown incident. Almost everyone had left, and Beverly treated the few who remained to a floor show involving a screaming monologue. 'Here I am, two months pregnant and playing Bessie Smith records. Here I am, thirty-six years old, I don't know what I'm going to do.' Then directly to Mailer after another party, 'You treat people worse than niggers in Georgia. You're just a bully! I want a divorce. I want it right now.' 'Put it in writin',' he replied, grinning. (Manso, p. 413). They had two black maids, Hetty and Alice Bradford, and Ecey heard from them that Mailer regularly ordered Beverly to undertake the same menial tasks as those performed by his employees. He 'treated her like a servant, unpaid'.

In 1965 Beverly made a tentative attempt to revive her career as an actress by setting up a company, Act IV, with theatre-connected friends from New York. Commendably, they wanted to specialise in one-act plays by emerging writers as a means of launching their careers. The project was effectively co-opted by Mailer. After its first production, *Dutchman* by LeRoi Jones, he announced that he intended to finance and stage a theatre version of *The Deer Park* and promised Beverly a key role. He managed to bring in the Hollywood actor Rip Torn to play the pimp Marion Faye, and Mickey Knox was given the role of the producer Munshin. Beverly was shocked when Mailer announced that he had invited his ex-wife Adele to read for the role of Elena. Quite how he had persuaded her to do so remains unexplained, given that she continued to harbour understandably bitter feelings following the stabbing. The experienced actress Rosemary Tory was eventually given the role, although Adele was asked to stay on as understudy. Beverly wanted to play Elena, but Mailer refused and insisted that she must be the beautiful, empty-headed Lulu.

Evidently the adaptation was becoming another dominion of the Norman Mailer empire, and this was clear also in his refusal to exchange the fractured syntax of the novel for something that sounded like authentic dialogue. On stage the performers often sounded more like figures from Beckett's *Play* than actual people speaking to each other. *The New Yorker* wrote that 'Mailer may have adapted his novel but he has not dramatized it, and he has drowned it in words'.

The play opened at the Theatre de Lys in the Village in January 1967 and ran for 128 performances. Beverly hated it. As Mailer later commented, 'It was a hit', but she thought that the whole enterprise was another instance of her husband's obsessive determination to control everything she did. Even when she went with him to weekend dinners with Barney and Fan he would quietly mock her ambitions, joking for his parents that game shows were the inevitable destination for failed actresses and implying that she should be grateful to him for putting her back, albeit briefly, into serious theatre.

Always a fan of William S. Burroughs, Mailer found himself during the summer of 1966 involved in a close reading of *The Naked Lunch*. Massachusetts was one of several states that had imposed a ban on the book for obscenity. Mailer, along with Ginsberg and the poet John Ciardi, had agreed to appear before the Superior Court in Boston to testify on the book's behalf. While the three men could not dispute the self-evident fact that various profanities and expletives, mainly involving sex, appeared on almost every page, they argued that it was a novel comparable with the landmarks of modernism, notably Joyce's *Ulysses*, and that as a contribution to American culture its execrations must be overlooked.

The compelling testimony, by Mailer in particular, that Burroughs' book would advance America's standing in the global literary league table, succeeded despite the fact that the judges were unfamiliar with terms such as stream of consciousness or interior monologue. It occurred to Mailer that Burroughs had come close to inventing a new language, made up of the composite materials of English but working in a very different way. This, he decided, was the model he would adopt for his novel on the wretched state of contemporary America, and he began *Why Are We in Vietnam?*, which he finished in four months. It was due to be published as part of his arrangement with Putnam, but the delay between completion and publication in 1967 was caused by the fact that it had nothing in common with the synopses for novels tentatively signed for. The advance of $25,000, half the agreed amount, also reflected Putman's case that Mailer was in breach of contract.

Shortly afterwards he took on a new agent, Scott Meredith, who arranged a series of contracts for forthcoming novels with the New American Library, which had previously made money from pulp fiction and paperback bestsellers. The shift in his fortunes was extraordinary, with an offer of $450,000 being made for a vaguely conceived 'large novel'. Initially Mailer turned it down because he was convinced that round sums, usually made up of tens or hundreds of thousands, were 'unlucky'. He settled for $448,000. Since *The Naked and the Dead* Mailer could rely on a regular if sometimes modest income. Now, despite losing two grand because of his bizarre superstition, he suddenly found himself, at least in the short term, able to support six children, various alimony agreements and two expensive properties.

Why Are We in Vietnam? opens with

Hip hole and hupmobile, Braunschweiger, you didn't invite Geiger and his counter for nothing, here is D.J. the friendLee voice at your service – hold tight young America – introductions come. Let go of my dong, Shakespeare, I have gone too long, it is too late to tell my tale, may Batman tell it, let him declare there's blood on my dick and D.J. Dicktor Doc Dick and Jek has got the bloods, and has done animal murder, out out damn fart, and murder of the soldierest sort, cold was my hand and hot.

And so on in similar paragraph-length 'sentences' for about two hundred pages. The narrator, Randy D.J. Jethroe, is the spawn of Joyce, Beckett, Burroughs and Shakespeare entrapped in the idiom of hard-nosed Texas masculinity. The story, such as it is, involves D.J. and his pal Tex Hyde on a hunting trip through Alaska, intent on killing grizzly bears, sometimes with the assistance of helicopters supplied by D.J.'s father, a millionaire cigarette manufacturer, who sponsors the hunt. The title becomes relevant only on the final page, when D.J.'s crazed aggression is revealed as a prelude to his immediate future. He has just been conscripted. 'Vietnam, hot damn,' he raves. Most reviewers thought Mailer had reached the apex of his ascent towards lunacy. *Life*: 'Is it worth reading? Only because the 16-year-old behind it is a 44-year-old named Norman Mailer committing atrocity on his talent.' *Saturday Review*: '[It struck me] not as a hoax, but a lark ... Mailer has grown a great deal in power of language since *The Naked and the Dead*. Why then has he been writing trivia and tripe for the past ten years or more?' The less begrudging commentators thought he had done something different ('the sensory event ... a certain directness', *The New York Review of Books*), but even they could not make up their minds about what the book was actually about.

With the benefit of hindsight, we might credit the novel as shrewd and prescient. Films such as *Platoon*, *The Deer Hunter* and *Full Metal Jacket* exposed the difference between patriotic support for the war in the mid-1960s and what actually happened in Vietnam, but we should remember that the films and other presentations of the conflict were based on hard evidence, often from soldiers, produced some time after America had made its humiliating withdrawal. When Mailer wrote the novel, differences of opinion were based more on ideology than facts. The liberal left told tales of the bombing and mass murder of peasants that came mostly from pro-communist propaganda sources, while the patriotic right presented the forces of Ho Chi Minh as yet another authoritarian incursion upon the free world which America was expected to protect. Mailer's perception of the conflict was governed by his affiliation with the former. He chose to present two maniacs determined to kill wildlife as symbolic of America's involvement in the war.

Over the five decades since the end of the conflict, American veterans have suffered greatly at the hands of the country they were supposed to be serving. After the conclusion of hostilities in 1973, the government treated most of them with indifference. GI benefits were minimal and difficult to obtain. It was as if the institution of the state was attempting to rid itself of the memory of an unwinnable conflict by forgetting the men they had sent to fight in it. Families of returning servicemen were sympathetic, but more often than not they found themselves protecting their kin from a growing sense of collective loathing. Even those who had not been actively involved in anti-war protests regularly hurled invectives at veterans, refused to serve them in bars or stores and sometimes spat at them. The war had been lost, with almost 58,000 Americans dead, an estimated minimum of 200,000 South Vietnamese fighters lost, and those who had survived were being held responsible. Mailer's presentation of the typical conscript as a psychopath fed into debates that immediately followed the end of the fighting. The title of the novel guaranteed the attention of those who wished to attribute blame.

The famous March on the Pentagon took place on 21 October, 1967. It was the largest anti-war protest on record, organised by the National Mobilization Committee to End the War in Vietnam; many of the Committee were writers, including Allen Ginsberg and Gary Snyder. It was estimated that at least 100,000 people were present when the protest began at the Lincoln Memorial. Mailer's participation had been arranged by Edward de Grazia, a legal advisor to the Committee. He had met Mailer before, when the latter had argued against the ban of Burroughs' *The Naked Lunch*, and he greeted him at Dulles Airport on the evening of the 19th.

The following day there was a dinner party at which de Grazia, the poet Robert Lowell, critic and writer Dwight Macdonald and author Paul Goodman were due to give speeches. Mailer volunteered as master of ceremonies and was asked to deliver the closing address.

Things seemed a little ominous once Mailer joined Lowell and de Grazia in a cab to the dinner. He poured as much of a bottle of bourbon as he could into a large mug, swigging from it regularly, and when Lowell praised him as the finest journalist in the country, he replied, 'Well, Cal' – Lowell's nickname used only by close friends – 'there are days when I think of myself as being the best writer in America', and took another mouthful of bourbon. Once they reached the Ambassador Theater Mailer left the group in pursuit of a lavatory. He got to the door but once inside was unable to find the light switch and in desperation urinated into his trousers.

Mailer went on stage unable to disguise or explain what had happened, and after Paul Goodman closed his speech, he introduced Dwight Macdonald to the audience. Mailer warmed up for his own performance with liquor from his mug and then delivered what amounted to an imitation of a character from his recent novel.

Opening with a shouted question to the audience – 'What are you, dead heads? ... Or are you all ... in the nature of becoming dead-heads?' – he then continued with a monologue of mangled syntax, abuse and obscenities. Those present, despite being largely indulgent and liberal, reacted with demands that he should leave the stage or be removed by security guards, but he was steadfastly out of control. 'We're going to try to stick it up the government's ass, right into the sphincter of the Pentagon.' Macdonald and de Grazia went onto the rostrum and tried to persuade him to bring the bizarre tirade to a close. He pushed them aside, stepped forward with his microphone and shifted into an accent that was a blend of Texas cowboy and Southern Confederate gent, beginning with a confession that he had missed the urinal and wet his trousers: 'But tomorrow, they will blame that puddle of water on Communists which is the way we do things here in America ... you know who I am, why it just came to me, I'm so phony, I'm as full of shit as Lyndon Johnson. Why, man, I'm nothing but his little old alter ego.' Randy D.J. Jethroe had stepped out of the book and onto the stage.

> This yere dwarf alter ego has been telling you about his imbroglio with
> the pissarooney up on the top floor, and will all the reporters please
> note that I did not talk of defecation commonly known as sheee-it! ...
> but to the contrary, speak of you-rye-nation! (Account of the speech
> by de Grazia and Macdonald in an interview with Mills, pp. 299–300)

The next day the protesters gathered at the Lincoln Memorial, crossed the Potomac into Virginia and were met by a line of soldiers of the 82nd Airborne Division in the spacious car park of the Pentagon, the headquarters of the US military. There is a press photograph of several of the more eminent representatives of the cultural establishment – notably Robert Lowell, Norman Chomsky and Mailer – in line and facing the soldiers. Each is wearing a decently tailored suit and tie, and Mailer has a thumb in his matching vest. Every face carries a contented smile, and they could be a group of well-educated professionals at an autumn garden party.

By contrast, the poet Ed Sanders stepped forward to perform a mystical exorcism on the building, proclaiming 'Out, demons, out', accompanied by Hari Krishna chants from fellow advocates of the new hippie counterculture – a blend of 50s hipsterdom, various types of Eastern philosophy and half-digested leftist mantras. This first wave of pacifist protesters was greeted by clubbings from soldiers and police and transportation to arrest areas in locked vans. The most prominent was Jerry Rubin, an anti-war, black-power and pro-legalisation of drugs activist, who was taken into custody in a rather dazed state after being floored by a rifle butt.

Lowell, Macdonald, Mailer, Chomsky and a few others stood dutifully behind a rope that marked the divide between the acceptable 'peaceful' protest and the assault on government property – at least until Mailer decided that he needed to cross the line, literally and figuratively, between left-liberal gesturing and the rough and tumble of mass protest. He tried to get himself arrested by running between two military policemen and was well behind the rank of armed soldiers before being picked up by federal marshals. They knew who he was and were not prepared to risk being photographed man-handling, let alone battering, one of the nation's most prominent literary celebrities. With a politeness worthy of a comic drama, they advised him to return to his friends on the safe side of the rope. He refused and made a few half-hearted attempts to push the officers away. Reluctantly, as if dealing with a grumpy infant, they found themselves with no choice but to restrain him and transport him to the temporary detention centre at the post office in Virginia. Once there he began to regret what he had done and called Beverly for help. She contacted de Grazia, who enlisted the lawyer Philip Hirschkop. After a night in custody, Mailer was sentenced to thirty days in jail with twenty-five suspended, one of the more severe of the penalties meted out for 'disorderly' behaviour. Hirschkop managed to have the four remaining days in custody suspended in return for a bail of $500.

On his release his speech to the press outside the courtroom was almost as bizarre as his performance two days before. This time he sounded like a gospel preacher cum deranged insurgent.

Today is Sunday, and while I am not a Christian, I happen to be married to one ... And there are times when I think that the loveliest thing about my dear wife is her unspoken love for Jesus Christ ... You

see, dear fellow Americans, it is Sunday, and we are burning the body
and blood of Christ in Vietnam. Yes, we are burning him there, and as
we do, we destroy the foundation of this Republic, which is love and
trust in Christ. (*The Armies of the Night*, p. 240)

Within a week of his return to Provincetown, the *Harper's* editor Willie
Morris contacted Mailer to ask if he'd write pieces on the march. His
declaration to the assembled media had been reprinted, or at least
summarised, in virtually all mainstream newspapers. Mailer contacted
Scott Meredith, who negotiated with Morris a series of articles,
amounting to twenty thousand words in total, for a payment of $10,000.
At the same time, Meredith agreed a contract with the New American
Library (NAL) for a book version with an advance of $25,000.

Morris visited Provincetown in late November to find that over
the previous six weeks Mailer had adopted a spartan lifestyle, with no
drink, and was every day producing page after page on the march. It was
over twice the agreed length, but after he'd read the bulk of it Morris
telephoned the managing editor, Robert Kotlowitz, stating that it was
'gold dust' and insisting that they must bring out the largest single volume
of a magazine ever produced, made up entirely of Mailer's account of
the protests in Washington. Kotlowitz agreed and Mailer continued to
write, completing a longer piece, to be called *The Armies of the Night*, by
early 1968. The *Harper's* edition, running to almost 90,000 words, came
out in March 1968, followed by the NAL volume in May.

Prior to this the record for a magazine article had been set by John
Hersey's account of 'Hiroshima' (1946) for *The New Yorker*. That came in
at just over 32,000 words, with the conventions of journalism – at least
in terms of space – being suspended, because Hershey had reported
on an event that had altered the destiny of the human race. Morris in
his phone call to Kotlowitz did not argue that a largely peaceful anti-
war protest was comparable with the first aggressive use of a nuclear
weapon, but he convinced his manager by claiming that 'I've just finished
reading a beautiful ninety thousand words … One of the great works
of American literature' (Interview with Morris, Mills, p. 306). The
selection committees for the 1969 Pulitzer Prize and National Book
Award felt the same way. His most enthusiastic fan was his mother.

> When I heard that Norman got the Pulitzer Prize for *The Armies of the Night* I said "*Umbashrien Got tsu danken!*" – which, freely translated, means "Keep the evil eye away." I was very thankful ... and then when he got two prizes, the National Book Award too, I said it again, a double *Umbashrien!* Still, I couldn't understand why he hadn't gotten the Nobel Prize. I figured he had a few enemies. I think he might've hurt somebody's feelings ... (Manso, p. 471)

If Morris's claims to his boss might seem exaggerated, they were outdone by the book's reviewers. Alfred Kazin in *The New York Times Book Review* compared him with Whitman. 'Whitman staked his work on finding the personal connection between salvation as an artist and the salvation of his country ... I believe that *Armies of the Night* is just as brilliant a personal testimony as Whitman's diary of the Civil War ...' Alan Trachtenberg in *The Nation*: 'A permanent contribution to our literature – a unique testimony to literary responsiveness and responsibility.' Richard Gilman in *The New Republic*: '... one of the most fascinating episodes of our recent cultural history'. Eliot Fremont-Smith in *The New York Times*: '... the best analysis yet of the politically and generationally splintered spectrum of the protesting left ...' Almost everyone loved it, but Gilman sums up the collective sense of Mailer as having done something extraordinarily original.

> The important thing is that Mailer has refused to leave history, actuality, to historians and journalists. Writing as he can, as part-inventor, part-observer, part-intervener, writing with gusto and vigor and an almost unprecedented kind of honesty ... Mailer has put us all in his debt.

All treated America's decisions to take military action in Vietnam as being of enormous significance. Young men were being killed and disabled at a rate comparable to the Second World War, but there was also the broader issue of the Cold War. Prior to Vietnam the communist bloc, now including China, was for most Americans the enemy, but the actual costs of involvement in an armed conflict were now inflicting themselves on small-town America and were not the exclusive concern of left-leaning liberals. Dozens of private and ideological dilemmas were wrapped into this, but Mailer had produced a book that appealed less to those with profound ethical mantras than to individuals whose sons or brothers might come home permanently disfigured or disabled, or not come home at all.

How had he triumphed while covering the same topic as his dreadful *Why Are We in Vietnam?* As Gilman put it, Mailer had displaced 'historians and journalists' from their routinely allocated roles by offering an account of one of the largest mass protests in American history in the manner of a novel. Notably, the vast majority of the reviewers who praised it unreservedly were, like Mailer, cultural mongrels with an investment both in literary writing and the more dispersed infrastructure of reportage, politics and social commentary. They cannot therefore be treated as unbiased given that since the Classical period literature had been treated as subordinate to all other discourses: at its best as an art form but sometimes relegated to the status of a form of recreation, even low culture. Reading the appraisals, it is evident that the reviewers are giving only a degree of concern for the subject of the book – though the vast majority are self-evidently sceptical about the pursuit of the war. Rather they are euphoric about Mailer's inauguration of a new brand of literature, one that sheds its junior role and competes at the same level with, say, the political or philosophical essay.

As Kazin puts it, 'Mailer's intuition in this book is that the times demand a new form. He has found it.' He does not claim that the new form will change anything, only that, by implication, literature has through Mailer been improved by the war. Similarly, Gilman:

... the artist who has to invent and the observer who has to prey on facts merge into the same person; the transcendencies of art and the imminences of action move toward each other's replenishment ...

The book is in the third person – in that Norman Mailer refers to the chief participant as 'Norman Mailer' – and it appears to be disarmingly candid. The other Norman's embarrassing drunken performance on the night before the march is described in unsparing detail. When 'Mailer' is reported as approaching the Pentagon, he apprehends 'floods of totalitarian architecture, totalitarian superhighways, totalitarian smog, totalitarian food (yes, frozen), totalitarian communications ...' (p. 199). Choose a passage at random from one of his political essays from the mid-1950s onwards, or his transcribed speeches, and any difference is imperceptible. Later, 'Mailer' broadens the perspective:

> The air between New York and Washington was orgiastic with the breath of release, some promise of peace and new war seemed riding the phosphorescent wake of this second and last day's siege of the Pentagon ... (p. 24)

As far back as 'The White Negro', Mailer had paraded 'the search after the good orgasm' as the impulse for political rebellion and revolt, and in *The Armies of the Night* it seems as if the release of 'orgiastic ... breath' from the protest has brought this close to culmination. *The Armies of the Night* was a reasonably faithful account of what the character 'Norman Mailer' had got up to, but it also imbued this figure with a special form of visionary wisdom enabling him to foretell the future and diagnose the dynamic relationship between the present and the past.

The critics who celebrated it as a unique combination of the novel and non-fiction missed out on its special significance for Mailer. It allowed him to have the best of both genres, to embed his sometimes deranged prophecies of the previous fifteen years within a portrait of America that seemed authentic. One has to wonder if the experience of recreating himself for the duration of the book as a different, quasi-fictional person, unaccountable to the real world, caused Mailer to lose track of what he felt free to do and what most people would treat as reasonable behaviour.

Roughly a week after the book appeared in May 1968, the weird effects of the non-fiction novel seemed to have found their way into the actual Norman Mailer. He appeared with Dwight Macdonald at a fund-raising event for students at Columbia University who were boycotting the campus and tearing up conscription cards. It was led by Mark Rudd, leader of the Columbia branch of the radical Students for a Democratic Society (SDS), which was a staunchly Marxist and prone to advocating violence. It was closely allied with the Black Panthers, some of whose members now carried firearms after an unarmed black man, Denzil Dowell, had been shot dead in North Richmond, California, in 1967. The atmosphere was heated, and Rudd read out testimonies from protestors claiming that police and prosecutors were systematically falsifying evidence against defendants. Mailer interrupted. 'I know that cops created evidence. They've done it to me. All cops are psychopathic liars. Your fight is to show that the people who run the country are full of shit.' (Jack Newfield's recollection in *The Village Voice*, 30 May 1968). The applause died as it became apparent that he was no longer talking about police responses to the civil rights and anti-war movements. He was describing in vivid detail the injustices visited upon him during the weeks after 'someone had stabbed my wife', as he put it.

A short time after, Mailer appeared on the Merv Griffin talk show. The journalist Pete Hamill was a fellow guest, and as the two men waited to go on stage Mailer launched several punches that missed Hamill's face by inches, announcing that 'Not hitting you, Pete, takes something out of my character', which confounded Hamill given that before this the two men had been on good terms. In front of camera, when asked to comment on the state of America, Mailer declared that 'the instances of faggotry have gone up in the country'.

Earlier that day, he had met up in a bar with Hamill, José Torres, Torres's trainer and Tom Hayden, an outspoken left-wing activist. They talked mostly about boxing until Mailer demanded that Hayden must set up a meeting between him and Fidel Castro. He went face to face with Hayden and screamed, 'I want a guarantee, man to man, that I can see Fidel. Or else, fuck him. I'm not taking any chances of going there and not seeing him. My time is valuable too.' (Mills, p 309). Hayden, while an active figure in the SDS, had never been in contact with Castro or anyone else in Cuba.

Hamill tells of how, around the period of the book's publication, Mailer choreographed his numerous New York parties as though he was planning a sequel to the night of the stabbing. 'God knows what he was anticipating when he'd put a guest list together, although drama may have been the criterion ... Generally it was at parties with literary types that Mailer made you nervous. I always felt it was some sort of "hoodlum goes to college" ... kind of thing that was operating' (Manso,

p. 469). One evening the novelist and critic Bruce Jay Friedman 'ruffled Norman's hair' as an amiable salute to the success of the book. 'Norman butted him with his forehead and said, "Let's go downstairs."' Friedman attempted to avoid violence, but Mailer followed him and, on the pavement, 'Norman put his head in Bruce's chest and went *boom!* Then I saw Friedman hit Norman in the body.' Once more Friedman tried to calm things by getting in his car, but Mailer began 'punching and head-butting the screen and windows' (Testimony by Torres, Manso, p. 469). Tom Quinn, boxing promoter and later stockbroker, recalls a night soon after this when Mailer demanded that Quinn go beyond the long-established routine of head-butting: 'he wanted to take me outside and fight ... "Come on outside, I'll tear your fuckin' head off. I'll kill you." I said, "No Norman ... that's it. I'm not gonna fight you."' (Manso, p. 470).

Mailer seemed to be living in a world unconstrained by notions of responsibility accepted by the rest of society. This might have been the psychological inheritance of *The Armies of the Night*, but, as would become clear, it was also a rehearsal for something even more bizarre, a film which Mailer directed and starred in as an even more maniacal version of himself.

While completing the book he had directed, edited and produced two films, *Beyond the Law* and *Wild 90*. The first is a hard-nosed representation of New York City cops on and off duty, and the second more experimental, with Mailer (The Prince), Buzz Farber (Cameo) and Mickey Knox (Twenty Years) playing Mafia hoods hiding from the police in a warehouse. Both productions were derided by critics and lost Mailer a fair amount of money, but they led to another project, which, in his view, would have emphatic relevance.

Maidstone was, supposedly, inspired by the assassination of two political figures. Martin Luther King Jnr was shot and killed in Memphis, Tennessee, in April 1968. He was planning the so-called 'Poor People's Campaign' which would result in a 'multiracial army of the poor' converging on the Capitol in Washington later that summer. It was estimated that the protesters would by far outnumber those who had marched on the Pentagon the year before. King and his co-organisers insisted that non-violence would be the benchmark of the event, but following his assassination riots broke out in several major American cities, prompted mostly by black people who believed that King had been murdered by a freelance gunman employed by government agencies. The new wave of protests were against segregation, racism and inequality generally but they had been given a particular energy by the assassination of King. The politician deemed responsible for quelling the disturbances was John F. Kennedy's brother, Senator Robert Kennedy. Kennedy had been persuaded to run for the presidency against Lyndon Johnson and during the early summer had become the intermediary between the political establishment and those involved with protests against Vietnam, the civil rights movement and broader calls for equality for the impoverished, irrespective of race. On 5 June, almost exactly two months after the death of King, Kennedy was shot and killed in Los Angeles by the Palestinian activist Sirhan Sirhan. As with John Kennedy, conspiracy theories almost immediately followed news of the killings, with the supposed assassins being treated as avatars for some plot devised by bodies not directly related to the government but dedicated to preserving a largely conservative status quo.

Maidstone would be advertised as Mailer's artistic, cinematic exploration of the American psyche in light of the assassinations. In truth it was *The Armies of the Night* on screen, starring the ego of Norman Mailer. The name of the film company he founded for the project might have raised suspicions: 'Supreme Mix' echoed 'Supreme Pictures', which he had invented as the degenerate, corrupt and successful studio in *The Deer Park*.

Maidstone was written, produced and directed by Norman Mailer, who stars in it as the film director Norman T. Kingsley. Kingsley divides his time between working on a sexually provocative film about prostitution – he specialises in pornography – and his campaign for the US presidency. On 18 July Mailer borrowed the spacious East Hampton estate of David and Elizabeth Brockman to address his cast. David was an immensely wealthy lawyer, the East Hampton House and grounds looked like something lifted from Renaissance England and Elizabeth enjoyed promoting the arts, particularly theatre. Mailer's performers were made up largely of personal friends, including Beverly, Adele and Jeanne; he had sent the latter first-class tickets for an Atlantic flight.

Carol Stevens was also present. His wives, ex and present, assumed she was a newly hired actress, but Mailer had in fact been having a relationship with her for more than six years. He would eventually marry her. An older woman, aloof, blonde and attractive, stood at the back. She too had been invited by Mailer, who was considering her for the part of Norman T. Kingsley's lover from his college days. Lois Wilson had of course known the real Mailer since 1947, and the notion of Mailer's furtive sweetheart from his early twenties playing Norman T.'s probably appealed to Mailer's idea of himself as despotic. Their affair would endure in secret almost until his death. In the end she left the set discreetly without having been introduced to other members of the director's harem. Any early sense of a blurring of boundaries between the actual and the invented was probably evident only to Norman T. and Norman M., but quite soon others involved in the venture began to suspect that they were guests in an open-air madhouse.

At this first meeting Mailer stood on a podium and addressed his cast members and production team.

It's going to be a film about a notorious movie director – Norman T. Kingsley ... He's a mystery even to those who know him best: some say he's the worst kind of monster imaginable; others call him a saint ... Kingsley is also running for President.

Mailer goes on to explain that the present real-life candidates – notably Nelson Rockefeller, Richard Nixon and Hubert Humphrey – have been 'knocked off', and that figures who might stand in their place, such as Sinatra, the conservative public intellectual William F. Buckley, Baldwin and Brando, are also likely to have been killed. 'Assassination is in the air.' Moreover, Kingsley is uncertain of whether he wishes to run, partly because 'politics bores him', and partly as he feels unsettled by the so-called 'Prevention of Assassination Experiment, Control' (PAXC), conducted by the CIA, the FBI and the Secret Service. Kingsley does not doubt the efficiency of these agencies, but he resents the possibility of being turned by them into a politically impotent stooge. He concludes by announcing that those who had not been assigned a role would draw lots to see if they will appear as members either of PAXC or 'the assassination party'. 'By the way,' he adds, 'Kingsley will be played by me.' (Speech reported by James Toback in *Esquire*, December 1968). We hardly need reminding that Kingsley was Mailer's middle-name and even during the opening speech those present were beginning to suspect that Mailer was finding it difficult to distinguish between his actual self and the one he'd mutated into as Norman T. Kingsley, controller of the fictional universe of the film

All of those listening knew Mailer well and picked up on the bizarre parallels between the movie and his personal history, including his one-time political ambitions and his tendency to act as a dictator at social events. As Toback wrote, the general view was that he had gone from 'commoner to Lord, from democrat to fascist, from neurotic to psychopath, from Marx to Nietzsche, from writer to hero'.

The apprehensions initially felt by all involved intensified during the next three weeks. The sets shifted between the neighbouring luxurious estate of the multimillionaire Robert David Lion Gardiner, the elaborately landscaped gardens of the sculptor and painter Alfonso Ossorio and the flamboyant home of the publisher Barney Rosset. No one complained about the beautiful settings, though how Mailer had persuaded his patrons to provide them remains a mystery, and the hotel accommodation for all involved was generous, to say the least.

The problem was that the film itself was becoming increasingly rudderless, and distasteful. Actors seemed to be switched between initially allocated roles to other parts almost at random, and worst of all Mailer appeared to have become possessed by his alter ego, Norman T. The presidential ambitions of the director within the film had gradually been sidelined by his taste for pornography, with Mailer asking various characters being asked to be filmed performing sex acts without any evident relevance to the plot. Only Mailer seemed to have any clear sense of what the movie was about.

The film's cinematographer, D. A. Pennebaker, recalled that 'there were too many things Mailer couldn't control ... the only focus that the film could take was the pornographic one. Everything felt that, and nobody knew what to do.' At a party on the Ossorio estate 'Norman was like a wild man ... He was suffering terrible paranoia about people in general.' (Interview with Mills, pp. 312–13). The party, held on the penultimate day of filming, was supposedly celebratory, but Mailer managed to have an argument with a young Provincetown bit-part actor who had dared to question the film's central themes, punching him and breaking his jaw. Torres mediated and Mailer agreed to pay all medical expenses, plus compensation, if he did not go to the police.

The final day of filming began with Mailer making another speech to all involved, in which he rejoiced in the success of the enterprise and celebrated his particular role as Norman T., the director in the film, and Norman Mailer, the director of everything. 'Master of the universe' was one phrase uttered, according to those present.

Most there would soon witness a freakish case of what can happen when the real becomes interchangeable with the fabricated.

Rip Torn had been allocated the role of head of the 'assassination party', or to be more accurate the role was assumed to be his following Mailer's sequence of improvised revisions of the plot and screenplay. Harold Conrad, sportswriter and recruit for a bit part that never materialised, sets the scene on the final day.

> The owner of the place, Gardiner, took us out in his forty-eight-foot motorboat. Beverly and Mara [Conrad's wife] and the kids and I, and also Rip. It was a beautiful day ... Gardiner's a bore, so I'm watching Rip sitting all alone in the front of the boat. I don't know if he's pissed or stoned, but he's deep into it. Nobody knows what the scene is going to be, since everything was ad lib. But there was something about Norman being killed at some point in the story – that was Rip's idea anyhow. (Manso, p. 485)

Interestingly, it remains unclear as to whether the 'Norman' due to be killed was the character being played by Mailer or Mailer himself. One might assume that the latter is unlikely, but all involved seemed to be flitting between performance and real life.

What happened a few hours later is well documented by several witnesses. Rip Torn attacked Mailer with a claw hammer, making several indentations in his head, and Mailer fought him off by first pushing him to the ground and then by biting off part of his ear.

The most fascinating aspect of the event was that those present, Torn included, were unclear about the status of the attack: was it an attempt to kill Norman T. Kingsley, a feature of the continually extemporised plot, or an attack on the director Norman Mailer, with murder in mind? For example, Pennebaker, as director of photography, had begun filming Mailer walking through the grounds before Torn went for him, and continued to shoot the scene as the two men fought and blood spurted in all directions. 'Beverly was yelling at him, "C'mon over here, *do* something!" … No one lifted a finger.' (Barney Rosset interviewed by Manso, p. 484). According to Rosset, even after the two men were taken away for medical treatment, no one was sure whether the altercation was supposed to be a grotesquely realistic culmination of the drama, something that would draw the untidy plot lines together, or if Torn had decided to take it out on Mailer for ruining the whole project. Beat generation poet and playwright Michael McClure spoke to Rosset. 'He told me that Rip had come up to him and said, "Let's go and kill Norman" – kill him, that is, within the action of the film.' But Rosset suspected that Torn had lost any sense of the distinction between Norman the director and Norman the quasi-fascistic presidential candidate. He replied, 'Michael, this is terrible. You have to go. It's your duty to be there to stop him.' (Manso, p. 485). But Rosset now realised that McClure himself was too far gone on dope – marijuana and heroin - to make sense of things.

Torn himself, speaking to Manso fifteen years after the event, offered a fascinatingly confused account of why he hit Mailer.

Norman must've told twenty or thirty people to set up a phony assassination attempt, because the film was supposed to be about assassinations … Also, I was worried because there really was a plot, I mean for real. Ten or twelve guys were so angry at Norman. They wanted to catch him and literally stone him. He'd made people very, very angry, and had done it deliberately … The more he played his character, the more he became the fascistic Norman T. Kingsley. But no one was going to face him one-to-one, except for dummy here, and I thought I was doing it for the film. (Manso, p. 486)

The police were not called, but had Torn been charged with assault he would probably have been the first person to be found not guilty by reason of postmodernism.

None of the figures involved commented on what now seems alarmingly obvious. The film project was a version of *The Armies of the Night*, with the same blurring of the actual and the make-believe. The only difference was that in the earlier work Mailer had made a home for himself in a world he designed, while in *Maidstone* he had dragged fellow performers into the madhouse run by Norman T. Kingsley.

POLITICS AND THE WOMEN

During the making of *Maidstone* Mailer had taken a few days off to visit and report on the Republican Party Convention in Miami. He recorded his impressions in *Miami and the Siege of Chicago* (1968), of how he was now 'getting tired of Negroes and their rights'; the book prophesied the release of 'immeasurable tides of rage ... in America itself', and he saw this with foreboding rather as the justifiable reaction of blacks against descrimination (p. 51). He expressed similar misgivings about the left in general; Yippies and anarchists of WASP background, 'too full of kicks and pot and the freakings of sodium amytol and orgy' to appreciate the 'individualism of the more rugged in America'. He was beginning to suspect that he was 'in some secret part of his flesh a closet Republican' (ibid). The difference between Mailer in 1968 and the activist behind 'The White Negro' and *The Armies of the Night* is clear enough. Norman T. Kingsley had also taken a sudden turn to the right before his presidential campaign had been brought to a close with an assassination attempt by claw hammer.

However, Mailer's feelings about the Republican nominees at the Miami convention were mixed, to say the least. Eugene McCarthy impressed him as a wit, shaking his hand when introduced in the restaurant but not standing. 'I remain seated,' he announced, 'because we poets must observe our natural precedence over the prose crowd.' He followed this by confessing his empathy with Robert Lowell after reading of his and Mailer's argument in *The Armies of the Night*. Later Mailer asked the journalist Joseph Roddy if the senator was joking. No, answered Roddy, providing him with references to verse published by McCarthy during the 1950s and 60s in prestigious literary magazines.

Hubert Humphrey, who wore make-up for his speeches, reminded Mailer of an 'embalmed corpse staring out of his coffin', and he detected in George McGovern a 'Christian sweetness ... like a psychic aroma ... It was excessive' (pp. 208, 122). Mailer was shocked most of all by his feelings about Nixon, whom he had previously loathed unrelentingly. Now, however, he sensed that Nixon had 'some of the dignity of the old athlete and the old con' and was capable of defending orthodox social and cultural ideals against the onset of self-regarding leftism.

There is no evidence that Mailer himself entertained the idea of re-entering politics when he was in Miami. The first discussion of it took place in his absence five months later, when Jimmy Breslin, Jack Newfield and Gloria Steinem met for drinks in a Manhattan bar called Limericks. Newfield was a journalist and documentary film-maker, Steinem a well-published feminist activist, and Breslin came from an impoverished background in Queens and had worked as an investigative journalist after leaving college without graduating. Breslin was thinking about running for either a position on the city council or as New York City mayor later that year. He would position himself as the man who had experienced poverty – his father had gone out for bread one morning when he was an infant and never returned – and who knew what life was like for members of the urban poor. The problem was that aside from his newspaper column, he was largely unheard of. Newfield mentioned that the previous night Barry Gray had discussed Mailer's *Miami and the Siege of Chicago* on his radio show and suggested, with heavy facetiousness, that the author should run for office. The three took it seriously and discussed the benefits of Breslin and Mailer on a double ticket, independents and not Democrats. Newfield phoned Mailer, who said that he'd go for it provided he could lose some weight before the campaign. 'The bum'll do it!' Newfield announced on his return to the bar. Soon the Republican sympathiser of the Miami convention and *Maidstone* would enter a bizarre coalition with the radical Mailer of old.

The first proper meeting of the campaign team took place in Mailer's Columbia Heights apartment on 31 March 1969, with Steinem, Newfield and Breslin in attendance. The left-wing element was represented by the lawyer Florynce Kennedy and by Jerry Rubin, and the writers Pete Hamill and Peter Maas went along as observers but left open the possibility of becoming involved. Drink flowed and chaos ensued. Kennedy proposed that Mailer and Breslin should step aside and make way for the mixed-race pastor Adam Clayton Powell, which was odd given that he was already the first black Congress from New York, as well as from any state in the Northeast. A black mayor of New York City would have impact, but expecting him to serve simultaneously as a member of the federal legislature seemed impractical. Rubin dismissed this as the 'Uncle Tom' option and argued that they should put forward a member of the Black Panthers, preferably one with a criminal record. Someone else moved that Steinem should become either campaign manager or candidate, the first trailblazing political feminist, but she declined. Mailer tried to calm things by proposing a 'hip coalition of left and right' and reminding those present that he and Breslin had invited everyone to the event to discuss their campaign rather than to replace them.

Order of a sort was restored the following day, in Foffé's restaurant, when Joe Flaherty, longshoreman-turned-journalist and political agitator, was appointed campaign manager, and it was agreed that Mailer should run for mayor and Breslin for president of the city council. The mood was cautiously optimistic in that the likely Democrat candidate, Mario Procaccino, was a hilariously bad canvasser. He had already addressed an assembly of African Americans, hand on chest, with the exclamation 'My heart is as black as yours', and despite his Democratic Party allegiance Procaccino was an ardent social conservative. The previous mayor, Robert Wagner, was widely despised, and the only other serious non-Republican candidate was the Puerto Rican Herman Badillo, widely respected but subjected to quiet prejudice by those who disliked Latinos as much as they did black people.

Remarkably, Flaherty had some knowledge of Mailer's campaign in 1960 but not of the event that brought it to a close. He shared his loss of innocence with his younger campaign staff.

I knew that Mailer had flirted with the idea before, but none of us knew the history. If we'd known that the party when he stabbed Adele was connected to his earlier 'candidacy', then we'd have said, 'Put a fucking ice bag on his head, he's off again. It must be an every-decade madness.' (Manso, p. 498)

Then he thought again. 'How many of you clowns got records?' he asked, and a lot of hands went up. 'What a fuckin' crew,' he said, smiling.

The official announcement of Mailer's and Breslin's campaigns took place a month later, on 2 May 1969, in the Overseas Press Club, the mid-town Manhattan, prestigious hub for the maintenance of standards in the American and International press. When asked about his political manifesto, Mailer hesitated and then went for 'free Huey Newton and end fluoridation'. Mailer had long held that fluoridised water led to impotence and cancer; Newton, co-founder of the Black Panthers, had been convicted of shooting the police officer John Frey (his conviction would be quashed in 1970). Breslin was appalled. His senior partner, he believed, would alienate voters of virtually all backgrounds and affiliations, aside from perhaps the most radical African Americans, and briefly he withdrew from the campaign. He was brought back by Flaherty, who persuaded him that over the next few months he would muzzle the deranged element of Mailer and coordinate a programme that was sane and attractive to lower- and middle-class voters.

Flaherty arranged events in colleges, high schools and universities, and even though some present would be below voting age, it was hoped that word of something new would spread among the young electorate in the city.

The principal proposal was that New York City be divided up into small self-governing units, rather like an urban version of the French communes, which could detach themselves from the central government of the city. If, argued Mailer, a suburb of Harlem wished to put up a statue of Martin Luther King, funded by residents, they would not have to ask for permission from any other body. Moreover, New York City would become the fifty-first state, far more autonomous than the rest; answerable to the federal government but in many respects independent. The key element here was the proposition that military decisions made in Washington would not necessarily pertain to citizens of the new state. Mailer felt that offering electors potential exemption from conscription would win hundreds of thousands of votes, but he had not gone into the practical details of how the constitution would be amended, particularly given that it would require a two-thirds majority in the Senate and the House of Representatives from politicians who would be allowing New York City liberties that their own states were denied.

Other campaign ideas became established during the early summer, and once more Flaherty was unable to prevent the press fixing on Mailer's more hair-brained schemes. These included citywide stickball competitions between the new self-governing districts, free-loan bicycles for commuters who preferred to avoid the subway and those who wished to exercise in city parks, no-charge day-care centres and nurseries, and markets for the sale of fresh fruit, vegetables and meat produced by farmers on the edge of the metropolis. All of this carried an air of the free-and-easy socialism of the Israeli kibbutz or Catalonia before the victory of Franco, but Mailer set it against other projects which encouraged individuality and what is now promoted as libertarian hedonism. Casino gambling would be legalised, even sponsored, with Coney Island envisaged as the Las Vegas of the East Coast. An annual Grand Prix involving expensive sports cars would take place in Central Park. Drug addicts would be provided with methadone, usually from police officers, who would be encouraged to live in areas they would generally only visit when on duty. This last strategy would, contended Mailer, enable local communities to absorb minor criminality rather than punish the criminally dispossessed.

The most controversial proposal was evolved by Mailer and Peter Manso. During each month there would be one 'Sweet Sunday'. All motor vehicles – including cars, lorries, vans and buses – would not be allowed on the roads. Airports would close because there would be no incoming or outgoing flights, and trains would remain in sidings. No one would enter or leave New York City and, with the exception of hospitals, all electricity would be turned off. 'New Yorkers', averred Mailer, 'could get a hint of fields or sea in the breeze on Sweet Sunday.' One of his earliest speeches on this was to an audience of John Adams High School in Queens, made up mostly of comfortably employed, university-educated parents. Flaherty was caught between the self-evident absurdity of the policy and the reverential silence observed by listeners, as if they had witnessed 'the second coming', as he later put it.

At Brooklyn College some were a little more querulous. One asked what would happen during a Sweet Sunday in high summer, with temperatures at 90 degrees-plus and everyone in need of air conditioning, if they could afford it, or at least a refrigerator. 'On the first hot day the populace would impeach me!' answered Mailer and moved on to the next questioner, who asked what would happen if ploughs could not shift the snow blocking numerous roads in the city, as had occurred during the previous winter. 'I'd piss on it,' he shouted back. By this point Breslin had his head in his hands, wearily aware of how his own constituency – dockers, manual labourers, city workers, etc. – would react to this vision of a quasi-anarchic nirvana. He left the campaign several times and was persuaded to come back by Flaherty, who, despite his initial enthusiasm, was himself realising that he had become part of an imminent catastrophe.

On 7 May a sufficient number of nomination signatures had been gathered, and Mailer arranged a party at the Village Gate, a jazz club. He drank more than half a bottle of whiskey, stood up, and greeted the campaign organisers as a 'bunch of spoiled pigs' with 'dull little vanities'. He replied to polite rejoinders with 'Fuck you!' Flaherty, Mailer and Beverly were driven back to the Columbia Heights apartment by a college kid, who during the journey went from being awestruck by his involvement with this cultural superstar to aghast by what he had let himself in for. Flaherty: 'Norman went into his lament in his broad Southern accent.' He said to Beverly, 'You ain't doin' shit in the campaign. You come into that bar, that motherfucker is puttin' me down, and you're jive-ass ...' Flaherty said, 'Fuck you, fuck the press. If there's one thing I hate, Mailer, it's a bully. You reduced this woman to tears for no good reason.' (Manso, p. 506). The college-kid driver was shocked enough to almost crash the car but said nothing. Flaherty, invited to their apartment, watched them make up and go to the bedroom where they had noisily enthusiastic sex; 'went to bed and fucked their brains out,' he recalled. 'That day,' says Flaherty, 'I had this mad fantasy of kidnapping Mailer and for the rest of the campaign never letting him out ...' (Manso, p. 507). Flaherty knew nothing of the *Maidstone* fiasco, but one wonders what he would have made of becoming Rip Torn, mark two, with kidnapping replacing the assassination attempt.

When the results for the Democratic primaries were announced on 17 June, Mailer came fourth, with 32,209 votes. Procaccino won with 233,483, and Wagner came second with 208,936. Some of Mailer's team felt guilty about the margin between Mailer and Badillo, who took 203,317. We will never know if Mailer's 32,209 votes would, in his absence, have gone to Badillo and given him a narrow victory over Procaccino, but Badillo never forgave him, seeing his campaign as an exercise in grandstanding rather than a serious attempt to improve the lives of the impoverished and under-represented. In the eventual General Election John V Lindsay, Liberal Independent, beat Procaccino by just over 5%

Roughly two weeks after the election, *Life* magazine contacted Mailer and asked if he would cover the imminent Apollo 11 moon-landing launch. His agent, Scott Meredith, opened by asking for $400,000 for an open-ended sequence of long essays of at least 10,000 words each. *Life* turned him down, and Mailer told Meredith to inform Thomas Griffith, the *Life* editor, that '[he] had something like fourteen people on his payroll'. Griffith contended in response that surely the mayoral team had disbanded; Meredith explained that the payroll involved his client's ex-wives, servants and parents. In the end, Meredith managed to negotiate three contracts totalling $400,000: $100,000 for the *Life* serialisation; Little, Brown would pay $150,000 for the hardback book; and the New American Library came up with $150,000 for the subsequent paperback.

Griffith had chosen Mailer because of his growing reputation as a prophet of the nation's destiny, especially in terms of the Vietnam War and the global struggle between the superpowers. Who then would be more suitable as the chronicler of a such a historic landmark, an American setting foot on another world? However, Griffith's perception of Mailer's temperament was flawed, to say the least.

Mailer hoped for what Tom Wolfe would go on to experience almost a decade later when he wrote *The Right Stuff* (1979). Wolfe had initially intended to do a documentary novel on the entire space programme, but, after speaking with those involved, especially the test pilot Chuck Yeager, he discovered that the men of tin of the 1940s and 50s – who wanted to adapt their skills as fighter and test pilots to handling rockets

– had something of a charismatic wildness about them, a joy in simply taking risks, that was snuffed out during the 1960s when the Apollo programme replaced skill with robotic discipline.

The first problem that confronted Mailer was the reluctance of NASA officials and lawyers to allow him to do one-to-one interviews with anyone directly involved with the programme. They knew his record and feared he would ask questions and, as Griffith put it, portray the astronauts as 'silly fly boys'. This was shrewd in the sense that Mailer wanted to find that the men going to the moon were the heroes of comic books on aerial warfare. The result, had he been allowed to talk with them, would have been worse. They would have come across as soulless technicians. The only astronaut he was allowed to meet was Charles 'Pete' Conrad, who invited him to a dinner party at his house. Conrad was not involved with Apollo 11 but would command Apollo 12, the next flight to the moon. They got on well enough and discovered a mutual taste for whiskey – more than 'half a bottle that night', according to Conrad – but there was no spark. By regulation Conrad could not answer Mailer's questions on the military implications of Apollo rockets, and he was not by his nature garrulous or outspoken about his job. Astronauts who did behave in this way would have been excluded from the programme during the selection procedure.

Mailer's most memorable encounter was with Dr Robert R. Gilruth, director of the Manned Spacecraft Center, who struck him as 'rather like a Chinese mandarin – completely pleasant, altogether remote ...' He was certainly a composed figure, but he was shaken by Mailer's opening question. 'Are you ever worried, Dr Gilruth, that landing on the moon may result in all sorts of psychic disturbances for us here on earth? I mean, many people seem to react to the full moon, and there are tides of course.' (*Of a Fire on the Moon*, pp. 20–21). He went on to ask if Gilruth was anxious about disturbing extra-terrestrial presences. Gilruth was dumbfounded, and Mailer portrayed him in *Life* and in the book as a buffoon.

More than half of the book reads as a technical guide to spaceflight. Mailer found that his Harvard studies in aeronautical engineering enabled him to appreciate what lay behind the NASA publicity, far more so than other members of the press corps. He even put together a meticulous guide to the fitness and dietary regimes of the astronauts, implying without quite stating that they had been transformed from human beings into machines.

In the end he claims that while there was applause and celebration at the landing, 'something was lacking'. 'Strong men did not weep in the street nor ladies copulate with strangers ... It was almost as if a sense of woe sat in the center of the heart.' (p. 386).

By the time the book was published in 1970, Mailer had other things on his mind. Midge Decter, editor of *Harper's*, had recently asked Irving Howe to review Kate Millett's *Sexual Politics* (1970) and was in a bar drinking with Mailer, who said to her 'I oughta write about it' – not just a review but an examination of the book as the culmination of the second-wave feminist principles that had developed over the 1960s. 'God, you certainly ought to', answered Decter, and she promised to contact him the following day for a piece for the magazine. This was the beginning of a sequence of articles that would result in *The Prisoner of Sex* (1971).

Irrespective of one's opinions on feminism in its various manifestations, Mailer's book can only be seen as intellectually stunted. He expresses his condescending support for the women's movement with some anecdotes from his own experiences of having to look after the children and the house while Beverly is elsewhere, sometimes for as long as several weeks. He appreciates that the rules allocated to women by social convention are restrictive and even slightly demeaning, but he also points out that the reallocation of, say, domestic duties should not cause us to overlook undeniable biological truths regarding the essential differences between the two sexes. He lists some questionable statistics, for example that during menstruation women drivers are twice as likely to have accidents as their male counterparts, and that periods greatly increase women's committal to mental institutions and their commission of crimes, especially involving violence. He does not blame women for this, but cites it as proof of a broader polarity in which physical difference is responsible for 'such abstract lands as seed and womb, vision and firmament, fire up a skyworks of sermon and poem to the incontestable mystery that women are flesh of the Mystery more than men' (*The Prisoner of Sex*, p. 59). As a small compensation for it being incomprehensible this sounds like an amusing caricature of a cult leader.

Without pausing for reflection, he moves on to the difference between male and female sexuality, dismissing abruptly the contention by some feminists that vaginal orgasms are a myth. His 'proof' that this is erroneous comes from personal experience: all of the women with whom he has had sex have had vaginal orgasms brought about the mesmeric power of his penis. He has no time for the alternative argument, that for many women the clitoris is the main site of stimulus. Generously he promises women who hold this belief 'a bit of male irony' on the difference between the clitoris and the penis, 'yea, as a pea, as a curled anchovy, as a shrimp to a cucumber' (p. 80).

It soon becomes evident why he is uneasy with the notion of a clitoral orgasm. It might exclude the male from the role as procreator, given that semen can be obtained without intercourse. But he regards the production of sperm via masturbation as would a fundamentalist preacher: pleasure without the possibility of conception is a sin against the sacred mysteries of creation and reproduction. Procreation by women without sex amounts to a quasi-violent assault against the timeless rule of maleness. To 'fail' at conception causes a man to grieve for his lost sperm. After this Mailer adopts an avuncular, condescending tone on how women do indeed deserve some kind of sexual liberation. 'She' might wish to 'cohabit with elephants', or 'fuck with Borzoi hounds, let her bed with eight pricks and a whistle … Let her travel to the moon, write the great American novel, and allow her husband to send her off to work with her lunch pail and a cigar.' But aside from all this, most of all, 'Let her conceive her children' only by intercourse with a man. (p. 233).

Gloria Steinem disclosed that Mailer had been evolving these ideas long before he made arrangements with *Life*. Indeed, she states that his opinions on women and race were what caused her to leave his mayoral campaign team:

His basic response to women of any race and men of color is that we're close to the earth and have this instinctive knowledge of which he is envious, an instinctive grace or athletic ability or sexual ease, but we don't have his intellect, his sense of strategy, political power, or ability to make things happen. (Manso, p. 502)

Characteristically, Mailer thought that despite his differences of opinion with Steinem on feminism, she qualified as a one-night stand. Speaking to Manso, she mocked his attempts at seduction. 'I said something like "Norman, I can't do that until you stop thinking your sperm is sacred." Looking crestfallen he replied, "I can't." ... There was something wistful about it ... and that was the last time I saw him for a long while.' (Manso, p. 525). Later, however, she admitted to her biographer Sydney Stern that she did sleep with him once simply to get him to leave her alone. He was also, she added, 'so vulnerable, in a weird way' (Stern, p. 176), a middle-aged man, now with an enormous paunch, who seemed obsessed with the idea of his powerful virility. As contemporary photographs show she was stunningly attractive.

The issue that prompted Mailer to write his book was Millett's accusation that key male authors – notably D. H. Lawrence, Henry Miller, Jean Genet and Mailer – disguised misogyny as art or unbiased representation. Mailer hit back by claiming that she deliberately misread key passages by overlooking their contexts. To an extent the case remains open with the exception of Millett's discussion of An American Dream, particularly the opening parts where, after killing his wife, Rojack takes self-evident pleasure in anally raping Ruta, the maid. Millett lets him off too easily, noting his 'obsession with machismo' and comparing him with 'a certain curio sold in Coney Island and called a Peter Meter', a means by which men could measure their penises and reassure themselves by equating 'excellence with size' (Millett, p. 330). She is right. The passages are a means by which certain types of male reader can, via Rojack, enjoy the prurient fantasy of using their penis as a weapon.

The so-called Theatre of Ideas organised an event for 30-31st March 1971, to be held at New York Town Hall, at which Mailer would defend his book against four feminists, including Jacqueline Ceballos, president of the New York Chapter of the National Organization for Women; Jill Johnston, lesbian feminist activist and regular contributor to The Village Voice, and Diana Trilling, more a conventional, left-liberal campaigner than an outright feminist. The woman whose presence ensured a full house was Germaine Greer, author of the recent, controversial The Female Eunuch (1970). Millett had been invited but declined on the grounds that the evening would degrade its ostensible topic by turning it into a sensationalist verbal brawl, and her prediction proved accurate. Tickets, sold out within a day of the event, the 'jet-setters were downstairs at $25 a ticket; but I don't remember whether it was $10 or $15 in the balcony' recalled Manso. In the audience were Jack Newfield, D. A Pennebaker, Stephen Spender, Arthur Schlesinger, John Hollander and Jules Feiffer. Adele and Jeanne were there, but Beverly was conspicuously absent. Her and Mailer's relationship was moving towards crisis point because she suspected that he was seeing one woman regularly, beyond his routine of one-night stands, and soon she found out that she was right.

Greer and Mailer were, as expected, the chief combatants, though during the evening neither added more to what was already known from their books. Thereafter, however, matters became farcical. Trilling, the closing speaker, had prepared her piece carefully, but before she began she became aware of whispering and movement to her side. Later she learned from friends that Greer had been passing notes to Mailer with a view to allowing him a special advantage during the debate. She was barely halfway through her given period of time when Mailer, taking on the role of Chair, asked her to bring things to a close. He wanted the argument to begin as soon as possible, but matters were interrupted as two lesbian friends of Johnston charged up the steps from the audience to embrace their heroine. All three were significant figures in the women's movement. That night they dressed in denim, and their display before the largely male audience was an example of feminism as a repudiation of male sexuality. They deliberately lost their balance, fell off the stage and then rolled around on the floor, hugging, kissing and making noises that sounded like expressions of sexual pleasure. Mailer stood up and commanded, 'Come on, Jill, be a lady!' Trilling sensed that he was moving forward to pull them apart and hissed at him, 'Don't touch them!' By now most of the crowd was whooping and cheering, some hurling obscenities, and when Johnston returned to the stage, accompanied by her two friends, Mailer moved close enough to the microphone for his quiet rejoinder to be audible throughout the hall. 'You can get enough prick and cunt as you want around the corner on 42nd Street for two dollars and fifty cents. We don't need it here.' (Manso, p. 522).

That marked the end of the seminar, which was followed by drinks in a Village bar for the speakers, their guests and various cultural celebrities. Mailer was self-evidently amused by how things had gone and seemed to have entered an alliance with Greer, which was sensed by Trilling. 'Greer looked at me malevolently but never said a word. She was wearing a floozy kind of fox fur that trailed over her shoulder to the floor.' (Manso, p. 520). Greer was famously uninhibited at social events or on the media and as attractive as Steinem. Trilling asked Mailer, 'Did you go to bed with her?', a question he regarded as a hilarious postscript to the evening, without replying to it. For many present it seemed as though Mailer had come through the whole thing as a wry stage-manager, capable of turning his chastening by four feminists into a pantomime.

The reason for the apparent empathy between him and Greer becomes clear enough from the combative hypothetical 'new women' of The Female Eunuch, for whom Trilling later offered a pithy summary:

> It would appear that in the service of the sexual impulse everything is well lost for Miss Greer: love, motherhood, the nurturing instincts, even the pleasures of a developing relation with the same lover. For Miss Greer sex is not sex unless it is *only* sex ... (Lennon, (ed.), Critical Essays on Norman Mailer, 1986, p. 108)

Clearly Trilling felt embittered by her encounter with Greer, but what is striking about her portrait of her as a rampaging sex maniac is its similarity to many of Mailer's heroes, notably Rojack and O'Shaugnessy. If, however, Mailer felt that he and Greer had formed a companionable attachment, he would soon learn otherwise.

Six months later she delivered the comeuppance she felt was due to him for the chaotic event in New York. She did an essay for Esquire called 'My Mailer Problem' (September 1971), which might have been more accurately entitled 'Mailer's Mailer Problem'. Greer discloses, brilliantly, that his defence of D. H. Lawrence against Millett is actually about himself, 'locked into the body of a middling male physique, not physically strong, of reasonable good looks, a pleasant to somewhat seedy-looking man, no stud' (Esquire, p. 90). Just as Lawrence dispossessed himself of his inadequacies by rewriting his past in his fiction, especially in *Sons and Lovers*, so Mailer, 'his mind ... possessed of that intolerable masculine pressure to command, which develops in sons outrageously beloved of their mothers, decided, in his writing, to live out his fantasies and ambitions', but, more importantly, also separated himself from the smothering affection of his maternal relationship. Hence his weird addiction to military metaphors and his relentless conflation of notions of sexuality, violence and political reform. 'One senses', writes Greer, 'in his petulance and in the spoiled airs of his impatient disdain ... a momma's boy, spoiled rotten.' At the post-symposium drinks party Mailer, grinning, introduced Greer to his mother as 'my secret ally'. Barney, Greer later recalled, was politely diffident, but she spent quite a while speaking with Fan, who praised Norman as possessed of genius beyond compare.

Mills interviewed Greer ten years later:

> There was a lot of feminist wrath around and he bought it. I mean [took it] in his chin. He wanted to be the subject of that rage and he courted it because it made him feel more masculine. It's the same reason he goes to dockside cafes and gets beaten up ... Mailer wants a woman who is stronger than him ... Norman accused me of not being tough enough. He thought I was going to be something of the archetypal rocky female. But I'm not tough, I'm ruthless, but not tough in the way that would excite him. (Mills, p. 357)

Given that Greer had known him for only a matter of weeks her assessment is very shrewd, particularly regarding his apparent inability to properly distinguish between anger and outright violence. She was, as she pointed out, 'ruthless', but she did not relate this to an appetite for getting 'beaten up' or visiting the same on others.

For some time, Mailer's relationship with Gore Vidal had involved precarious mutual respect, though Vidal had treated him more with patrician tolerance than as a friend. Things came to a head shortly after the publication of *The Prisoner of Sex*. Vidal was an avid supporter of feminism and during the various TV and radio coverages of the Theatre of Ideas evening he had made quips about Mailer's seemingly obsessive concern with maleness in general and his own machismo in particular. Mailer hit back with a letter to the fashion magazine *Women's Wear Daily* on Vidal's puzzling disinclination to court women, let alone marry or procreate. Vidal's homosexuality was common knowledge within the intelligentsia, and Mailer had sent the gossipy, insinuating letter to a magazine concerned mainly with clothes because it had already been rejected by every other mainstream outlet. Soon afterwards Vidal responded in a review on a book by Eva Figes in *The New York Review of Books* on 22 July 1971. He digressed: there had been a 'logical progression' from notions of manliness represented first by Arthur Miller, then by Mailer, and then epitomised in the acts of Charles Manson. He concluded that the 'Miller-Mailer-Manson man ... has been conditioned to think of women as, at best, breeders of sons; at worst, objects to be poked, humiliated, killed ...'

Mailer did not initially respond to this and kept himself to himself until he found that he and Vidal would appear together live on the Dick Cavett Show on 2 December 1971. In the green room, where interviewees prepared themselves with the help of free drinks, Mailer decided to slap Vidal on the cheek. Vidal returned the gesture unaggressively, more to mock his assailant than as an act of revenge. Mailer treated this as insultingly effeminate and head-butted Vidal. Luckily for Vidal, Mailer had been drinking long before he arrived at the studio and thus failed in his attempt to knock him unconscious. 'You're absolutely mad,' declared Vidal. 'You are violent.' Before this he had regarded Mailer's reputation as a brawler as part of a pantomime performance; now he had encountered a man who really wanted to hurt him.

When they appeared on the show little improved, as Mailer seized from Cavett the role of host and introduced Vidal as a 'shameless ... weak' writer and 'no more interesting than the contents of the stomach of an intellectual cow'. Mailer then pulled a clipping of Vidal's *New York Review of Books* piece from his pocket and demanded that Cavett make Vidal read it aloud. Cavett refused, and after a commercial break the show descended into a state of anarchy. Mailer accused Vidal of murdering Jack Kerouac, adding that 'You bragged about what you did to Jack Kerouac, after all'. Vidal replied that 'He didn't die', but Mailer insisted, 'Well, he did.'

The audience would have known that Kerouac had died in 1969 in hospital in Florida. The cause had been announced as an oesophageal haemorrhage, which doctors were unable to treat because his liver was so severely damaged by alcohol abuse that his blood would not clot. Mailer's allegation that Vidal had murdered him thus seemed macabre and absurd, but the audience were listening to a heavily abbreviated version of a private quarrel that had been taking place since the late 1950s. Then, Vidal had commented, nonchalantly, to Mailer that he had once had sex with Kerouac. Mailer was driving the two of them back from a New England party and was so appalled by the disclosure that he came close to crashing the car. At the time Mailer saw homosexuality as a perversion, and sexual acts between men as a cross between rape and indoctrination, involving an active participant and a victim. He did not doubt that Vidal – the intellectual grandee – was the former, who had coerced the innocent poet into homosexuality and driven him to alcoholism.

For the audience Mailer seemed to have become deranged. Janet Flanner, journalist and veteran of the Paris-based Hemingway–Fitzgerald set of the 1920s, was the third guest. She, Cavett and Vidal appeared calmly bemused by Mailer's ravings while he, now standing, was pleading directly to the studio audience. 'Can I reach you; can I talk to any of you, or is it hopeless? I do have a thing to say, believe it or not.'

Next, he took issue with Millett's comments on the opening of *An American Dream*, explaining that Rojack had not 'buggered' the maid but 'entered her another way', insisting that anal intercourse between men was debauched, implying a man doing the same to a woman was entirely acceptable.

The chuckling in the audience was met by Flanner, who protested, 'Oh, goodness's sake!', and Mailer responded that because she had lived in France for so long she was not aware that it was 'possible to enter a woman another way as well'. The audience was now convulsing with laughter. Cavett signalled for another commercial break and cancelled what would have been the concluding part of the show. Fifteen years later Mailer would invite Vidal to his apartment to declare, for the gossip columnists, that the two of them had made up, which was in truth a promotional exercise for their respective writings. In the interim their rare encounters at parties or launches were toxic, mostly because Mailer seemed determined to provoke Vidal into a violent response. Drink was thrown, furniture overturned, abuse hurled, and Vidal would remain urbanely calm. Most famously, at a party following the National Book Awards in 1978, Mailer approached Vidal from behind and pitched him onto a buffet table. Vidal stood up, brushed himself down and offered a withering rephrase of his comment the farcical Cavett show of 1971: 'Well, Norman, once again words have failed you.'

13

THE BIOGRAPHER'S SONG

Mailer had met Carol Stevens in 1962. She was a singer, then performing at Smalls Paradise nightclub in Harlem. Their affair overlapped with three of his marriages, and he only made it public when she became pregnant. In 1971 they rented a house in Vermont, and in 1972 he bought a property in the pretty village of Stockbridge, Massachusetts, where their daughter, Maggie, was born. Were it not for her pregnancy she would have continued as a member of his private harem of conveniently available lovers. Many had put up with this; and at least two were doing so even when he set up home with Carol in Stockbridge. Beverly and Mailer had separated in 1969, and she assumed that they might at least consider repairing the break. She was told of what was going on with Carol by Barbara, but her husband had said nothing. He had simply disappeared and set up home with his new, pregnant partner, and for the next few years Beverly did her best to undermine Mailer's most recent exercise in replacing wives as though they were automobiles.

Mailer's secretary, Anne Barry, recalled,

I didn't meet her [Carol] until I went up to visit them in the house they bought in Stockbridge ... I couldn't read Carol very well. She was quiet, and either she walled me out or there was nothing there ... She puzzled me, she didn't fit in with the rest of his wives. It didn't seem to me that it would last, although I couldn't put my finger on why.

She goes on to comment on the house, which Carol had chosen and furnished.

I thought it was terrible ... upstairs off the long hallway were lots of rooms that were just cubicles ... And downstairs there was something painful about the parlour. Carol had got it up with Victorian furniture, little loveseats and the lady's chair and the gentleman's chair ... It was so stiff no one would dream of sitting there. (Manso, p. 531)

Adeline Naiman Lubell who'd known Mailer since the 1940s, commented that while she liked Carol, she 'couldn't understand why Norman continued to get himself into these insane relationships in which his fantasy was to shape the woman' (Manso, p. 531).

The Mailer that Carol thought she knew during the ten years before they openly became a couple turned out to be very different from the assembly of alter egos she came across a few months after their move to Stockbridge in September 1972. The couple met Anne Edwards, a moderately successful biographer, and her future husband, Stephen Citron, owner of a local bar. Carol became interested in the dance classes Anne organised for other early middle-aged cosmopolitan women in the district and suggested to Anne that singing might accompany recorded music, which led to her being invited to perform on her own at Stephen's local inn called Orpheus Ascending. She was delighted to return to a career she thought was over, albeit in a modest parochial setting. The first evening was going well, until Mailer heard comments from two slightly drunken men seated close to him on the physical qualities of the performer, notably her being very 'well stacked'. Mailer asked them to be quiet but they upped the volume. Suddenly, the most outspoken found that his ears had been grabbed and within a second felt a shattering blow as Mailer's forehead crashed into his own. The crack was loud enough to turn the heads of all present, and when Carol looked toward Mailer, she saw a man unconscious on the floor and his companion being punched in the face and chest by her partner. She shouted over that unless Mailer left them alone, she would leave him. Edwards took her upstairs, and when she returned, she found that Mailer and the man he had knocked out were hugging and toasting each other with bourbon. (Lennon, p475).

Carol had never seen anything like it, and when she spoke of it later to friends of Mailer she learned that the man with whom she hoped to have a long-term relationship had spent much of his adult life settling disagreements with violence. Further unnerving discoveries would await her. She found herself puzzled by his behaviour following Barney's death from cancer on 12 October 1972. Mailer told her that she was not invited to the funeral service because it was a family event. She was, she assumed, now part of the family, despite the fact that they were unable to marry because of Beverly's refusal even to discuss a divorce settlement. His reluctance to let her come to the service and interment at Long Branch was part of his policy of keeping aspects of his life secret from his new partner.

In late October and early November he had been riding the wave of publicity from *The Prisoner of Sex* and his encounters with feminists. On one occasion in the University of Berkeley, he began his talk by asking those in the audience to hiss at those who opposed the women's movement, a somewhat hypothetical grouping since none were present, but many hissed, and he smiled and called them 'obedient little bitches'. What followed included his observation that 'a little bit of rape is good for a man's soul'.

He would, he decided, accuse the press of having made up or distorted his words if Carol read reports in the papers, but in truth he wanted to ensure that Carol had no knowledge of his tour for another reason. He was accompanied by a woman called Suzanne Nye, with whom he'd begun an affair shortly before Carol's pregnancy. He planned to spend one more week with Suzanne following Barney's funeral. Also, he knew that with Barney's passing would come embarrassing disclosures of his financial chicanery. Notably, an elderly woman arrived at Fan's apartment shortly before the funeral with an unpaid notarised loan for $26,000 that he owed. Mailer paid.

Carol would not learn of the unpaid loan until 1975, but she directly experienced the ranting Norman Mailer on 5 February 1973 at the celebration of his fiftieth birthday, which had taken place on 31 January. Friends organised the event at the Four Seasons restaurant in Manhattan, sending invitations to several thousand people. These stipulated that the maximum capacity for the restaurant was five hundred and that attendance required purchasing a ticket at $30 a person, $50 per couple, on a first-come, first-serve basis. This seemed rather grandiose, but within two days of the invitations going out in December the party was fully booked. A number of Mailer's old friends, family members and ex-wives, specifically Adele, Jeanne and four of his seven children, were guaranteed places, and they too had to pay. Celebrities and stars who knew him mainly by reputation were keen to appear at what was regarded as the social gathering of the year: Shirley MacLaine and Jack Lemmon booked places, as did Jessica Mitford, Andy Warhol, Lily Tomlin, Bernardo Bertolucci, Princess Diane Von Furstenberg and Senator Eugene McCarthy. Correspondents and editors from *Time*, *The New York Post*, *Newsweek*, *The New York Times* and *The Village Voice* all attended, along with freelance journalists such as Pete Hamill, George Plimpton and Murray Kempton. Fan regaled the press corps with celebrations of her son and his uniqueness. 'Other children had that sameness about him, but not Norman ... Norman was not an ordinary child. He was just different.' What occurred shortly afterwards fully justified her claims.

About half an hour into the party his erstwhile electoral running mate, Jimmy Breslin, introduced him as 'one of the half-dozen original thinkers in this century', and Mailer mounted the podium carrying a large bourbon, having already downed at least half a bottle. He announced that he had recently discovered why Richard Nixon was president: 'He has gristle behind his retina.' Listeners laughed in the expectation of a ribald punchline. Instead, Mailer appeared insulted that his guests had not appreciated his diagnosis of the president and turned his attention to his own life, specifically involving intimate disclosures on 'my ex-wife', her 'new lover' and the unbecoming nature of their sexual organs. He was met with boos, and Joe Flaherty, his one-time campaign manager, muttered wearily, 'Here we go again.' He concluded the performance with a submission that did hold the attention of his guests, some because they thought he was losing his mind. 'What happened in Dallas?' he asked. 'What about Martin Luther King? The real story behind Watergate? How many plots are there in America? Two? Three? None?' 'None' was swept aside in his assertion that from John Kennedy's murder onwards the CIA and FBI had been conspiring against and manipulating the American public. He did not explain what these two agencies expected to achieve by assassinating figures who were generally popular but went on to advocate for a 'democratic secret police', 'a people's FBI and a CIA', which would have a mandate to investigate 'the other two'. (Mills, p. 375).

Chaos descended. Carol left the hall, not to be seen until the next day, and Adele was overheard by a reporter saying, 'I don't understand what the whole thing was about.' Mailer, having retired to the Pool Room, was followed by a small group of journalists determined to learn whether he had genuinely discovered something about the security services or was hallucinating. Memorably, an old lady in leather bikers' gear, who had not been invited to the event, declared that 'I'm not gonna be your gumshoe'. Which puzzled him since he had not asked her to be his gumshoe or met her before. 'I've thought years about the manipulation of history,' he replied, followed by 'Let go!' She had flung her hands around his neck while continuing to promise that she would save him and declaring her unrelenting love for him.

Carol's impressions of the performance were supplemented by the hour or so she spent in the company of Adele and Jeanne, during which both offered wry guidance on what they, and indeed Bea, had experienced. Mailer was, they explained, genuine in his declaration of unsparing love to the women who had replaced his previous wives, but there was a caveat. Usually within a year of his new official relationship he would exchange his previous passionate extra-marital affair for another. This struck a note of suspicion with Carol which she would soon promptly follow up on. That he had recently taken on a woman called Suzanne Nye as his occasional assistant and typist, even providing her with a small flat in the Brooklyn brownstone to undertake her duties in comfort, seemed initially a matter of business. But soon Carol began to sense something untoward about the fact that Suzanne accompanied him on every journey when he was due to deliver speeches or cover political conventions.

Eighteen months after the party Carol heard that Beverly had filed an order against Mailer and assumed, with qualified relief, that she was finally suing for divorce and seeking alimony. Soon she found that while there was a request for a financial settlement – $30,000 a year, including custody costs for their children – the primary case in the suit was a restraining order.

Mailer, Carol learnt, had recently been involved in a physical altercation with his ex-partner/present wife. In July 1974 Mailer had arranged to look after his and Beverly's sons in the Provincetown house while Beverly was supposedly in New York. It had been agreed that Carol would not go to Provincetown even if Beverly was absent. Mailer had actually arranged to meet Suzanne off the train and to spend at least ten days swimming from the beach and picnicking in the dunes with a woman who he had convinced his sons was their aunt. When he and Suzanne arrived, Beverly was in the house with no plans to leave. Mailer raged at her: 'No, you leave. It's *my* house. *You* get out of this house.' He moved closer to her and hissed 'Wouldn't it be funny if Suzanne wound up with this house?' – not his partner Carol, but his mistress. (Dearborn, pp. 326-7). Beverly, in front of their sons, called him a filthy debauchee and was rewarded with two blows from his fists, which left her with a black eye and swollen cheek. She called the police, but Mailer and Suzanne left before they arrived, and she decided that financial vengeance would be the best policy.

Before Carol learned the full story of what had prompted the divorce suit and restraining order, she herself had already had an experience of his darker side. As was sometimes the case Beverly and their two sons would stay overnight in Stockbridge, and in June 1974 Beverly went to a local nightspot to listen to Carol sing. Mailer closed the event by thanking his 'wife' for a great performance, and Beverly stood and shouted to them that she was the 'only Mrs Mailer'. Back at the house Carol, feeling humiliated, refused to go on to a late-night party with Mailer, Beverly and others. He hurled abuse at her, threw a glass of lemon in her face and banged her head into the side of a cupboard. She fell on the floor, stunned and bleeding. Fan, who had agreed to look after the children, came downstairs and asked, 'Are you all right?' Carol rolled onto her back but before she could reply found that Fan had addressed the question to her beloved son. By the end of 1974 Carol had decided that their relationship was over, and she was relieved of the difficulties of announcing it to him by his news that she would have to leave Stockbridge before the end of 1975. She assumed that her replacement was Suzanne – who she now knew was more than a secretary – but was surprised to be introduced to a complete stranger. Like a magician pulling a rabbit from a hat Mailer announced the presence of Barbara Norris, whom he'd met in 1974. Barbara would become his full-time partner after the departure of Carol and, once he and Beverly agreed a divorce five years later, his wife, the final Mrs Mailer.

It would be wrong, however, to regard Carol, Suzanne and Barbara as the only women who shared Mailer's attentions in the early 1970s. In autumn 1972 he fell obsessively in love with the late Marilyn Monroe. Robert Markel, editor-in-chief of Grosset & Dunlap, had since the spring of that year been planning what amounted to a visual biography of the late actress made up of photographs by, among others, Milton Greene, Henri Cartier-Bresson, Eve Arnold, Philippe Halsman, and Lawrence Schiller, who would edit the volume. Already there had been immensely popular exhibitions of up to five hundred photographs of Monroe in thirty American cities and Markel anticipated a coffee-table bestseller. He contacted Scott Meredith regarding a writer to do a lengthy preface, and Meredith did not hesitate to recommend his client Norman Mailer. Markel accepted his argument that Mailer knew more of the shifting contours of American post-war culture than any other non-academic writer. Markel's account of his first meeting with Mailer in his office is illuminating (Mills, pp. 380–81). 'He wasn't just looking at the picture,' Markel recalled. 'He was looking at her and thinking about her right there. He was meeting her, in a sense, for the first time.'

Meredith agreed that Mailer would receive $50,000 for a twenty-five-thousand-word preface, but within two months the editor was informed that he had already reached sixty thousand words and 'was not yet on to Miller' (Arthur Miller, Monroe's last husband). Markel had accepted that the preface would be mainly chronological, as would the illustrations, but it was now clear that Mailer was writing a book, not an introduction. Later that year Meredith renegotiated the contract, and Mailer's life of Monroe was published separately with fewer photographs in 1973.

Soon after the book appeared and shortly before its British release with Hodder & Stoughton, several reviewers and two of Monroe's previous biographers, Frederick Guiles and Maurice Zolotow, accused Mailer of plagiarism. Zolotow went so far as to sue him, but both authors withdrew their allegations after the provision of very generous copyright costs from Grosset & Dunlap. In interviews during and following the dispute Mailer vehemently denied the charges despite the fact that alongside the quotations he had acknowledged, large amounts of text that were supposedly his came close to being paraphrases of passages from Guiles and Zolotow.

As Mailer saw it, his meeting with Monroe in Markel's office was cathartic and transformative. She had sashayed out of the photographs and become part of his life, his possession. The fact that Guiles and Zolotow had put together accounts of her based on empirical evidence and interviews was immaterial. Their books were unemotional, factual. His would be about a woman he knew intimately, so he felt no need to apologise to men who saw her only from a distance.

Some, such as Carl Rollyson, have claimed that the book is a landmark in the history of biography. This would be true if Mailer had deliberately set out to do something new with the genre, but that was not his concern. He was indulging a fantasy in which the actual Norman Mailer would be the only true, redemptive lover of Marilyn Monroe, overlooking the fact that she had died a decade before.

The most unsettling chapter is on her marriage to Arthur Miller. Mailer's style is ruthless and energetic. His intention is to ridicule Miller as a literary fraud and overreacher and introduce himself as Monroe's true partner, the soaring intellectual figure who matches her unique screen presence and sexuality. Of Miller, Mailer states that he had 'only a workmanlike style, limited lyrical gifts, no capacity for intellectual shock ... his verbal ideas were banal' and goes on to claim that he was living off his wife's money from Hollywood, that she was 'his talented slave'.

There is a particularly unnerving passage in which he sounds as though he is on the set of *The Misfits*, appalled at Monroe's treatment by John Huston and the man who wrote the screenplay, Miller. He blames Miller particularly, but at one point he also describes the moment when Monroe's character wakes after spending the night with Gay Langland, the middle-aged cowboy played by Clark Gable. There is, he tells us, 'only a sheet to cover her nakedness' (p. 261). Then:

Should they release the film with the shot of Monroe's nude breast? Monroe, no surprise, is for it. 'I love to do things the censors won't pass. After all, what are we all here for, just to stand around and let it pass us by?' Huston replies, 'I've always known that girls have breasts.' (p. 261)

There is no evidence that any of this took place, but Mailer implies that he witnessed it first hand and goes on to refer to the bared breast on three further occasions. Rollyson calls the book a 'novel biography'. Verbal masturbation would be a more accurate description.

During the bad-tempered discussions between Schiller, Markel and Mailer on whether the publication should be an illustrated biography or a book of photographs, Mailer said to Schiller, 'Larry, you don't know a damn thing about laying out books', and Schiller answered 'Well, what do you know about Marilyn Monroe? ... At least I fucked her, and you didn't.' Markel recalled that Mailer had to be hustled out of the room, 'apoplectic ... ready to take a swing at [Schiller]' (Manso, p. 543).

When he was speaking with Markel at their first meeting, Mailer said, 'But what about Robert Kennedy?', and the editor assumed he was suggesting a different book on the life and death of the senator. But what became evident when the Monroe biography was completed was Mailer's suspicion that she had not committed suicide, that the official findings had been faked to cover the involvement of government agencies in her killing. He was convinced that she'd had affairs with John and Robert Kennedy and that the intelligence services, particularly the FBI and CIA, had murdered her to hide the involvement of the political aristocracy in the kind of sexual relationships that many heterosexual male moviegoers craved. His perception of her as a victim of the political establishment is the principal topic of the book's concluding chapter, the same conspiracy theories that lay behind his address to the audience at his fiftieth birthday party when the book was in press.

He never quite left Monroe alone. Almost ten years later he produced a shorter, 50,000-word version of the biography called *Of Women and Their Elegance* (1980). It was a first-person autobiography spoken to the reader by Monroe, in which she replies to and justifies the version of her life that Mailer had produced in 1973. On numerous occasions in *Marilyn: A Biography* Mailer insisted that she would be reincarnated, that her magnetism and sexual energy could not die with her. In *Of Women and Their Elegance* he brought her back to life, a verbal resurrection of the woman he had always wanted. Showing a polite respect for Mailer's reputation the mainstream press reviewers largely ignored it.

Within a few months of the publication of *Marilyn* Mailer began a two-month regime of hard exercise. He gave up alcohol, restricted his diet and mixed punch-bag training with short half-mile jogs. Having lost roughly twenty-five pounds, dropping from 190 to 165, and he told *Time*, 'I've really gotten to a point where I'm like an old prize-fighter and if my manager comes up to me and says, "I've got you a good fight with a good purse" I go into the ring' (*Time*, 16th July, 1973) and six months later he was overjoyed to learn of the forthcoming heavyweight championship fight between Mohammad Ali and George Foreman, the so-called 'Rumble in the Jungle', in Kinshasa, Zaire. It was originally planned to take place on September 25th 1974 but was postponed until October 30th because of Foreman's eye infection following a sparring injury. Mailer had decided that, like his life of Monroe, he would become as much a participant as an observer. His fitness programme was designed to turn him into a version of the two contenders for the heavyweight title. Mailer was also now treating each of his books much as a past-his-peak boxer saw the next fight as financial investment, a contest between what he could pay and what he owed. His 'manager', Scott Meredith, had recently lent him almost $200,000, which would be deducted from the agent's percentages. He was still paying regular alimony to Adele and Beverly, supporting seven children and spending in total a quarter of a million a year to get by, including the private expenses of his life with Carol and monies paid and quietly given to Suzanne Nye, his secretary and live-in lover.

In desperation he found time to write a book called *The Faith of Graffiti* (1974) for $35,000, a hymn to the aesthetics of New York's graffiti 'artists'. He praises them much as he did the hipsters of the 1950s, treating the offence caused to the establishment as a guarantee of a spray-can vandal's talents, irrespective of the distress caused to people obliged to live with the mess on their buildings and subway stations.

Meredith persuaded Little, Brown to pay his client $1 million for his next novel, which testifies to his skill as an agent, since Mailer seemed once again to have given up on conventional fiction. Agents are generally perceived as being concerned more with money than aesthetics, but in this instance Meredith trod a cautious path between the two, ensuring that the contract was worded in a manner that seemed innocuous enough to the publisher but in reality was devilishly ambiguous. The so-called novel would be about 'the whole human experience', in other words anything at all. More significantly, bar one exception, the term 'novel' was replaced with 'work' throughout. This was a standard formula for publishing contracts, but Meredith was aware that Mailer's growing reputation as a man who produced literary hybrids, blends of fiction and documentary, fabrication and truth, would protect him against any charge of being in breach of contract whatever he chose to deliver. The million dollars was safe, and Mailer received $200,000 shortly before flying to Zaire. He resented having to cover his own expenses from an advance for a later work, but again Meredith came to the rescue by negotiating a sub-clause whereby *Playboy* would come up with a further $200,000 for a serialisation of the Foreman–Ali fight, inclusive of Mailer's travel and accommodation.

In *The Fight* (1975), its author appears as 'Norman', and we are reminded of the eponymous author of 'The White Negro' of two decades before. The consensus was that while Ali had speed and almost balletic timing something about Foreman made him all but indestructible.

> Foreman's hands were as separate from him as a kuntu. They were his instrument, and he kept them in his pockets the way a hunter lays his rifle back into its velvet case ... Foreman ... might as well have been a contemplative monk. His violence was in the halo of his serenity ... One did not allow violence to dissipate; one stored it. Serenity was the vessel where violence could be stored. (p. 48)

This comes close to being ludicrous in that Foreman's habit of keeping his hands in his pockets was treated by those who knew him as an inconsequential quirk rather than a quasi-mystical token of ferocity.

Covering the press interview, Mailer reflects on a book by Marcel Griaule, a French anthropologist who compared speech patterns in West Africa with the weaving and creation of a thread. Mailer detects something similar in Foreman's exchanges with the press, 'a real sense of the delicacy of what he might be weaving, a fine tissue, strong in its economy, a true cloth to come out of an intelligent and uneducated man ...' (p. 55). A less entranced reader of the interview transcript might, however, regard the 'web' of Foreman's concise, sometimes monosyllabic responses as a sign of his boredom with the journalists' vacuous queries.

Mailer's mood of awe is by degrees condescending and mildly racist. Foreman and Ali are now, he implies, creatures unfettered by their Western legacies. They are African brutes confronting each other in their element. It is noticeable that Mailer sheds his mood of reverence when dealing with other black Americans who are present but not directly involved as fighters. Drew Bundini Brown, Ali's trainer, comes across as a bit-player at a pantomime, perhaps since he is not as beautiful as the contenders but more likely because he 'corrupted his African purity' by marrying a Russian-Jewish woman and later converting to Judaism. The showman and loud-mouthed promoter of the event, Don King, is mercilessly ridiculed. He tells reporters of his self-education while serving four years for manslaughter.

> 'Read Freud. He almost blew my mind. Breast, penis, anus. Powerful stuff. Then Masters and Johnson, Kinsey, and . . .' He hesitated. 'Knee's itch, I read a lot of him.'
> 'Who?'
> 'Knee's itch. Nigh zith.'
> 'Nietzsche?'
> 'Yeah.' (pp. 118–19)

According to Mailer, King also professed to have read Kant – 'that helped my head' – Sartre and Karl Marx, 'a cold motherfucker'. No other record of King's claims to erudition exists. It does, however, resemble the intellectual life-record of Norman Mailer, without the comedic mispronunciations. Mailer implies that characters such as this, especially African Americans, become inadvertent self-parodies when they attempt to assimilate to the high culture of Europe and America. Bitterness underpins Mailer's account too because King, like Bundini Brown, had assimilated by showing that he could make as much money, just as ruthlessly, as whites.

The most famous passage in the book is Mailer's description of jogging with Ali and his coaches. To his satisfaction he stays at their pace for a

mile and a half and then makes his way back to the accommodation area
during what is still a pre-dawn morning.

> Just then, he heard a lion roar. It was no small sound, more like
> thunder, and it opened an unfolding wave of wrath across the sky and
> through the fields ... He could never reach those lights before the
> lion could run him down. Then his next thought was that the lion, if
> it chose, could certainly race up on him silently, might even be on his
> way now. (p. 91)

For a moment he recalls being in his sailing boat off Provincetown
when another formidable presence, this time a whale, reminds him of
his fragile mortality. He places himself alongside Melville in the list of
American writers challenged by insuperable nature, and then he brings
to life Hemingway, whose 'own lion [has been] waiting down these years
for the flesh of Ernest until an appropriate substitute had at last arrived'
(p. 92). Hemingway crops up frequently in the book as the hunter who
relished confrontation with the massive carnivores of West Africa, albeit
armed with his high-calibre rifle.

Mailer's exercise in self-aggrandisement is rooted in his sense of
the location, and the fight, as the fulcrum for all kinds of unfettered
savagery. These black people, he implies, have returned to their
origins, a gloriously uncivilised hinterland where one of the world-
championship contenders runs through countryside occupied by other
savage brutes.

His inclination to blur the line between farce and vanity reminds
one of another event in which an animal made Mailer fear for his
safety, specifically the evening he returned from the New York streets
bloody-nosed and concussed after a sailor had dared to call his poodle
'queer'.

In 1975, three months after his return from Africa, Mailer was
involved in a gruelling tour of Southern US universities, giving lectures
and holding seminars mostly for students with ambitions to become
writers. He loathed the routine, but between advances for books,
payments negotiated by Meredith from mostly private universities
offered him a regular income.

After delivering a lecture at Loyola University in New Orleans, Mailer took a flight to Little Rock, Arkansas, where his old friend Fig Gwaltney picked him up. Gwaltney had persuaded Mailer to do a question-and-answer session on creative writing at Arkansas Polytechnic College, where he taught. The remuneration would be small, but Fig and his wife, Ecey, were two of Mailer's oldest friends, and he looked forward to their customary hospitality. After Mailer had talked with students, he met members of faculty at the Gwaltneys' house for drinks, during which Ecey took a phone call from a local art teacher who had designed the cover of one of Fig's novels. Was it true, she asked, that Norman Mailer was staying with them, adding 'Could I crash?' She arrived less than fifteen minutes later, wearing tight blue jeans and a cotton shirt tied at her waist. Ecey noted that her auburn hair now had blonde highlights. She was six feet two, with a stunning figure and a beautiful face. Walking straight up to Mailer she asked, 'How are you, Mr Mailer?' Without replying Mr Mailer stepped back to make the most of the woman facing him and then left the room.

Barbara Norris taught art at the neighbouring Russellville High School and was famous in the area as a woman so attractive as to turn heads in local bars and restaurants. She seemed to be from another world, likely Hollywood. Ecey said later that while Barbara had heard of Mailer, the only book of his she had read was *Marilyn*. She had planned their encounter carefully, seeming to step from the pages of the book he had recently published, a woman as sensational as the one that Mailer enshrined as his own. And she succeeded. Mailer confessed to Gwaltney that he had left the room because he was 'riveted', too shocked even to speak with her.

He said to Gwaltney that once he'd calmed himself he would go back inside, and that evening he and Barbara talked for hours. Barbara was twenty-six, only eight months older than Mailer's firstborn, Susan. She told him of her background, from a humble Baptist family in Arkansas; her father taught basic engineering at the local Job Corps Center and her mother co-ran a beauty salon. Before studying art at the Arkansas Polytechnic College she worked in a pickle factory and after graduation married her high-school boyfriend, Larry Norris. The marriage ended soon after his return from service in Vietnam, apparently suffering from post-traumatic stress disorder, and when she met Mailer she was looking after her only child on her teacher's salary. She was not a movie star, but as a woman with spellbinding looks who had come from nowhere there were parallels with Monroe, and Mailer was captivated.

Barbara offered him the story of her albeit brief life as something far more complex than would be expected of a small-town girl. As a member of a fundamentalist Free Will Baptist community, she had gone to church at least three times a week and been taught to regard the Bible as a rule book for morality, which she regarded as ludicrous, especially after her break-up with Larry. Then she made a point of dating, and sleeping with, various men in the area, one of which, she informed Mailer, had recently lost the election for the House of Representatives by only two per cent of the votes and was soon due to become Attorney General of Arkansas. At the time Mailer had not heard of Bill Clinton. Her commitment to painting involved more than a steady wage. She adored the realist mannerisms of Edward Hopper and Andrew Wyeth as 'quintessentially American' and told Mailer that she had once hitch-hiked more than a hundred miles to see a small exhibition of the latter's work. Though she never hoped to match either artist, she admitted that her own large oils involved at least 'an aspiration' to record something of small-town America. Having first enrolled to read English at Arkansas she had changed to her real love, art, but she read as much as she could, remaining a member of the book club which had recommended *Marilyn*.

For the first time in Mailer's long career as a lothario he did not attempt to sleep with his new crush on their first meeting. For one thing, Barbara's son, Matthew, was being looked after by neighbours, and she had promised to return home by midnight. Norman flew north from Arkansas the next day, having promised to write to her. He gave her a post-office box address so that her replies would not raise Carol's suspicions, and three days after his departure she received a crate containing every one of Mailer's hardback publications, signed by him. She managed to read all of them in little more than three weeks, feeling that she now knew the man with whom she had spent an evening at the Gwaltneys. She met him again in Little Rock shortly after reading *The Fight*. They rented an apartment in the city, spending most of four days and nights in bed. In June 1975, she joined him in Chicago, where he was doing promotional events for *The Fight*, and they went on together to New York, spending two weeks in the Brooklyn brownstone and planning their future. The crate of his books also contained a velvet box carrying a silver sing with a blue sapphire stone and a note stating that he loved her.

Barbara suggested that she would sell her house, enrol at the Rhode Island School of Design and try to make a living as an artist, but Mailer persuaded her that her beauty and poise would secure a better income, and contacted his friend the photographer Milton Greene. Greene met her and insisted that she would do very well as a model if she lost a few pounds. She flew back to Arkansas, went on a crash diet and announced to her parents that she was resigning from her job, moving to New York and leaving her son in their care for the time being. By the end of the year, she was working for the Wilhelmina modelling agency and appearing regularly in advertisements for high-class jewellery, perfumes and clothes in a number of fashionable upmarket magazines, including *Vogue*. Her agency thought Norris was too small-town a name for a metropolitan model, and Mailer suggested Church as a double-barrelled attachment, a snide riposte to her strict Christian upbringing. He was enjoying his Pygmalion role. In the end she chose Norris as her first name.

During 1975 Mailer's personal life was complicated, to say the least. He would not sever his ties finally with Carol until early 1976. They were not married but they would marry and divorce in a near record time in 1980 to legitimize their child. Beverly was still his wife and insisting on an extortionate divorce settlement and Suzanne Nye remained his lover while being unaware of the existence of a fourth partner, Norris, who would soon cause her to be dismissed as the unofficial member of the Mailer's hectic love-life.

Fan Mailer liked Norris and found her an apartment on Willow Street near her own, but by February 1976 she was persuaded by Mailer to move into the brownstone with him permanently. Her son, Matthew, would join them periodically between spending time with his father and maternal grandparents.

Throughout this period Mailer was working on the long novel for Little, Brown, an arrangement that Meredith renegotiated later in 1976.

It was an astonishing deal given that periodic payments to him prior to delivery of the so-far unnamed piece of fiction were guaranteed for an indefinite period. He would receive $150,000 per year, paid monthly, but this was not conditional on the date of delivery or, for that matter, on the nature of material delivered. Mailer could, technically, draw a regular income from the publisher until his death without actually doing any writing. Today that would amount to an annual salary of almost $720,000, or around 350,000 sterling. Bing Crosby's 1949 song 'Busy Doing Nothing' comes to mind, but while the amount received by Mailer sounds extraordinary, it enabled him to only just avoid being taken to court by his ex-wives, his creditors and the IRS. Shortly after moving Norris into the brownstone, he sold the Stockbridge house for $100,000 to cover some accumulated back taxes. Carol moved out with nothing. The new owners were *Screw* magazine, who planned to use the property to shoot soft-core pornography.

A regular income did, however, enable Mailer to set aside the promised novel and deal with a proposition put to him by Larry Schiller. Schiller had worked and argued with him during the *Marilyn* project, and Mailer at first treated with caution large packages of official transcripts, photographs and typed interviews from Schiller that started to arrive in February 1977 – at least until he began reading them. Like virtually everyone else in America, Mailer had read newspaper reports on 18 January 1977 of the first judicial execution in the country since 1967. Gary Gilmore, found guilty of murder in Utah, had relinquished all stays of execution, and his wish to be shot by firing squad rather than hanged was fulfilled on the morning of the 17th.

Schiller had bought the rights to do a book or a film on Gilmore shortly before his execution, and he convinced Mailer that a book, by him, would be a bestseller. They went to Howard Kaminsky of Warner Books and persuaded him that despite Mailer's ongoing commitment to Little, Brown for the novel, a book on Gilmore would make a vast amount of money. Newspaper sales had rocketed because of ghoulish interest in the reintroduction of capital punishment, and it was clear, they argued, that a book which offered an account on Gilmore's life and death, turned by Mailer into a noirish horror story, would sell. Kaminsky contacted Little, Brown, and it was agreed that they would pay $25,000 for the hardback, on condition that Warner's paperback edition, which would sell far more, would come out almost simultaneously. Kaminsky offered half a million to be divided equally between Schiller and Mailer.

Mailer needed the money, but other things attracted him to becoming the custodian of the life and death of Gary Gilmore. He found from letters that Gilmore believed in reincarnation and was profoundly attracted to the notion of karma, the concept that our destiny is determined by our previous actions and inclinations.

> He appealed to me because he embodied many of the themes I've been living with all my life long before I even thought of doing a book on him ... I felt here's a perfect example of what I've been talking about all my life ... (John Aldridge's interview with Mailer, *Partisan Review*, Spring 1980)

He saw in Gilmore a lower-order version of himself, a man whose mood shifts would take him rapidly from withdrawn contentment to unmotivated attacks on those he hardly knew. The difference between them was that Gilmore had had an appalling childhood; he was frequently beaten and sometimes abused by his father, Frank Gilmore, who also attacked Gary's siblings and his mother, Bassie.

In various interviews Mailer later reflected on the dilemmas he faced when planning a book that is based on indisputable facts but written in the manner of a novel. First of all, he tried out a weird variation of Mailer the narrator of *The Armies of the Night*, on this occasion a 'big ungainly man', a recently divorced American writer now in Paris with suitcases full of Gilmore interviews and other documents. He confided in Norris, who reminded him of the difficulties of shaking off the actual Norman Mailer.

> Look, sweetie. What would happen if you were free and alone in Paris? You'd be walking down one of the boulevards and you'd sit at a sidewalk café to have a cup of espresso. A pretty girl would walk by and you would give her one of your twenty-five cent smiles. She would smile back and stop to talk. (*A Ticket to the Circus*, p. 253)

The girl would join him for coffee, added Norris, go with him to a museum and then to dinner. They would sleep together and soon afterwards she would be living with him, pregnant, '... and you wouldn't be free and alone in Paris anymore, would you?' It is a beautifully pitched account of how Norman Mailer could never cease to be Norman Mailer, as a writer or a philanderer.

Instead he becomes an omniscient third-person narrator who records the speech, thoughts and perceptions of the characters, which one would expect in a novel. But these were real people. When Gilmore's cousin Brenda Nicol collects him from prison following his release after his sentence for armed robbery, we read of her private impression of his 'nice voice, soft spoken, twangy, held back. A lot of feeling in the center of it.' And we have no reason to suspect that the account of their drive back to Provo isn't also a reflection of her sense of the countryside. 'In the mountains, the snow was iron gray and purples in the hollows, and glowed like gold on every slope that faced the sun. The clouds over the mountains were lifting with light. Brenda took a good look into his eyes and felt full of sadness again. His eyes had the expression of rabbits she had flushed, scared-rabbit was the common expression ...' (p. 16). It is quite possible that Brenda experienced something like these moments of lyrical romanticism as she drove through the mountains, but all surviving evidence casts her as kind-hearted and semi-literate. She might have felt what is described in the book, but it is unlikely that she could have expressed it in this way, at least without the assistance of Mailer as her upmarket stylistic proxy.

With Gilmore and his fellow inmates Mailer has fewer problems, reverting to a jail idiom that involves both reported speech and third-person accounts of his progress towards execution.

The book won Mailer his second Pulitzer Prize. It is an extraordinary piece of work, not least because it records a crossroads in the history of the American justice system. The decade prior to the execution of Gilmore was the only period in the history of the country, including the century and a half before the Revolution, when judicial killing was effectively prohibited. It was the era which coincided with protests for racial equality and the acceptance of women's rights as a prerogative for social improvement, and most on the liberal left assumed that America had joined the majority of Western European democracies in abandoning capital punishment forever.

Mailer does not mention this explicitly in the book, but coverage in the press on debates within the judiciary and among politicians would have left him in no doubt that his account of Gary Gilmore would resonate far beyond the man's insistence that he should be executed. Interestingly, Part 7, the section which covers events that occurred immediately after the shooting of Gilmore, involved some verbatim press reports along with dramatized accounts of the activities and thoughts of some individuals directly involved, Schiller included. No space at all, however, is given to the storm of discussions in the media on the long-term consequences of what had occurred. Implicitly, advocates of capital punishment had been handed a victory.

Nicole, Gilmore's girlfriend, tells us that 'With her eyes closed, she had the odd feeling of an evil presence near her that came from Gary. She found it kind of half agreeable. Said to herself, Well, if he is the devil, maybe I want to get closer.' (p. 106). Mailer describes the murder of Max Jensen with unadorned detachment, telling us nothing of his history or of what is going through Gilmore's mind as he kills him. All we can do is watch.

> Gilmore brought the automatic to Jensen's head. 'This one is for me,' he said, and fired.
>
> 'This one is for Nicole,' he said, and fired again. The body reacted each time.
>
> He stood up. There was a lot of blood. It spread across the floor at a surprising rate. Some of it got onto the bottom of his pants.
>
> He walked out of the rest room with the bills in his pocket, and the coin changer in his hand, walked by the big Coke machine and the phone on the wall, walked out of this real clean gas station. (p. 224)

The Gilmore we intuit from the impressions of those closest to him is by degrees unhinged and magnetic, someone not quite normal but because of that enthralling.

Two years after the book came out Mailer offered his own opinions on the death penalty in 'Until Dead: Thoughts on Capital Punishment'

(*Parade*, 8 February 1981). Judicial execution, he contends, 'may be one of our last defences against the oncoming wave of the computer universe', something that will restore to us the primitive instincts that a mechanised, computerised society seems to have extinguished. 'Living amid all the blank walls of technology, we require a death now and again, we need to stir that foul pot.' He had once said something similar about rape. He did not recommend that executions should be performed in public, but the whole article carries an air of capital punishment as satiating the same appetite that once drew enormous crowds to such events.

Halfway through his preparation of *The Executioner's Song*, Mailer received a letter via his agent from Jack Henry Abbott. Abbott was a near facsimile of Gilmore. Like him he was, as he described himself, a 'state-raised' convict; a half-Chinese, half-Irish product of a broken home, various foster homes and juvenile institutions. For all but ten months he had spent his entire adult life in jail, and when he first wrote to Mailer he was serving twenty years for murdering a fellow inmate. He was thirty-seven, and what impressed Mailer was Abbott's intellectual gravity. 'Abbott's letter', he later commented, 'was intense, direct, unadorned, and detached – an unusual combination ... I felt all the awe one knows before a phenomenon. Abbott had his own voice. I had heard no other like it ...' (Manso, p. 621). From the moment Mailer replied to him they exchanged letters virtually every other day. In his own *In the Belly of the Beast* (1981), Abbott summarises his disclosures to Mailer: 'state-raised' criminals, he explained, envisage rather than actually experience emotions; they 'emulate ... a fanatically defiant and alienated individual who cannot imagine what forgiveness is, or mercy or tolerance, because he has no *experience* of such values' (p. 13). Abbott in his letters would re-emerge as Gilmore in Mailer's book.

On 18 April 1979, Mailer wrote to Abbott:

Well, I finished the book [*The Executioner's Song*] ... part of my understanding of [Gilmore's] experience has come from our letters and I think you'll feel the echoes of some of the things you wrote to me in Gilmore. But I believed he would share your sentiments ... I do not think I could have come to understand him without

the letters you've written to me … And in your thought, I find
his, except you underline what he could never quite bring himself
to admit, which is that the logic leads to violence and violence,
indeed, is the only outcome of the logic … I know some violence is
one of the fundamental emotions in all human behavior, one of the
ineradicable ones, like sex and a passion for justice. (18 April 1979,
   Selected Letters)

It is unlikely that Mailer's presentation of Gilmore as an existential anti-
hero would have been of much comfort to Jensen's relatives. The most
striking feature of the letter, particularly the last sentence quoted here,
is its almost verbatim return to the homilies of 'The White Negro'.
Abbott and Gilmore embody perfectly Mailer's 1957 notion of the
'philosophical psychopath' with an 'unreasoning drive' and who can
'remain in life only by engaging death'.

Critics who saw themselves as occupying the intellectual high ground
celebrated *The Executioner's Song*. Christopher Ricks stated that it
'promulgates no ideas or theories, though it contains a great many, as
well as intelligent speculations, all voiced or thought by others' (*London
Review of Books*, 16 March 1980). In short, Mailer had adopted the
legacy of Wordsworth's *Lyrical Ballads*, with the condescending literary
ventriloquist using simple-minded figures to voice earnest metaphysical
principles. Joan Didion compared the two halves of the book with 'two
long symphonic movements', respectively female and male (*The New
York Times*, 7 October 1979). The most famous article was published
ten years later by Mark Edmundson, who sums up the consensus of
responses of 1979–80: 'from the point where Gilmore decides that he
is willing to die, he takes on a certain dignity … Gilmore's effort, from
about the time he enters prison, is to conduct himself so that he can die
what he would himself credit as a "good death"' (*Contemporary Literature*,
Winter 1990). Again, one has to wonder how the families of Max Jensen
and Bennie Bushnell, his second murder victim, would have felt about
Gilmore being idolised as a redneck Heathcliff. This is highbrow idiocy
at its worst. Mailer played a game of smoke and mirrors. He did not
quite alter the facts of Gilmore's life, crimes and eventual fate, but he
turned them into a spare, existential artwork and therefore embargoed

the question of whether he was just a small-minded narcissist who killed people because he felt like it.

Reality would revenge itself on Mailer via Abbott. In early 1980 he showed Mailer the manuscript of *In the Belly of the Beast*. It had no chronology or any particularly coherent structure; instead, it was made up of the letters that Abbott had sent to Mailer over the past year. Abbott's prose is brutally energetic and strikingly well-constructed. Mailer had of course already read these letters, but now, put together as a single work, it was as though Abbott had made a pact with his literary sponsor. Without shedding anything of his authentic savagery – let alone showing remorse for his acts – he had crossed the boundary between the rough-house subject of a book and the existential dignity of its writer. There is a long tradition of the brooding, dangerous Byronic hero in literature, but Abbott is the first to author his own work. Mailer sent it to Erroll McDonald, an editor at Random House, who offered Abbott an advance of $12,500. The book was scheduled for publication in June 1981.

Abbott faced the parole board in April of that year, and the news that his book was in press with a major publisher played a part in the panel's sense of him as a reformed figure. Luckily, for him, they had not read it. He presents 'dangerous killers' as figures who 'defend their principles with acts of murder … this is the state-raised convicts' conception of manhood, in the highest sense' (p. 13). He was saying to the American society and its judicial institutions: you are to blame for how I am and what I do. Nonetheless, the parole board did see a letter from Norman Mailer, the man who had once advertised this notion of justified violence. Mailer informed them that Abbott had been of enormous assistance to him during his research for *The Executioner's Song* and that after release he would be offered free accommodation and $150 a week as his personal assistant and researcher.

Against the odds Abbott was paroled and met Mailer at Kennedy Airport on 5 June. A month later his book was published and greeted with first-class reviews. 'An exceptional man with an exceptional literary gift,' wrote *The New York Times Book Review*; 'his voice is like no other, his language sharp-edged and hurling with rage.' It was a repeat of the reception of *The Executioner's Song*, except now the brutal genius had been admitted in person to the highbrow elite rather than exhibited as a fascinating curiosity.

Two weeks after the publication, in the early hours of 18 July, Abbott visited a restaurant on East 5th Street named the Binibon and stabbed to death Richard Adan, a twenty-two-year-old Cuban whose father-in-law owned the restaurant. Photographs of his young wife, widowed at twenty-one, featured prominently in newspaper reports. Adan was an actor and dancer, but on the night of his encounter with Abbott he was working as a waiter in the Binibon. The reason for the stabbing, at least according to Abbott's testimony, was a dispute between the two men over whether customers or staff only were allowed in a particular washroom.

Subsequent events carry an air of noir comedy, except that few involved would find them amusing. The *New York Times* review, the most enthusiastic of all, appeared the day after Abbott killed Adan (though the event was not yet in the news), and the *Soho News* had already compared Abbott with Solzhenitsyn. Both, argued Abbie Hoffman, had confronted the implacably unjust prison systems of 'totalitarian states'.

Shortly after the murder, Abbott called Mailer from a payphone. Mailer was hungover, and before Abbott could explain why he wanted to talk, Mailer promised to call him back and hung up. After returning briefly to his halfway house for parolees, Abbott decided to visit the apartment of Jean Malaquais, to whom Mailer had introduced him. He accepted coffee, seeming apprehensive, and then without informing Malaquais of what had just happened went to the bus terminal. Travelling via Chicago and Texas he made his way to Louisiana, where he found work on the oilfields under the assumed name of Eastman.

During his nine weeks there the only person he contacted regularly was Scott Meredith, who was now his agent. Abbott was keen on learning of whether later reviews were as enthusiastic as the first wave – they were, Meredith assured him – and how the book was selling. After two months it had made him more than $100,000 in royalties, a satisfying figure given that he was being paid only $4 an hour as a labourer. Neither he nor Meredith spoke of his other claim to fame, as a renowned debut author now on the run and suspected of murder.

By various means Bill Majeski, the New York detective assigned to the case, tracked him down, and Abbott was arrested by the Louisiana

State Police on 23 September. He was tried in January 1982, and Mailer testified on his behalf, mostly on how impressed he was with Abbott's previous history of rehabilitation. Little of this was reported in the press, but the newspapers were transfixed by Mailer's comments to them when he left the court. He began with platitudes regarding the 'absolute tragedy' and 'hideous waste' of Adan's death and was then asked by the *New York Times* reporter, 'What will happen if Jack Abbott gets out of jail and kills again?' Mailer replied that he would 'take that gamble ... I am willing to gamble with certain elements of society to save this man's talent', as if one more victim would be a worthwhile sacrifice for further masterpieces. On the Adan family's demand for the death penalty, he stated that 'blood atonement' was a primitive ritual, adding that 'All I have to offer is my psychic blood', whatever that meant. 'Adan has already been destroyed,' he pointed out, 'but at least let Abbott become a writer.' He went on to claim that imprisoning people like Abbott – artists – and forgetting about them is 'the ground floor of fascism. A democracy involves taking risks.' The America which disposes of writers at the expense of spurious notions of deterrence or retribution reveals itself as 'fascist [state, where] the rich are getting richer and the poor are getting poorer'. Photographs of Mailer on the steps of the courthouse show him in a crouched fighter's position with fists clenched and teeth bared.

Mailer seemed to have overlooked the fact that the murdered Richard Adan too was an artist. A Cuba born actor and dancer of considerable repute, he had recently toured Spain, performed in a drama series for public television and completed a a play about the Lower East Side for production next season by the La Mama experimental theater group. In Mailer's perception of things he was just a waiter, which brings to mind the portrayal in 'The White Negro' of the killing of the store owner as an act of existential, artistic grandeur. As a despicably mediocre figures both got was coming to them.

The exchange that threw the generally indulgent, liberal press corps into a state of rage came when Mike Pearl of *The New York Post* asked, 'What elements are you willing to gamble with? Cubans? Waiters? What?' Mailer replied vacuously, 'Society has got to take certain risks.' (Transcript of Mailer's address in Lennon's files, 21 January 1982).

In an interview with Mills from prison in Missouri, Abbott seemed to side with Pearl.

> [I] was so far away from his experience that he couldn't understand it. It's a social drift ... but Mailer isn't aware of any of this. He doesn't want to believe it. I would say that ultimately Norman and I are enemies, we're class enemies ... He doesn't know this other world. He always wants to but he always wants to do it in such a way that he pulls them into his world. (Mills, p. 32)

Abbott was right. Mailer had used him in the same way he had used Gilmore: as a literary trope, a means of seeming to cross the border between the world of criminals and the dispossessed and the high-cultural uplands. His ludicrous aesthetic had blinded him to the fact that glorifying violence by writing about it didn't make bad men any less bad.

The jury found Abbott guilty of manslaughter, and he was sentenced to fifteen years to life. In 2002 he hanged himself in his cell.

14

PHARAOHS AND TOUGH GUYS

Norris found out that she was pregnant in summer 1977 and gave birth to John Buffalo on 16 April 1978. Immediately afterwards Beverly began a divorce suit and when the Provincetown house was sold to the IRS in 1980, she appealed for a more generous settlement, but this was rejected by the court on 25 September and Mailer was free to marry again. He did so, but not to Norris. He and Carol were espoused in a civil ceremony in the chambers of Judge Shirley Fingerhood on 8th November. On the 10th the couple flew to Haiti for a divorce that would be recognised by the US civil court. The marriage had lasted little more than two days but their child, Maggie, was now legitimate. On 11 November Mailer and Norris were married by a Brooklyn rabbi and John Buffalo too became an official member of the Mailer clan.

Beverly, however, refused to go away. For the next two years she mounted civil actions accusing Mailer of trigamy, on the basis that she had not agreed to his divorce from her and that his two subsequent marriages were effectively criminal offences. She gave up only in September 1982 when the Supreme Judicial Court of Massachusetts concluded that his divorce from her was legitimate, though the decision was by a small majority of judges rather than unanimous. Beverly's sense of outrage was fuelled partly by Mailer's tendency to display Norris as a painter and a model who outshone all of his previous partners. Soon after Norris moved into Columbia Heights, Beverly drove to the brownstone and demanded to see Mailer on the street. She could not tolerate the presence of this new woman in a building where she'd lived only as an occasional visitor. When Mailer leaned into the car window to talk, she wound it up and stepped on the gas pedal in an apparent attempt to decapitate him. He escaped with lesions on his chin and the back of his head.

Once they had settled into Columbia Heights, Norris divided her time between working on the draft of a novel set in Arkansas in 1969 (the period of her first marriage), a children's book she was co-authoring with Mailer, and managing displays of her paintings at the prestigious Central Falls gallery in Soho. She also organised dinner parties which were far more genteel than the raucous evenings of Mailer's previous marriages. She would appear in glamorous, glittering dresses that matched her long auburn hair while Mailer held court as the East Coast gentleman in his tailored Brooks Brothers suits and Gucci shoes. Their class of guests was decidedly upmarket too, including Gloria Vanderbilt, the fashion designer Oscar de la Renta, the media millionaire Bill Paley, and the last of the three, politically ambitious Kennedy brothers, Ted, and his wife, Joan. After riding out the Chappaquiddick scandal of 1969, Kennedy lost the Democratic nomination for the presidency closely to Jimmy Carter in 1980 but remained active in the top tier of American politics. Mailer's fantasy of becoming part of the most exclusive dynasty of the post-war era, the Kennedys, endured. Old friends such as Roger Donoghue and José Torres were still made welcome, but usually on different nights, and they rarely featured in the countless celebrity-crowded photographs that frequently illustrated society magazines.

Mailer's many children were regular visitors, and the only other permanent residents were John Buffalo, followed shortly by Matthew, Norris's son, whom Mailer unofficially adopted, and soon after that by Fan, who had given up her own apartment.

Mailer had since the early 1970s been working on his 'groundbreaking' novel for which his agent had secured a Little, Brown advance that was more like a salary. *Ancient Evenings* would be completed in 1982. In 1974 he had visited Egypt to imbibe the atmosphere of a civilisation that largely predated recorded history. Cairo was in a state of chaos, following the defeat of the country by Israel in the brief Yom Kippur War of the previous year. The Nile region, including the pyramids, was still officially classified as a 'war zone', in fear that the Israeli Defense Forces might launch air attacks in the west of the country while the precarious

UN ceasefire still held. Despite bribing a taxi driver and then a guard, Mailer succeeded only in climbing one of the pyramids without hope of entry and with his vision of the spectacle blurred by smoke and exhaust from Egyptian military trucks.

Five years later, in a letter to Abbott in prison, Mailer reprimanded him for his statement 'there's Israel doing the lackey's work for the US against the bold, brave Arab nations'. Mailer stated that while he was not a full-blooded Zionist, Israel was the last refuge for those Jews who had survived the Holocaust. 'Just as I don't know what it is to be a convict, you the fuck don't know what it is to be a Jew. You don't know what it is to have six million of your people killed when there are only twelve million of them on earth.' (18 April 1979). One has to wonder if Mailer was not even slightly distracted from his ascent of the pyramid by Egypt and Syria's recent effort to complete the project begun by the Nazis. The Arab states did not explicitly espouse Nazi anti-semitism but their objectives were clear enough: they intended to destroy Israel. His only comment on his experience in Egypt appears in *The Fight*. Cairo disgusted him as a 'collision of overflowing new wealth and scabrous poverty' for which Anwar Sadat was responsible. He said nothing of the president's attempt, shortly before he arrived, to wipe Israel off the face of the earth.

As always Mailer's literary calling distracted him from everything else, in this case his portrait of a civilisation that predated Judaism by several millennia.

Ancient Evenings begins with the unnamed narrator investigating the pharaohs' tombs; he eventually discovers that he is Menenhetet Two ('Meni II'), one of the occupants of the burial chamber. He is not quite a ghost but rather an example of a belief shared by ancient Egyptians and Norman Mailer: reincarnation. Soon he meets his great-grandfather, Menenhetet One, or to be more accurate he discovers him via a flashback, which also enables him to see himself as a six-year-old boy. Menenhetet One is 108 years old, or at least this is the age of the corpse encountered by Meni II, but since time is a fluid concept there is no fixed notion of his age. For the six-year-old Meni II he is sixty, Mailer's age when he completed the novel, and for all we know he will reappear more than two centuries after his biological birthday – such are the limitless delights of reincarnation. Generally speaking, four generations of the Meni dynasty feature in the novel, but there are so many shifts between fixed points of time, not to mention the intrusions of other narrators from the mythology of the period, that we lose track of how many incarnations of Menenhetet there are.

The novel's only thematic keystone is a preoccupation with incest, sexual violence, sodomy and scatology. The description of Menenhetet's buggery by Ramses II is the length of a short story; elsewhere Meni II's penis is referred to as his 'Sweet Finger', while Menenhetet One is equipped with a 'battering ram' or 'sword'. An unnamed copulator at an orgy makes use of his 'thighbone of sweet wisdom'. Queen Nefertiti cries out 'My little *cemetery, unite* with Me, *copulate* with Me' as 'his obelisk … float[s] on her river'. Cannibalism is described in excruciating detail with and counterpointed against the delicious, spiritually uplifting aroma of excrement.

Some passages are almost hilariously terrible. Menenhetet is at one point treated by the Royal Lion, Hera-Ra, to some intimacies. The lion 'rolled over on his back, spread his legs, showed me the depth of his anus … rolled over again, got up, and burped in my face to give me a sour whiff of all the [battle-field] blood he had drunk …' Menenhetet follows the lion into the field of battle which often mutates into an orgy. 'Occasionally the lion would trample over a group of copulators, squeezing their grapes, so to speak, and many a soldier … would lose his erection for this night and more.' Shortly afterwards Hera-Ra eats a dead man's liver ('I think he was dead, though he twitched'). Following the hungry creature's example Menenhetet allows himself a taste and is impressed by its 'intoxicating effect'.

In another episode, an obese concubine called Honey-Ball has her toe amputated, the standard punishment for insulting a pharaoh. Menenhetet is passionately obsessed with her, and after placing her damaged foot in his mouth discovers that the gap left by the missing toe is effectively her second, more sensitive, clitoris.

As the old cliché has it, reviews were mixed. It is astonishing that anyone found it publishable let alone readable, but the pro-modernist elite of critics who thought that literature should be defended from such vulgar encroachments as coherence or comprehensibility deemed it wonderful. Harold Bloom in *The New York Review of Books* thought it was the best novel in English since 1939, and Anthony Burgess was similarly adoring. Others, possessed of something close to common sense, disagreed. Benjamin DeMott in *The New York Times* wrote that 'describing the book simply as a failure – a near-miss earning respect for noble ambitions and partial triumphs – will not do ... It is, speaking bluntly, a disaster ...'

While *Ancient Evenings* was going into paperback in summer 1983, Mailer completed another, uncontracted novel in just over two months. He sent the draft of *Tough Guys Don't Dance* to Little, Brown in September, assuming that they would extend the generous contract of his Egypt novel to include this new one, furnished with a delivery advance which would be negotiated by Meredith. They rejected it, stating that it was more appropriate that he should send it to another publisher. This was a polite disclosure of their knowledge that over the previous four months Mailer, via Meredith, had agreed a deal with Random House involving a $4 million payment for four novels to be delivered within the next nine years at $250,000 a year on the understanding that he would deliver, 'on average', a novel every four years up to just beyond his seventy-sixth birthday. This was an even more generous arrangement than the long-term annual payment of $1 million from Little, Brown, which a bright lawyer might claim had been brought to a close with *Ancient Evenings*. Notably, the new one-novel-every-four-years was an 'expectation' rather than a contractual obligation, and Mailer had tried to sell *Tough Guys Don't Dance* to Little, Brown just before he signed the Random House agreement. Appropriately enough the star of the novel is a louche criminal.

It is difficult to summarise a plot where little makes sense and few of those involved care too much. The principal character is Tim Madden, one-time bartender and drug-dealer, who once served time for narcotics smuggling. He is, as the novel opens, trying to make a living as a writer in his house in Provincetown, having recently been left by his wife. Three weeks after her departure he wakes up hungover with an unexplained tattoo and no memory of recent events. The interior of his car is stained with blood, and after a warning from the Acting Chief of Police, he checks the place where he has his harvest of cannabis. There, he finds the severed head of a very attractive blonde woman. Other corpses turn up in and around the town, and the nature of their deaths remains largely unexplained. All of this adds to Madden's notion of the region as haunted by a centuries-old 'spiritual vengeance'. He imagines the previous inhabitants of his old house: 'whores and smugglers, and whalers with wages hot in their pockets' (p. 64). His current though absent wife, Patty Lareine, his ex-wife Madeleine and her husband, the corrupt policeman Alvin Luther Regency, a local barfly, Spider, and his friend Stoodie – each with criminal associations – and Patty's occasional lover, Bolo, referred to by Madden as 'Mr Black', all appear to be guilty of something, ranging from adultery to potential murder. They are not so much bad or unreformed as demonic prisoners of a 'gray New England winter, gray as the spirit of my mood', as Madden puts it.

During the mid-1970s Mailer became friendly with three men who exemplified his abiding sense of the criminal underworld as something that could energise the moribund orthodoxies of American society. Robert Rowbotham, Richard Stratton and Buzz Farber were all involved in smuggling drugs from Europe and the Middle East to the East Coast of America. Stratton co-owned an old farmhouse in Phillips, Maine, in a town frequented by wealthy second-home owners from cities further south, quietly mocking the well-behaved gentility of the region by using it as a base for shipping imported marijuana and harder drugs. He shared ownership of the property with Norman Mailer, and the question of how Mailer avoided prosecution remains a mystery. The parallels with Madden's Provincetown are clear enough. All three men were arrested, and Mailer testified at their trials, memorably informing the jury that it would be 'bad for the cosmos' and 'bad karma' to convict Rowbotham. He, along with the other two, was found guilty and given a lengthy jail sentence.

Shortly after Rowbotham's trial the Columbia Heights building was broken into. Nothing was disturbed or stolen, but Mailer found his own bag of cannabis, which he had carefully hidden, placed in the centre of his bed, which fuelled his belief that he was being continually monitored by the FBI. It was not the severed head of a beautiful woman, but given that he and Madden shared an addiction to pot and sex the opening of the novel spoke for itself. Madden's proudest boasts were his success as a Golden Gloves boxer and getting a woman into bed only six minutes after meeting her. Both were exaggerations of Mailer's machismo self-image, to varying degrees. As a boxer he was useless, though even José Torres was too polite to point this out; and it is unlikely that he succeeded in seducing a woman in only six minutes, but there are many recollections by others of him doing so in less than an hour.

During the period of negotiations for the lucrative Random House contract Mailer took out several mortgages on properties in Provincetown, most notably 627 Commercial Street, a large house which he would partly let to Ellen Hawkes and Peter Manso. Hawkes was writing a book on Ginny Foat, accused of being an accomplice in a murder committed by her former husband, arguing that she was tried for being a woman who had the courage to stand up for herself. Its provisional title was *Feminism on Trial*. Manso was preparing a 'biography' of Mailer that was made up exclusively of interview testimonies by people who had known him from his childhood onwards, including those who had witnessed the stabbing of Adele, and Adele herself.

It was as if various aspects of Mailer's past had conspired to return to him in Provincetown. To complicate matters his children were regular summer visitors to the Provincetown house, and although there were only a few conspicuously noisy arguments, the place seethed with bitterness. The children were learning, from Manso, more and more of their mothers' histories with their father, and Manso himself began to become dismayed by the new image of his one-time hero. Later, when the book was about to come out, he stated that Mailer was 'no rebel … [but] an opportunist' who played '"house nigger" to wealthy East Side reactionaries' (*Provincetown Arts*, Summer 1987). One of these was the lawyer Roy Cohn, who had worked for and socialised with Senator McCarthy as well as senior figures in the Mafia. Later he represented and mentored the then real estate developer Donald Trump. At the time Mailer was beginning *Tough Guys Don't Dance*, Cohn had arranged to move into a neighbouring house in Provincetown. Manso had done press profiles of Cohn and warned Mailer that a conspicuous friendship between the two men would draw the attention of the police or FBI. Mailer thanked him for his advice and kept quiet about the fact that Cohn had for some time been doing him favours behind the scenes. The most recent involved Cohn's involvement with Si Newhouse, the owner of Random House. Through Cohn's hands-on manipulative skills, the publisher came up with the offer of annual payments that Mailer was delighted not to refuse, to adapt the famous phrase from *The Godfather*.

One begins to see why Mailer, via Madden, perceived Provincetown as a place of secrets and ominous rumours, if not hidden corpses. Madden at the beginning of the novel confesses to his failings as a narrator: 'my memory is damnable' (p. 24); 'My dreams were now as reasonable as my memory, or my memory was as untrustworthy as my dreams. In either event, I could not tell them apart'. As Manso bombarded Mailer with testimonies from his past, Mailer found himself forced into a corner. He had sanctioned the book and could only hide from the recollections of others by adding what amounted to his own footnotes, neither denying what they had said nor rebuking them for saying it. He simply, like Madden, provided a rather blurred counter-narrative of private reflections. Madden was more candid than his author about those aspects of his past he might prefer to forget. At one point he asks himself, 'How many times over these last few years had I come to the edge of battering Patty Lareine with my bare hands?' (p. 159). This is a question that Mailer faced on numerous occasions when Manso's interviewees confronted him with his acts of violence and cruelty, especially towards women. Mailer's refusal to address these accusations meant that Manso left them out of the book. Mailer later said that *Tough Guys* was the 'weakest' of his novels, a case of 'what happens when you have to do what is necessary' to make money. (Interview with Christopher Bigsby, BBC Radio 3, *Third Ear*, 12 November 1991). As a piece of quasi-autobiographical fiction it is probably his most revealing. Apart from the fact the Provincetown in 1984 seemed to be crowded with noisy ghosts, Mailer was also in fear of something far more dreadful in the imminent future. He had dedicated himself to Norris as the final, singular love of his life, but she was behaving strangely, asking obtuse questions about why he had decided to visit this or that place and who had gone with him.

15

A CLANDESTINE WORLD REVEALED

Mailer began *Harlot's Ghost* (1991) about six months after *Tough Guys Don't Dance* (1984) was published. It took him almost half as long to complete as *Ancient Evenings*, but he devoted much more attention to it, in maniacal daily bursts. For one eighteen-month period he gave up drink and other indulgences completely and locked himself into his Provincetown study, and when he delivered the draft to Random House it was one of the longest novels in American literary history, coming in at 1,310 pages in print. It would have been around a hundred pages longer than that, and difficult to bind, had not the typesetters added an extra line to each final galley page. He described it to friends as his 'spy novel'.

In August 1985, when it was still at planning stage, Fan died. She was crippled with arthritis, almost blind, plagued by loss of recent and distant memories but probably not quite the victim of what we presently understand as dementia. When she commented to her Jamaican maid that 'I just wish I was dead', her domestic asked, seemingly without irony, 'Would you like me to help you?' Fan replied sharply, 'No need. Drop dead yourself!' Telling friends of this later, Mailer added proudly, 'That was my mom.'

The people who had brought him into the world and helped him in his earliest attempts to make sense of it were now gone forever, and this lent his new novel a special energy. It would be about figures whose pasts were not so much shared as privately reconfigured.

There were two principal distractions from Mailer's work on this massive book. He directed a film version of *Tough Guys Don't Dance*, starring Ryan O'Neal as Madden. It was not intended as a comedy, but a cinematic version of a book with apparently as many unidentified corpses as live protagonists seemed to most audiences an attempt at laugh-a-minute surrealism. The Cannes Film Festival audience guffawed heartily, thinking it was a modern caricature of the Humphrey Bogart PI genre.

In February 1989, when Mailer was well into the draft, Ayatollah Khomeini, the Islamist dictator of Iran, issued a decree against Salman Rushdie for having written *The Satanic Verses* (1988). It was, he proclaimed, blasphemous. Two million six hundred thousand dollars would go to an Iranian who killed Rushdie and a million dollars to anyone else who took his life. Mailer was one of the signatories of a PEN letter declaring that literature was the vital, last refuge for free speech, and appeared at several events and in the news media. He mounted the stage at a PEN rally and quoted Christopher Hitchens's depiction of King George III as equally fitting for Khomeini: 'an old, mad, blind, despised and dying King'. It was, in its way, a courageous statement but ludicrously naïve. Khomeini's fundamentalist regime in Iran would go on to sponsor many of the anti-Western, Islamist terrorist groups that still plague Western society today.

As with many of Mailer's novels, *Harlot's Ghost* divided critical opinion. Some deemed its rambling gigantism and its failure to reach anything close to a conclusion unendurable, while others found in this a soaring grandeur; Lennon calls it his 'unfinished cathedral'.

In the opening, the most bearable part of the book, we get to know something of the three principal characters and their interrelationships. The central figure here and in the rest of the work is Herrick (Harry) Hubbard, a second-generation CIA operative, who idolises Hugh Tremont Montague – the 'Harlot' of the title – an urbane, ruthless top-level official in the agency. Hadley Kittredge Gardiner (referred to throughout as 'Kittredge') is a Radcliffe graduate and scion of a distinguished academic family who works for the CIA as their psychanalytic/intellectual guru. She was once married to Harlot, until a rock-climbing fall resulted in the death of their son, Christopher, and condemned Harlot to life in a wheelchair. Kittredge, seemingly with as much emotion as someone moving house, divorces Harlot, whose disability appears to have rendered him impotent, and marries Harry. Their lovemaking is 'fabulous', 'a sacrament', though Harry occasionally cheats on her.

The prologue closes in 1983 as a decomposing body is fished out of Chesapeake Bay. Its fingers have been chewed to the bone by fish and little is left of the head following its close encounter with a double-barrelled shotgun. This last creates a link between Mailer and Harry; both idolised men who shared this fate, in Mailer's case Hemingway. Dental analysis suggest that the corpse might be Harlot, but several uncertainties endure. Did he kill himself, was he murdered, or has he faked his death, perhaps to defect to the Soviet Union?

Other strange things occur, the most bizarre being the appearance of the ghost of Augustus Farr, a previous owner of the Chesapeake house, who communicates with both Kittredge and Harry. A hallucinating CIA agent is disturbing enough for the security of the state, but the fact that two of them are able to communicate with the same spirit indicates that the KGB has little to worry about. Dix Butler, a murderous, icily fascinating figure, arrives. He enjoys killing prisoners, but torture is his speciality. Kittredge sleeps with him and comments, 'With Dix Butler, I can't explain why, I feel very close to Christ.'

The rest of the novel, more than one thousand of its pages, is given over to the recollections and speculations of Harry. He continually ponders the possibility that Harlot is alive, probably in Moscow, but the narrative mostly takes us through Harry's life, from his graduation from Harvard onwards. He is recruited and trained by the agency in Washington, serves in Berlin and Montevideo, and is involved, when based in Miami, with the Bay of Pigs affair, the Cuban Missile Crisis and a plan to assassinate Castro. He has an affair with thinly disguised version of Judith Campbell Exner, the lover of John F. Kennedy, Frank Sinatra and Sam Giancana, the Mafia boss. Harry too flies to Moscow, and we leave the novel with him in the Metropole Hotel having supplemented his earlier tales with shady speculations on his organisation's involvement in the assassination of President Kennedy, the death of Marilyn Monroe and the Watergate scandal. All of this could have been made very exciting if rendered in around 300 pages, but strewn over close to three quarter of a million words it saps our will to remain awake, let alone to read on. As the *New York Times* review put it, 'He comes closest to another highly gifted, overexuberant ex-Harvard man, Thomas Wolfe ... What he lacks is his editor.'

The possibility that Mailer was attempting to demythologise the thrill of spying as usually rendered in fiction can be rejected. He does not try to present intelligence work as gruelling and patience-sapping. Rather, the figures who are recruited seem to be part of an East Coast gentlemen's club (ladies included, notably Kittredge), enjoying expenses-free excursions across the globe.

In truth, the intelligence community fascinated Mailer because he saw in it similarities with something in his personal history he was not quite prepared fully admit to but to which, in interviews on the book, he offered tantalising clues.

> I have an umbilical connection to *Harlot's Ghost* because I've been obsessed with questions of identity all of my life ... I've always been fascinated with spies and actors and people who take on roles that are not their own and then take on that role more than they might like to.
> (*The Guardian*, 5 October 1991)

The seeds for the book can be found in his 1976 essay 'A Harlot High and Low', in which he ponders the psychology of spying: '... facts are wiped out by artifacts; proof enters the logic of counterproof and we are in the dream; matter breathes next to antimatter.' Of the possibility that CIA operatives might have been responsible for the assassination of a president but would never in any circumstances admit to it, perhaps even to themselves, he asks, 'Where is the root of identity in that kind of man?' (*Pieces and Pontifications*, p. 160). Crucially, he admits that 'I could have been in the CIA. And I probably would have been very good at it.'

Harlot's Ghost is not really about the CIA; rather the organisation he imagined and presented, made up of endless uncertainties and deceptions, plots and counterplots, is a labyrinthine extension of Norman Mailer.

His fascination with conspiracy theories on who exactly killed Kennedy and Monroe, attempted to kill Castro and engaged in other terrible endeavours resurfaces in Harry, but he was doing more than extrapolating these fantasies to the book. Rather, he had found in his fictionalised world of espionage parallels with own lifelong addiction to cheating and infidelity.

Mailer inhabits the book like a man hooked on a drug he has invented exclusively for his own use. Norris wrote in her memoir:

> He said his double life started when he began researching that book ... The timing was about right. All the clandestine talking on pay phones, making secret plans, hiding and sneaking around, were perfect spy maneuvers. He said he needed to live that kind of double life to know what his characters were going through. (*A Ticket to the Circus*, p. 322)

He confessed this to her shortly before the novel went to press. Over the previous few weeks she had quizzed him several times on his accounts of trips recently made.

> 'Sweetie, there were several charges in Chicago this month. I thought you went to Los Angeles.'
> 'Oh, I did, but I didn't tell you I had to make a stop in Chicago to see Saul Bellow about a project we might do.'
> 'Saul Bellow? No, you didn't tell me.' (Ibid., p. 315)

Norris continued to probe him, on the nature of the 'project' and what had come of his discussion with Bellow, until his improvised fabrications became self-evidently ludicrous. Eventually he came clean. 'Okay, I'll confess. I stopped off to see an old girlfriend', insisting that it was a friendly visit, without sex. 'He swore it was the first time he had ever done anything like that.' The more he insisted on this the more Norris looked into phone records and compared them with his reports of what he had been doing and with whom. 'I became obsessed with finding out the truth ... [I] found a lot of calls to Chicago, going back months and months. There were calls to California, too, and other odd calls, to Washington, to Florida.' (Ibid., p. 316). Norris goes on to report that he affirmed that he had been faithful to her during the first eight years of their relationship, 'his grand experiment in monogamy', as he put it, that his exercises in deceit during his research for *Harlot's Ghost* were undertaken as a harrowing obligation to the novel, and that, while he had met women, their encounters were no more than exercises in pretence. He did not want sex, merely to experience what it felt like to go under cover. Initially she seems to have believed him, but when the truth came out, she was horrified and enraged.

Bound proofs of the novel were being scrutinised for review between June and October 1991. This might seem an extraordinarily long period for the run-up to publication, but few reviewers could give themselves over to the two-week period of attention demanded by more than 1,300 pages of dense narrative. Parts of the book were being sold for serialisation in weeklies, including *Rolling Stone*; Mailer conducted a tour of the country, giving more than thirty-five interviews in two months; he was appointed 'New York State Author' at Albany University and gave the inaugural address for his two-year tenure; and on his travels wrote numerous articles hinting that the CIA were involved in unseemly activities, notably John Kennedy's assassination.

His absence for most of the second half of 1991 provided Norris with the opportunity to look for more evidence. She made use of a licensed private detective to seek out specific places, dates, times and, crucially, names from her bulky collection of credit card slips and charges, phone records involving numbers she did not recognise, booking references for restaurants and motel and hotel rooms, slips on his cheque book, airline and train tickets left in his suits and luggage, and any other pointers towards what he might have been doing, where and with whom over a period of years well back into the early 1980s, before he had begun work on the novel. By the end of the year, she had knowledge of his regular liaisons with Carole Mallory, an occasional film actress and cover model for *New York* and *Cosmopolitan*. It was evident that he had been seeing her before he started work on *Harlot's Ghost*, and his claim that his other life was an attempt to replicate a CIA clandestine lifestyle further unravelled when Norris discovered that Scott Meredith, his agent, had been diverting funds to Mallory on a monthly basis for some time before Mailer had thought of the book.

Another name that appeared regularly on restaurant and hotel charge slips was Eileen Frederickson, closer to his age than Norris was. Norris went through Mailer's Provincetown office drawers and found letters between them. Frederickson was a receptionist at the Drake Hotel on Lake Michigan where he had stayed when promoting *The Executioner's Song* in 1979. They slept together the night they met. While Mailer insisted that now Norris knew of both affairs he would end them immediately, he continued to meet up with Frederickson until a year before his death and ended the relationship only because he was then physically incapable of having sex.

Other records disclosed his regular meetings with Lois Wilson. Lois was his talisman of infidelity. Their relationship began when he was with Bea in 1947 and endured through all of his subsequent marriages. Once more he assured Norris that their marriage was strong enough for him to leave the women he'd been with, albeit intermittently, for two thirds of his adult life. He lied, and, as with Frederickson, Wilson followed him into the 2000s as a token of promiscuity as rejuvenation.

In late August 1991 Mailer returned to Provincetown as a break from his publicity tour, and Norris confronted him with original paper documents, photocopies and computer printouts provided by her private investigator. Mailer's sister, Barbara, witnessed their altercations one afternoon. '... Norris came down in a fury. She presented him with some stuff she'd found, I think, on the computer or something ... And then she left.' (Lennon, p. 655).

During the next two weeks Norris bombarded him with further proof of his misbehaviour, no part of which he was able to refute. In September she returned to New York with John and Matthew and asked him to leave. Assuming she needed time to digest the disclosures and, perhaps, consider reconciliation, he packed some bags and gave her the spare keys to his study, asking her to place there a box of books and files. When in the brownstone, she unlocked his office and searched his desk drawers, which were bulging with love letters, many of which involved other women outside the trio of Frederickson, Wilson and Mallory.

Since Norris and Mailer had met, he had joked about the fan mail he regularly received from women, but the ones in his desk included luridly specific references to sex acts between him and several correspondents – although the despatches from Mallory outnumbered all of the rest.

Whether his handing over of the keys was by way of a confession, or if he thought she would not presume to go through his papers, will remain a mystery.

Susan Mailer offers a clue.

> My father was in love with the excitement of seduction. As much as
> he loved Norris, he probably chafed under the domesticity of their
> daily routine. It killed the passion that fuelled his life … it wasn't
> surprising that he'd cheated, then left the evidence for her to find.
> That of course would have made it all even more exciting. When Aunt
> Barbara asked why he'd done it, he said, 'Life was getting too safe.' (*In
> Another Place*, p. 258)

In September 1991 Mailer admitted to all of Norris's accusations. There
was little else he could do. He assured her that his lifelong addiction
to philandering was now over forever, but he showed little remorse.
Sometimes he seemed obsessed with confessing, offering Norris minute
details of his meetings with the three women with whom he'd had long-
term affairs for most of their marriage and sometimes adding accounts
of his liaisons with others; places, dates and his alibis included. On one
occasion they took the elevator from the Brooklyn apartment, and found
a cab to take them to a Manhattan restaurant for dinner. At no point
during the journey did Mailer pause in his seemingly limitless catalogue
of disclosures. Halfway to the restaurant Norris felt that she was about to
faint, ordered the driver to stop and insisted on walking. To her distress
Mailer too left the cab and accompanied her on the sidewalk, continuing
his monologue.

Painful though it was to her, she convinced herself that the obsessive
revelations involved a form of self-cleansing, and gradually she agreed
that they would return to being a married couple, at least for an
experimental period of several months.

On 31 October she accompanied him to a Random House launch party
at the New York '21' Club, hosted by the publisher Harold Evans. Halfway
through, Carole Mallory arrived with a squadron of photographers
and hack journalists and insisted on having her photograph taken with
Mailer while declaring herself to be the woman who had 'inspired' the
novel. Mailer pushed the photographers away, and Carole found herself
being instructed quietly by Norris that this was the last time she would
see Norman so she should make the most of it. She was right. She had

last slept with him in June in Los Angeles, and under instruction from Mailer the monthly payments to her arranged by Meredith had been cancelled for good a week before the launch party.

In January 1992, Mailer was invited to Langley, headquarters of the CIA, to give a talk on *Harlot's Ghost* and discuss it with an audience of around five hundred members of the agency. He received several ovations, mainly in response to his praise for the CIA's work during the Cold War and what he saw as the challenges it faced afterwards, mostly from rogue states with nuclear weapons and links to terrorist groups. A disconnection between him and the audience became evident when he expressed his approval for 'wet jobs' already undertaken and required in the future. The term was a euphemism for state-sanctioned assassinations against those thought to pose a threat to the stability of America and the West. As far as his listeners were concerned this was part of a noir fantasy indulged only by thriller novelists, but Mailer seemed to believe that the men and women he was addressing had been involved in or at least knew of such acts. One agent commented later that 'What did he expect? Guys with guns?', and another, after reading the novel, said that its lugubrious and neurotic characters 'would never have passed the polygraph'. E. Howard Hunt attended the event. He was the most senior figure in the CIA who had been brought into the novel as a character. He stated that 'the writer who presumes to reveal the inner world of espionage without having experienced it is comparable to a young man haunting a brothel exit and asking patrons what it was like' (Quoted by Elaine Sciolino, *The New York Times*, 2 February 1992).

Hunt had stumbled on a half-truth. Intelligence work might have had little in common with Mailer's routines of infidelity, but when sex was involved, keeping secrets was his lifelong raison d'être. His affairs with Frederickson and Wilson endured for a further fifteen years. Despite, or rather because of, his manic confessions, Norris never suspected that he also continued to see Suzanne Nye following his apparent break with her in 1975. In her memoir, Susan Mailer confesses that Mailer visited her at her home in Chile for a month in 1986. He was to come alone and 'incognito' to avoid being presented as sympathetic-by-association with the Pinochet regime. Susan was thus surprised to find that in place of Norris he had brought Suzanne. Nor was Norris aware of his occasional encounters with Barbara Probst Solomon, a friend of his sister; their casual relationship began at Harvard and continued well into his marriage with Norris. His friend Robert Lucid, Professor of English at Pennsylvania University, had introduced him to Carol Holmes, his graduate student, in the 1970s. Holmes was attracted by Mailer's status as a controversial literary celebrity, she was outstandingly attractive, and he was unable to resist her. Mailer's machinations were tactically astute, if morally questionable, and went far beyond the levels of physical exertion that most could endure. He bombarded Norris with a white noise of detail that concentrated largely on the three women she knew of and several one-night stands. This effectively blinded her to suspicions regarding anything or anyone beyond that. Susan thought his being found out made his serial infidelities 'all even more exciting' for him, but along with the excitement came a good deal of calculation.

At the close of *Harlot's Ghost* Mailer wrote 'To Be Continued', which many reviewers greeted as a dismaying threat. He knew too that he would never write another book in which the characters of the first would discover or reveal the secrets that surrounded them. The novel was too tightly bound into his own world of interwoven pretence and lies for that.

During the months of autumn and early winter 1991, when he and Norris were attempting to return to a stable relationship, she took revenge and subjected him to something similar to what he had done to her. She had known a young man at high school in Arkansas who was now a surgeon based in Atlanta. In later interviews refers to him as 'Benicio'. He saw some of the press coverage of the *Harlot's Ghost* launch, including gossip that the Mailer marriage was on the rocks, called her and later in November they met in Georgia and had a brief affair. (Lennon, pp. 662-3). On her return she went to dinner with Mailer, told him what she had done and asked about practical arrangements that had taken place following his previous marriage break-ups. He had never been through this before, had always been the transgressor and the suitably patrician organiser of the outcome. Now Norris had seized the initiative and shown him what his earlier wives had put up with. Others in the restaurant later reported that he banged the table and howled 'No, no, no, no, no. ... We are not breaking up!' A week later she announced to him that she had had a one-night stand with another man in New York, who remains anonymous, his name deleted from all free-access papers. She was victorious, to an extent, in that Mailer was for the first time in his life begging his partner for the survival of their marriage. What she did not learn was that he accepted humiliation as a suitable penalty for his continued life of infidelity.

16

RETIREMENT: WITH PICASSO, OSWALD, CHRIST AND HITLER

Mailer's short biography of Picasso, *Portrait of Picasso as a Young Man*, was completed in early 1992, during the months following his near break-up with Norris, but was not published until 1995. His publishers were dumbfounded by the first draft, and it took Meredith almost three years to persuade them to bring it out. The main problem was that Random House were also publishing the second part of John Richardson's massive four-volume authorised biography, the first part of which had appeared in 1991. Richardson was one of the most celebrated art historians of the mid-twentieth century and had become a close friend of Picasso in Provence in the 1950s. Jason Epstein was editing the work of both men. He felt he must defer to Richardson's opinion on Mailer's project and showed him the draft. Richardson, in the manner of a donnish gentleman, praised Mailer as an enthusiastic amateur but at the same time refused to allow him even to quote from his own book. Epstein foresaw a terrible response by the critics and refused to publish Mailer on the grounds that the draft was 'unsuitable', a word inserted into the contract as a standard get-out clause available to all publishers. Meredith instead placed it with Grove/Atlantic.

It is by equal parts bad and revealing. Despite Mailer's own occasional attempts at painting and his conversations with Norris, his ignorance of the history of visual art is starkly evident. His claim that his decision to trace Picasso's artistic life only up to his development of Cubism because that was the zenith of his achievement is fatuous, mainly because he shows that he has no real understanding of what Cubism involved. Mailer was not interested in Picasso's work. Rather he saw in the painter's personal life parallels with his own, particularly his attachment to his mother and his addiction to infidelity. He was writing about himself and projecting his image onto that of the most celebrated artist of the twentieth century. He seemed to think that sexual incontinence united them in greatness.

Larry Schiller is a very real photojournalist, but in *The Executioner's Song* Mailer turned him into a figure energised and transformed by the narrative, without significantly altering his actual involvement with Gilmore. Schiller was beguiled by the experience of reading about himself and by what Mailer could manufacture from the truth.

In late summer 1992, just after the completion of the Picasso book, Schiller phoned Mailer and suggested that they co-operate in a project he knew he would be unable to resist. He reported that he'd recently been in contact with members of the KGB and suggested he and Mailer meet in a bar, a place that would not be bugged, for a quiet discussion.

They did so the following day, and Schiller explained that he had got to know Ludmilla Peresvetova, who had worked for the head of the KGB, Vadim Batakin. Batakin had offered to introduce him to Aleksandr Sharkovsky, the KGB head of operations in Minsk, who had access to the files that Soviet intelligence kept on Lee Harvey Oswald, the man most non-conspiracy theorists treated as Kennedy's assassin. Mailer had his doubts about Oswald's guilt, and the prospect of disclosing the truth excited him greatly. Oswald had lived in Minsk for two years before returning to America in 1962. On 22 November 1963 he was arrested for firing the shots from the Texas School Book Depository that killed Kennedy as the presidential motorcade passed through Dealey Plaza in Dallas. Two days later a nightclub owner, Jack Ruby, shot Oswald dead, curtailed a trial and prompted decades of speculation on what had really happened.

Schiller explained that he could arrange visas for the two of them to visit Minsk and Moscow and could set up one-to-one exchanges with KGB operatives. Glasnost had since 1991 become the policy of a Soviet federation that was rapidly fragmenting into quasi-independent nations, including Belarus, of which Minsk is the capital. State operatives, spies particularly, feared for their futures, and some were willing to accept money in exchange for their confessions to Western media.

In terms of official investigations on the Kennedy assassination, little had been added since the Warren Commission Report of 1964, and the most meticulous recent research on the shooting had been done by Gerald Posner for his book *Case Closed* (1993). Posner dismisses all the conspiracy theories that had circulated during the previous three decades and concludes that Oswald was a dysfunctional loser whose only discernible motive for killing Kennedy was his own unhinged solipsism. Mailer began writing up his version of the events shortly after Posner's book came out, and his early research work undertaken with Schiller makes for a fascinating story in its own right.

During the eight months between September 1992 and April 1993, Mailer and Schiller lived in Minsk and Moscow, with Mailer taking a few short return visits to the US. The contrast between his experiences in Russia and Harry Hubbard's self-exile to the Metropole Hotel in the Soviet capital might be seen as hilarious, though Mailer was not amused. In Minsk they rented a two-bedroom flat in one of the hastily assembled *Khrushchyovka*, low-cost three- to five-storey blocks dating from the early 1960s. Theirs was an improvement on the originals, given that they did not have to share a bathroom with their neighbours.

Nominally, Belarus had been independent since the dissolution of the Soviet Union in 1991, but it remained a member of the Commonwealth of Independent States, and the border with Russia amounted to little more than a line on the map. Most significantly, its security service, run by the State Security Committee, was effectively the old KGB renamed, and all of its files from Oswald's period in the country were intact.

Though the economy was no longer collectivised by statute, little had changed over the previous twelve months aside from there being even less to purchase than in the communist era. Restaurants could be owned as private enterprises, but no one seemed to know how to buy let alone run one. During their first two weeks Mailer and Schiller trailed around the city in search of a cooked meal but found little more than pork stew, without the pork, potato cakes that lacked the traditional ingredient of bacon, or borscht made up only of root vegetables. They decided to cook their own food and managed to live on vegetable soup flavoured with stock from bones, scrambled eggs on dark rye bread and, when finding black-market sources, tuna, which they ate with fried cabbage and potato. There were, however, seemingly limitless supplies of vodka: Ludmilla, their translator, informed them that she knew of no other means of survival or enjoyment. As autumn gave way to winter the temperature rarely rose above zero and darkness fell in mid-afternoon, enduring for as long as eighteen hours. Of nightlife, even bars, there was none. For most of his life, even during his later, reactionary years, Mailer had cultivated an affection for Soviet Russia, and in a letter to Mickey Knox from Minsk he observes, bizarrely, that 'it made me realise how Russian I am ... one gets a sense of what life was like in the old Soviet Union'. (Lennon, p. 667). This is probably the only known recommendation of communism as a form of masochistic penitence.

Norris visited for two weeks – mainly to check that her husband was not returning to his habits as an ageing gigolo – and managed to exchange dollars for gristly stewing beef and chicken. If only Mailer had an inclination for wry self-caricature, his visit to Belarus and Russia could have become one of his best books. He and Schiller met Sharkovsky on several occasions but were offered hardly anything of significance on Oswald, at least until the ex-KGB man invited them to rent a small office in the Minsk KGB building for $1,000 a month in cash, most of which went into Sharkovsky's pocket. Even the fragments of the Oswald file then released to them were largely inconsequential. The only significant disclosure was that after his arrival, Soviet security assumed that Oswald was a spy, a mole who would acclimatise himself to his new circumstances before sending information on the day-to-day workings of communism back to the CIA. After Oswald married Marina Prusakova in Minsk, the KGB bugged their flat and installed tape recorders in the one above it, collecting every sound for twenty-four hours a day, sex included. Mailer was not given access to the tapes but did contact Marina's aunt, Valya. All she required in return for an interview, at which she told them no more than they'd already surmised, was comfortable Western shoes. Her request was, by various means, communicated to members of the security services who also craved decent footwear. Schiller arranged a delivery of shoes and boots, for men and women and ranging through the standard sizes, from Austria. Some in Minsk now walked more comfortably, but the two American investigators seemed only to stumble further into a morass of confusion and petty corruption.

Sharkovsky did excite them by telling of how his team of watchers suspected that Oswald had been sent by the Americans to blow up a new hotel where Nikita Khrushchev was due to stay. Oswald had visited the building and then been followed through various shops, where he purchased items such as a wireless circuit board, electrical switches, wiring and batteries. This was it, thought Schiller and Mailer. Oswald was a CIA agent who had been caught on his bombing mission, 'turned' by the Soviets and persuaded to return to America to assassinate the leader of the country which had despatched him to the East. But Sharkovsky kept them guessing until finally he smiled and revealed that Oswald was building a toy for the child of Marina's friend.

They spoke to workers at the factory where Oswald had been employed and to friends and relatives of Marina, and none had anything interesting to say beyond their surprise at being joined by this quiet American who had chosen to live and work within the Soviet system. He seemed feckless, failing to become more than half-fluent in Belarusian and Russian, and a little introverted, though the latter was less to do with his temperament than his inability to conduct proper conversations.

After six months of strenuous research and several thousand pages of notes the two men had proof of hardly anything.

Their final interview with Sharkovsky was preceded by Schiller briefing Ludmilla in an attempt to get him to open up. She was to compare Mailer with Pasternak and Solzhenitsyn and convince Sharkovsky that if he handed them all the files he would go down in history as the man who had disclosed the truth about the killing of America's most enthralling modern president. Sharkovsky shook his head. Several days later Schiller announced to Mailer that he had made contact with another official at KGB headquarters, who would hand over the files for $10,000. Mailer exploded, pointing out that each of them would be likely to receive long prison sentences, or worse. They fought in the stairwell of the *Khrushchyovka*, and then Schiller explained how he had planned things. He would be the likeliest suspect and would leave for America from the most tightly monitored airport, Moscow. Mailer would fly from Minsk and Ludmilla from Leningrad. Ludmilla too, asked Mailer? Yes, Schiller explained; they had married the previous day.

All three of them escaped without even having their bags checked. The two men pored over the files back in New York, with Ludmilla as translator, and discovered little more than they already knew.

The final part of the odyssey took the two men to Texas, where they conducted interviews with Oswald's widow, Marina, in a Dallas hotel room. She was reasonably fluent in English, but in the absence of Ludmilla Schiller brought along an enormous Russian–English dictionary. He also played bad cop to Mailer's calm, avuncular presence, but after a week of interviews they were left only with a replica of her testimony to the Warren Commission. In desperation Schiller began to raise questions about her sex life with Oswald, including the truth or otherwise of the account of a blood-stained bedsheet that proved her virginity on their wedding night. What this had to do with the shooting of Kennedy remains unclear, but by this point Schiller and Mailer seemed to have lost any sense of logic, had become the equivalent of hack reporters in hot pursuit of anything that would excite the prurient interest of their readers.

Mailer had no proof that Oswald had acted on behalf of any state or agency, and there was nothing at all to suggest that he had cultivated a private ideological grievance against Kennedy. What he did was to turn him into an avatar for several philosophical traumas that plagued America at the close of the 1950s. There were rumours voiced following the Warren Commission Report, without any basis in the Report itself, that Oswald might have been gay, and Mailer plays on this: 'it might be all for the best if Oswald turned out to be homosexual. That would have the advantage of explaining much even if it explained nothing at all.' (Oswald's Tale, p. 379). He goes on to speculate that even if he was not homosexual, the pressure of a society obsessed with aggressive masculinity forced him to play out macho roles, especially as a Marine. This echoes Mailer's 1950s ruminations on homosexuality, and it was his stepping stone to another Mailerism. 'In the profoundest sense, as Oswald saw it, he had located the tumor – it was that Kennedy was too good.' (Oswald's Tale, p. 781). It had been some time since he had fixed upon cancer as an all-inclusive metaphor for political and social deterioration, but he is now back on home territory. 'The world was in crisis and the social need was to create conditions for recognizing that there had to be a new kind of society … An explosion at the heart of the American establishment's complacency would be exactly the shock therapy needed to awaken the world.' (*Oswald's Tale,* p. 781). Oswald, then, is Mailer's quintessential visionary malcontent, the hipster of 'The White Negro' and Rojack of *An American Dream*.

Oswald's Tale (1995) sold badly, as did the life of Picasso, and Mailer blamed the performance of the former on Random House's $30 pricing, but production costs for a non-fiction volume of more than 800 pages left the company with little option. Privately he conceded that his attempt to present Oswald as a human being rather than an embodiment of vileness had alienated those for whom Kennedy was the emblem of the American idyll.

Mailer's long-term agent, Scott Meredith, had died in 1993, and Mailer had become a client of the Wylie Agency. Andrew Wylie had in the early 1990s arrived as the writer's hero, the strong-arm bully who managed to fill publishing houses with trepidation and sometimes fear. Mailer's financial situation was once more nightmarishly complicated in that his advances and royalty payments were always in lieu of unrecovered debts from contracts with the publisher, arrangements inherited by Random House or other organisations and demands from the ever-vigilant IRS. On top of this he had mortgages on two homes, alimony payments for five ex-wives, plus college and school fees for his children. Wylie arranged for him to receive $30,000 per month from Random House for the rest of his life, provided that he committed all single-authored book-length projects to them. Cleverly Wylie excluded from this any income from screenplays, interviews, speeches, magazine pieces or 'consultations', while securing for him exclusively an income from 'other earnings' that would cover the (roughly calculated) $300,000 per year needed to look after his properties and family. He was one of the wealthiest writers in the world, at least in terms of recorded income, but what he earned disappeared into a black hole of private debts and family commitments. More significantly, in order to maintain the equilibrium between income and outgoings he would need to produce an enormous number of books and articles. It was a literary life sentence.

In November 1994 Mailer appeared on a shared French-German television network with Jean Malaquais. Malaquais, irrespective of the failure and eventual collapse of the Soviet Union, remained a hard-line Marxist and said to Mailer on air that 'Being a celebrity is your infantile malady', going on to accuse him of abandoning his commitments to any kind of political creed for money and fame. It marked the end of their already precarious friendship. Mailer returned to his room in the George V Hotel, Paris – Norris had stayed in the US – remained awake with a bottle of Irish whiskey, and read the New Testament of a Gideon Bible available for guests in the night table.

At Harvard passages from it had featured on the 'World Literature' course. Now he started to read the Book of John, the best-known account of the life and death of Christ, later commenting that he 'couldn't make head or tail of it'. His main problem was that the only editions of the Bible then available were the King James translation into English of 1611, done in a manner familiar to literate contemporaries of Shakespeare but jarring for most twentieth-century readers. By the time he returned to Provincetown he had mastered the idiom and was busy comparing the account in John with those in the three other Gospels. He had not suddenly acquired an interest in Christian theology. What fascinated him was the nature or rather the absence of Jesus Christ. His experiences were described and some of his utterances quoted, but the more one searched for a three-dimensional figure with a particular temperament the more elusive he became. He seemed to be made up of doctrinal abstractions. Mailer later stated in an interview that 'I wanted to retell it the way all writers want to retell a classic story ... There are easily one hundred writers who could do a better job [than Matthew, Mark, Luke and John], and I'm one of them.' (*Washington Post*, 10 May 1997).

He had promised Random House a sequel to *Harlot's Ghost*, and by the time his editor, Jason Epstein, enquired about this in the late 1995, Mailer confessed that he had been working exclusively on his fictionalised life of Christ for six months. He decided that the 'better job' would be done by allowing the main character to tell his own story. There had been several novels about Christ, the majority written by religious evangelists as reader-friendly versions of the New Testament. Others, such as Robert Graves's *King Jesus* (1946) and Anthony Burgess's *Man of Nazareth* (1979), allowed scripture to give way to imaginative reinterpretation, but Mailer was the first to turn to the son of God into a first-person narrator. This was audacious even for a Jew, given that the founder of the world's largest religion did not speak directly to the readers of the Bible and was not expected to hold court in this way, at least until the second coming. Mailer does not so much alter the narrative of the Gospels as make us question the authenticity of the New Testament accounts. For example, in the completed novel Jesus says of Sermon on the Mount, 'They had me saying all manner of things, and some were the opposite of others. Matthew put so many things together, indeed, that he might as well have had me not ceasing to speak for a day and a night, and speaking out of two mouths that did not listen to each other.' (*The Gospel According to the Son*, p. 111). These collisions between different versions of the ultimate truth are important, according to Jesus, because they would eventually result in disputes that led to war, notably following the Reformation.

Most of all, the novel is a meditation on the relationship between truth and fiction, an unresolved and unresolvable conflict which appropriately enough informs Norman Mailer's career as a writer, not to mention his private life. He was, like his version of Christ, addicted to reframing the real world as by parts myth and fiction. Since *The Naked and the Dead*, there had always been a blurred line between what he reported and invented, and as he showed in *The Executioner's Song* he could manipulate the truth simply by writing about it.

Once, when he visited Norris's father's house, he was invited to say a few words at the local Baptist Sunday School. James Davis was a Baptist Deacon, his daughter's husband was the first Jew he had ever encountered and he wanted his Sunday School attendees to meet a man descended from the tribe of Jesus of Nazareth. Encouraged by Davis to speak as if he had a special affinity with the Galilean Jew who was betrayed by his own, Mailer did his best to bring the New Testament to life for the audience. The episode seemed for most innocuous, even comedic, but it prompted Mailer to believe in his suitability as Christ's literary spokesman. As a non-Christian, he thought more and more about the relationship between his private ethnic legacy and the civilisation which had co-habited with and just as frequently despised Judaism; he felt he had unique access to the dialogue between the two cultures. It is likely that Jesus spoke Aramaic, but with Mailer in the novel we come very close to listening to a mid-to-late twentieth-century American Jew, albeit of the self-deprecating variety. Constantly he questions his own statements, and often there is an implied degree of drollery in his reiteration of familiar tales. Of Joseph and Mary's journey to Bethlehem: 'This is the truth of why we took that journey, and it is also true that I was born in a manger by the light of a candle. As we all know by now, there was no room at the inn.' (p. 15). In a film adaptation Woody Allen or Mel Brooks would have been well-suited to the role.

Mailer spent most of his final decade in Provincetown until 2007, when, a few months before his death, Norris insisted that they move to Brooklyn where they had easier access to emergency medical help.

Some things did not change. The worst appraisal of *The Gospel According to the Son* appeared in *The New Republic*, by James Wood. The review was called 'He Is Finished'. Mailer fumed but bided his time. In 2005 he spotted the magazine's editor, Martin Peretz, in a Provincetown restaurant. He went outside, waited until Peretz's party left, and punched him twice in the face.

His weight plummeted and surged. In 1999 he managed to shift downward to 170 lbs and upward before the end of the year to 240. From the late 1990s onwards, he was continually tested for various cardiac disorders, and by 2003 it was decided that a bypass operation was necessary, though Mailer ignored all advice until relenting in 2005. Given that he felt well enough to hit Peretz after leaving hospital we should assume that the operation was a success.

One preoccupation endured from 1998 onwards, twelve months after the publication of *The Gospel According to the Son*. It began with Mailer reading Rob Rosenbaum's recently published *Explaining Hitler: The Search for the Origins of His Evil*. Rosenbaum was a literary critic and journalist who had spent ten years interviewing historians, biographers and psychologists in an attempt to track down something uniquely evil in what was known or could be surmised about Hitler's life. Conclusions elude him but he seems to imply that if someone so unremarkable as Hitler could cast so hideous a shadow across the twentieth century then so might anyone else. The notion that a man held to be the ultimate personification of evil was a blend of the dysfunctional and the mundane excited Mailer. He did not necessarily agree or disagree with Rosenbaum but went on to read more traditional, evidence-based accounts, notably Franz Jetzinger's *Hitler's Youth* (1958) and August Kubizek's *The Young Hitler I Knew* (1953). Then he shifted his attention to a lateral study of the Germanic character, familiarising himself with the ideas of Nietzsche, Schopenhauer and Herder, the literary work of Rilke, Heine and Goethe, and the music and prose writings of Wagner. Elke Rosthal, his friend in Provincetown, was invited over three times a week to teach him to read and speak German.

Mailer's novel on the early life of Hitler, *The Castle in the Forest*, was published a few months before he died in 2007. The narrator is Dieter, an agent of Satan disguised as an SS officer, who has witnessed, indeed guided, Hitler (or 'Adi'), from his conception to his later teens. There are very few direct references to the events that carried Hitler from rural obscurity to Nazi dictator, beginning with his service in the First World War, but what we encounter is still very unappetising.

He is the product of an incestuous marriage between his father, Alois, who tells his wife, Klara, with sleazy satisfaction, that she is his niece, knowing that she is in truth his daughter. Adi sometimes listens to the farmyard noises emitted by his parents when they have sex in the bedroom above, but Dieter, as a direct witness, treats the reader to an untempered description of their habits. Alois enjoys 'burying his nose and lips in Klara's vulva, his tongue as long and demonic as a devil's phallus ... Klara turned head to foot, and put her most unmentionable part down on his hard-breathing nose and mouth, and took his old battering ram into her lips', only to find it 'as soft as a coil of excrement'. (p. 68). This passage won *The Literary Review* 'Bad Sex in Fiction' Award in November 2007 three days after Mailer's death. He remains the only author to have won the prize posthumously. Faeces feature persistently in the novel, particularly in relation to Adi, who has difficulty controlling his bowels. Klara has to change his nappies well into his childhood and when doing so she discovers that he has only one testicle. As some kind of legacy from his years of incontinence, in his early adulthood Adi develops a body odour that some find unbearable and others addictive. Adi enjoys masturbating, during which he begins to 'practice holding his arm in the air at a forty-five-degree angle for a long time'. His one relatively normal fascination is with his father's beehive, which becomes 'contaminated', resulting in its inhabitants being gassed and inspiring in him a mixed sense of exhilaration and glee.

None of this is rooted in the albeit patchy historical facts surrounding Hitler's childhood and youth, which means that once more Mailer had set a record for literary insurrection. Numerous critics and thinkers had declared that the Holocaust should never be the subject of literary writing, the most-quoted mantra coming from Theodor Adorno, who is supposed to have written that 'To write poetry after Auschwitz is barbaric.' The exact wording of the statement fluctuates according to different translations from German, but it is clear that his notion of 'poetry' encompassed other literary genres. Adorno's point is that while the Nazis' act of mass extermination can and must be researched and recorded it would be an insult to its victims to render it in a genre that was at best an art form and worst a means of entertainment. Despite this there have been a vast number of novels and even poems on the Holocaust and the Nazi regime, but few, if any, can match Mailer in allowing invention and the imagination to intrude upon undisputed truths.

Even towards the end, Mailer has Dieter address the reader while posing questions to himself, asking amongst other things, where exactly the castle of the title, or rather the concentration camp, is situated. Dieter explains to his audience that *das Waldschloss* means 'the castle in the forest' in German and is the name given by a group of Jews to their particular concentration camp, from which no trees are visible, let alone a castle. (p.465). It is sited on the empty plain, an abandoned potato field with nothing of interest on the horizon. These Jews, he explains with half-hearted respect, have not surrendered their sense of irony, their badge as the brightest of their tribe. 'It should come as no surprise that [these] ... prisoners were from Berlin.' This is the closest Mailer comes to directly engaging with the Holocaust, and it is pure fiction. No group of Jews in any concentration camp conjured such ironies from their horrific plight.

Perhaps Mailer felt that, as a Jew, he was licensed to play games with the history of the Holocaust, but if so, what was his intention? By presenting its architect as a grotesque, smelly, one-ball masturbator, born out of incest in an agrarian community where bestiality seems endemic, what is he hoping to achieve? Even if his portrait of young Hitler was authentic, which it is not, would it explain, psychologically, what he became, or offer some retributive comfort to those who survived or who mourned those who did not? Common sense informs us that the answer to both questions is no.

Over the ten years that he worked on the novel there was no point at which he became resigned to it being his last. Indeed, on several occasions he promised a sequel to it and to *Harlot's Ghost* for Random House. But as mortality and decrepitude intruded ever more frequently as factors he could never avoid the book took on even greater importance.

It brings to mind the infamous passage in 'The White Negro' involving the hypothetical murder of the middle-aged shopkeeper by two hoodlums, what he called 'daring the unknown', 'trying to create a new nervous system'; through shock, causing the reader to inhabit rather than simply condemn or avoid the nature of violence, and therefore better understand it.

But this time Mailer's shock tactic of introducing us to Hitler as an awful freak is misguided and revealing. He chose to write about Hitler because he had exhausted all other exhibitions of literary self-aggrandisement. He had done the son of God so now he must deal with the 'agent of Satan', and he probably expected John Milton to beam down expressions of admiration.

During 1999 and 2000 Norris was diagnosed with several types of cancer. Her fallopian tubes were removed, and following chemotherapy and radiation treatment her flowing auburn hair fell out. Before she met Mailer she had written a basic draft of *Windchill Summer*, a murder mystery, and it appeared with Fourth Estate with reasonable reviews and sales in 2000. She had wanted Mailer to suggest improvements, but he politely declined, stating that it was her work, not his. In truth, the understanding between them was that neither knew when her cancer might return, and he did not want further delays in getting the book into print.

The following year George Plimpton sent Mailer the script of a play he'd written with Terry Quinn called *Zelda, Scott and Ernest*, about the uncomfortable friendship between the Fitzgeralds and Hemingway. Plimpton would play Scott, Mailer Hemingway and Norris Zelda. They opened in Provincetown to acclaim and full houses and decided to take the production to Europe, finding equal popularity and praise in several major cities, including Paris, London and Berlin. The tour took place during spring and early summer 2002, and while on the surface all three enjoyed themselves, the whole project carried an air of gloom. After Scott's death in 1940 Zelda had existed in a state of limbo for a further eight years, part of her husband's legacy but little else. Even though Mailer was not playing Norris's husband, there was a memorable incident in Berlin when a member of the audience howled in despair every time Zelda spoke. Norris walked to the front of the stage and addressed her. "'Sweetheart,' I drawled, 'I know just how you are feeling. I have been a little deranged myself, from time to time ... But I need you to stop yelling while I'm talking, because poor Scott is about to die, and I need to finish this play so we can all go home.'" (*A Ticket to the Circus*, p. 358).

She went home, briefly, to New York, and then south to her parents', where her father was seriously ill with a heart condition. He died on 21 July 2002. Gaynell, her mother, had diabetes and several other debilitating conditions. She could not drive and had never written a cheque, and was flown north to the Provincetown house. For Norris the subsequent twelve months felt as if she had taken on the role of receptionist in a waiting room to eternity. Mailer too had now given up driving due to his poor eyesight and knee-joint problems. At almost eighty he felt a danger to himself, his passengers and other road users. Norris had to ferry her ailing mother and husband to doctors and hospital appointments, as well as running the home. Gaynell knew of Mailer's past and treated the house as a monument to licentiousness. She was a devout Baptist who did not read books, apart from the Bible, and refused to have the television switched on in any of the rooms where she would sit. She regarded it as sinful, even demonic, and despite Mailer's commitment to Norris, he felt that her mother had been sent to him as a retributive agency.

It is for this reason that Mailer was so enthusiastic about an early reading by members of the Provincetown Repertory Theater of George Bernard Shaw's *Don Juan in Hell*. He would play the eponymous debaucher, and Norris his one-time paramour Doña Ana. He emailed Gore Vidal at his home in Ravello in Italy to ask if he would fly to America and rehearse for the role as the Devil.

Vidal at first wondered if it was a joke but decided to call Mailer's bluff, sent him an enthusiastic note of acceptance and stated that he would book a flight to New York within the next few days.

Vidal could walk no more than thirty steps at a time and only with a stick. Mailer was by then using a Zimmer frame. They joked for once about having a great deal in common, disposed of their mobility aids only when on stage, forgot their previous antipathies and treated one another with a respect that verged on affection. When the production opened on 12 October 2002 the theatre was bulging with spectators from as far away as New York, hungry to witness this dramatised encounter between two of America's most famous writers, who had spent the previous half-century cultivating an atmosphere of mutual contempt, often involving acts of violence instigated by Mailer.

Much of the play is made up of a dialogue between Don Juan and the Devil, and Vidal was acknowledged as the star turn, even by Mailer. He appeared with his blazer turned inside out, its red silk lining as alluring as his performance. Mailer had made some revisions to Shaw's text and there are close resemblances between the figure played by Vidal and Dieter of *The Castle in the Forest*, each exhibiting a mixture of quiet erudition, slyness and shameless contentment with their roles.

There are parallels too between the play, the novel and the DIY theology of *On God* (2007), Mailer's final work of non-fiction. God, proclaims Mailer, probably exists but as a fallible and certainly not omnipotent entity. He is, rather, more human than organised religion would admit. Equally Satan has a certain charm and is not the ineradicably vile figure of scripture. There is a little of us in him too.

Performances of the Shaw piece would have continued, but Mailer and Norris had booked other venues in Europe for full productions of *Zelda, Scott and Ernest*. Mailer interrupted these to visit the site of Dachau concentration camp, which Dieter has its victims call *das Waldschloss*. Mailer took note of the landscape of the region as part of his remythologising of it for the novel. He also went to Hitler's Berchtesgaden refuge and the villages where he grew up in Austria.

Shortly after their return to America, Norris's cancer recurred. Once more she survived, following surgery in early 2003. Acting with Plimpton, she had grown to appreciate him as one of Mailer's kindest and most sensitive friends. He promised to return to Provincetown for Christmas but died in September.

Mailer's final swipe at establishment complacency was *Why Are We At War?* (2003). He presents the Bush administration's military interventions in Iraq and Afghanistan as colonial enterprises and nothing to do with their ostensible motive of halting the growth of anti-democratic Islamist violence, both in terms of state-sponsored terrorist groups and outright military antagonism by the likes of Saddam Hussein.

His thesis was an echo of his past. Sixty years before, he had presented the Soviet bloc as a false enemy invented by a materialist, soulless capitalist state determined to bring the rest of the world into its stockade, and he extended this to his anti-Vietnam War campaign. This time the counterfeit threat came from Islamism rather than communism, but on both occasions he had little interest in the facts. If any threat, even falsified, was against the status quo, he rejoiced in its ability to make the American establishment panic.

The book was a user-friendly version of opinions he had expressed shortly after 9/11. Initially he said that the Twin Towers attack was on par with previous events that had radically altered perceptions of the here and now, including the assassinations of the Kennedy brothers and Martin Luther King. He added soon afterwards that the hijackers should be applauded for bringing down an 'architectural monstrosity', and that had not thousands been killed the Islamists would have been praised as 'brilliant' cultural strategists (*New English Review*, March 2009; publication of an interview with Ibn Warraq, conducted eight years earlier). In various interviews he presented America as a 'cultural oppressor', the 'most hated nation on earth' which was now being rewarded for wrecking its own social, cultural and architectural homeland and threatening to impose its ghastliness upon the rest of the world, notably against Muslim states. (Interview with Ann Treneman, *The Times*, 13 September 2001).

In 'The White Man Unburdened' for *The New York Review of Books* (17 July 2003), Mailer argued that Bush's response to 9/11 reflected a feeling of political and sexual impotence among white American males. Women, specifically feminists, had humiliated them, and black people had shown, in sport, that the WASP was physically inferior. Latinos, apparently, would soon be gaining ground in politics and art. It was 'The White Negro' revisited, and it credited Islamic radicals as the ones who had finally destroyed the ancien régime of white supremacy. Clearly,

he had forgotten his enthusiastic support for Salman Rushdie, who had
been sentenced to death by Islamists for literary free speech.

If one is tempted to treat this as an example of Mailer reborn as a
cultural relativist, suddenly alert to the importance of traditions that do
not comply with Western liberalism, forget it.

Michiko Kakutani was probably the most merciless literary critic in
America from the late 1970s onwards. She undermined the esteem of
members of the US cultural elite by writing reviews of their work that
were brilliantly convincing cases for the prosecution, and Mailer was
one of her regular hapless defendants. Interviewed by Douglas Brinkley
in 2005, Mailer called her a 'threefer ... Asiatic, feminist and, ah ...'
('The Last Buccaneer', *Rolling Stone*, 30 June 2005). He intended to say
lesbian but a sudden influx of common sense caused him to recognise
the danger of revealing himself as a homophobe as well as a racist. In any
event nothing was publicly known of her sexuality and in a millisecond
he caught a glimpse of a libel suit.

He knew that, a month later, he would have his quadruple bypass
operation. He was becoming angry and reckless, states of mind that
informed his novel as he hastened to complete it.

Why Are We At War? is admirably researched, at least in that Mailer
had read a good deal of material available on Islamist militarism and
terrorism. What he appeared to ignore or blind himself to was that
the terror groups and the states who sponsored and protected them
were outspoken in their intentions to destroy Israel. We should not
treat this as an example of anti-Zionism on his part, which is why his
final novel on Hitler, by a Jew, is so bizarre. The Holocaust is shuffled
into the wings and Norman Mailer takes over as the choreographer
between Satan and his mortal agent. It is not about Hitler and what
Hitler and his vile accomplices did. It is about Norman Mailer, who,
as an artist, regards himself exempt from charges of cheapening the
most horrible event of recent history. *Why Are We At War* was a non-fiction
polemical counterpart to *The Castle in the Forest*. In the former, the raging
troublemaker of old announces to fellow Americans, and by implication
all western democracies, that what totalitarian states – grounded
in fundamentalist theology or otherwise – get up to is none of their
business. In a similar vein he presents the architect of the Holocaust

not so much as the ultimate personification of evil but as a grotesque, lacking decorum, basic notions of hygiene, and one testicle. He did not really care about the nature of his argument. His intention was to shock and fix the reader's attention to the alchemist who could so effectively cause offence – Norman Mailer. As pieces of writing both books have their qualities – Mailer to the end was a punchy, belligerent stylist – but in all other respects they are atrocious.

Norris recalls that the last truly happy episode of their time together was in late summer 2007, when Maggie, his daughter with Carol, was married near the beach in Provincetown. 'The boys somehow got Norman down the stairs to the chairs on the beach, and Maggie and John were married ... on a clear, sparkling day in September. Then Norman struggled back up the stairs, had a polite glass of champagne, posed for a few pictures, and went to bed.' (*A Ticket to the Circus*, p. 388). Since June Mailer had regularly visited hospitals to have fluid drained from his lungs; often he could hardly breathe. In October 2007 he was admitted to Mount Sinai Hospital in New York with what appeared to be a collapsed lung. Norris: 'He knew his time was up and so did I. I was sitting beside his bed crying one day when he said, "You're crying. You must really love me" ... "Of course I do, you silly old coot! Why else do you think I've stuck around all this time?"'

> 'I'll be right behind you,' I told him. 'So have all the fun you can before I get there.'
> He smiled and took my hand. 'Remember the Taxicab Kiss?' he said.
> 'Like it was yesterday.'
> 'It's gone by fast, hasn't it?'
> 'Yes, it has.' It surely had. (p. 389)

This is his last recorded conversation. Shortly afterwards he had a tracheotomy, which alleviated his worst discomforts but prevented him from speaking. He never left the infirmary and died on 10 November 2007, aged eighty-four. His death certificate recorded the cause of death as acute renal failure.

He and Norris, who died in 2010, occupy the same burial plot in Provincetown cemetery.

BIBLIOGRAPHY

SELECTED WORKS BY NORMAN MAILER

Advertisements for Myself New York: Putnam's, 1959.
An American Dream. 1965. Reprint, New York: Dell, 1970.
Ancient Evenings. Boston: Little, Brown, 1982.
The Armies of the Night: The Novel as History / History as a Novel. 1968. Reprint, New York: New American Library, 1968.
Barbary Shore. 1951. Reprint, New York: Signet, 1951.
Cannibals and Christians. New York: Dial, 1966.
The Castle in the Forest. New York: Random House, 2007
Deaths for the Ladies (and other disasters). New York: Putnam's, 1962.
The Deer Park. 1955. Reprint, New York: Berkley, 1967.
The Deer Park: A Play. New York: Dial, 1967.
The Executioner's Song. Boston: Little, Brown, 1979.
Existential Errands. Boston: Little, Brown, 1972.
"A Folly Repeated. On Conviction and Creative Martyrdom, as Reflected by the Salman Rushdie Controversy". *Writer's Digest,* July, 1989.
The Faith of Graffiti. New York: Praeger / Alskog, 1974.
The Fight. 1975. Reprint, New York: Bantam, 1976.
Genius and Lust: A Journey Through the Major Writings of Henry Miller. New York: Grove, 1976.
The Gospel According to the Son. New York: Random House, 1997.
Harlot's Ghost. New York: Random House, 1991.
"Jackie, the Prisoner of Celebrity", *Esquire,* December, 1983.
Maidstone: A Mystery. New York: Signet, 1971
Marilyn: A Novel Biography. New York: Grosset & Dunlap, 1973.
Miami and the Siege of Chicago. 1968. Reprint, New York: Signet, 1968.
Mind of an Outlaw. Selected Essays. Ed. P. Sipiora. New York: Random House, 2013.
The Naked and the Dead. New York: Rinehart, 1948.
Of a Fire on the Moon. Boston: Little, Brown, 1970.
Of Women and Their Elegance. London: Simon and Schuster, 1980

On God: An Uncommon Conversation. With J. Michael Lennon. New York: Random House, 2007.

Oswald's Tale: An American Mystery. New York: Random House, 1995.

Portrait of Picasso as a Young Man: An Interpretive Biography. New York: Atlantic Monthly, 1995.

Pieces and Pontifications. Boston: Little, Brown, 1982.

The Presidential Papers. New York: Putnam's, 1963.

The Prisoner of Sex. Boston: Little, Brown, 1971.

Selected Letters of Norman Mailer. Ed. J. Michael Lennon. New York: Random House, 2014.

Tough Guys Don't Dance. New York: Random House, 1984.

A Transit to Narcissus. New York: Howard Fertig, 1978

Why Are We At War? New York: Random House, 2003

Why Are We in Vietnam? New York: Putnam's, 1967.

SELECTED BIBLIOGRAPHY AND RECOMMENDED FURTHER READING

Aaron, Daniel. *Writers on the Left.* New York: Harcourt, Brace, 1961.

Abbott, Jack Henry. *In the Belly of the Beast.* New York: Random House, 1981.

Abel, Lionel. *The Intellectual Follies: A Memoir of the Literary Venture in New York and Paris.* New York: William Morrow, 1987.

Abrams, Gary. "For Mailer, A 'Tough' Job: Pounds for His Thoughts." *Los Angeles Times,* September 23, 1984, 1, 21.

Adams, Laura. "Existential Aesthetics: An Interview with Norman Mailer." *Partisan Review* 42 (1975), 197.

_____. *Existential Battles:* The Growth of Norman Mailer. Athens: Ohio State University Press, 1976.

_____. *Will the Real Norman Mailer Please Stand Up?* Port Washington, N.Y.: Kennikat, 1974.

_____, comp. *Norman Mailer: A Comprehensive Bibliography.* Metuchen, N.J.: Scarecrow, 1974.

Agee, Philip. *On the Run.* Secaucus, N.J.: Lyle Stuart, 1987.

_____, and Louis Wolf, eds. *Dirty Work: The CIA in Western Europe.* Secaucus, N.J.: Lyle Stuart, 1978.

Aldridge, John. *After the Long Generation: A Critical Study of the Writers Two Wars.* New York: Noonday, 1951.

_____, "From Vietnam to Obscurity." *Harper's Magazine* (Feb. 1968), 183.

Atlas, James. *Delmore Schwartz: The Life of an American Poet.* New York: Farrar, Straus & Giroux, 1977.

Bailey, Jennifer. *Norman Mailer, Quick-Change Artist*. New York: Barnes and
   Noble, 1979.
Baldwin, James. "The Black Boy Looks at the White Boy." In *Nobody Knows
   My Name*. 1961. Reprint, New York: Vintage, 1993.
Bloom, Alexander. *Prodigal Sons: The New York Intellectuals and Their World*. New
   York: Oxford University Press, 1986.
Bloom, Harold. "Norman in Egypt." *The New York Review of Books*, April 28,
   1983, 3-4, 6.
Bosworth, Patricia. *Montgomery Clift: A Biography*. New York: Harcourt Brace
   Jovanovich, 1978.
Bower, Brock. "Never the Champion, Always the Challenger." *Life*, Sept. 24,
   1965. 94.
Boyum, Joy Gould. "Tough Guys Don't Dance." *Glamour*, November 1987,
   249.
Braudy, Leo, ed. *Norman Mailer: A Collection of Critical Essays*. Englewood
   Cliffs, N.J.: Prentice-Hall, 1972.
Brenner, Marie. "Mailer Goes Egyptian." *New York*, March 28, 1993, 28-38.
Brightman, Carol. *Writing Dangerously: Mary McCarthy and Her World*. New
   York: Clarkson Potter, 1992.
Calisher, Hortense. *Herself*. New York: Arbor House, 1972.
Campbell, James. *Talking at the Gates: A Life of James Baldwin*. New York:
   Penguin, 1991.
Clavir, Judy, and John Spitzer, eds. *The Conspiracy Trial*. Indianapolis: Bobbs-
   Mer rill, 1970.
Clemons, Walter. "Mailer in Egypt." *Vanity Fair*, May 1983, 61-64.
Conrad, Harold. *Dear Muffo: 35 Years in the Fast Lane*. Introduction by Budd
   Schulberg. Foreword by Norman Mailer. New York: Stein and Day, 1982.
Cooney, Terry A. *The Rise of the New York Intellectuals: "Partisan Review" and Its
   Circle*. Madison: University of Wisconsin Press, 1986.
Crouse, Timothy. *The Boys on the Bus*. New York: Random House, 1973.
   Dickstein, Morris. *The Gates of Eden: American Culture in the Sixties*. New York:
Basic Books, 1977.
Edwards, Anne, and Stephen Citron. *The Inn and Us*. New York: Random
   House, 1976.
Elman, Raymond. "Tough Talk: A Conversation with Peter Manso."
   Provincetown Arts (Summer 1987), 23-25.
Epstein, Jason. *The Great Conspiracy Trial: An Essay on Law, Liberty, and the
   Constitution*. New York: Random House, 1970.
Epstein, Joseph. "Mailer Hits Bottom." *Commentary*, July 1983, 62-68.
Ehrlich, Robert. *Norman Mailer: The Radical as Hipster*. New Jersey: Scarecrow,
   1978.

Dearborn, Mary V. *Mailer. A Biography.* New York: Houghton Mifflin, 1999.

Farbar, Buzz. "*Viva* Interview: Mailer on Marriage and Women." *Viva* 1 (Oct. 1973), 75.

Farber, M.A. "Killing Clouds Ex-Convict Writer's New Life." *The New York Times,* July

26, 1981, 1, 26.

Flaherty, Joe. *Managing Mailer.* New York: Coward-McCann, 1969.

Fuller, Edmund. "Mailer in Egypt: Neck-Deep in Nile Mud." *Wall Street Journal,* April 23, 1983, 30.

Gerson, Jessica. "An American Dream: Mailer's Walpurgisnacht." In Daniel Walden, ed., *Studies in American Jewish Literature,* vol. 2. Albany: State University of New York Press, 1982, 126-31.

_____. "Norman Mailer: Sex, Creativity, and God." *Mosaic* (June 1982), 1-16.

Gilbert, James. *Writers and Partisans.* New York: Wiley, 1968.

Gilman, Richard. *The Confusion of Realms.* New York: Random House, 1969.

Gilmore, Mikal. *Shot in the Heart.* New York: Doubleday, 1994.

Gingrich, Arnold. *Nothing But People: The Early Days at "Esquire," A Personal History.* New York: Crown, 1971.

Goodman, Paul. *New Reformation.* New York: Random House, 1970.

Gordon, Max. *Live at the Village Vanguard.* New York: Da Capo, 1980.

Glenday, Michael K. *Norman Mailer.* New York: St Martin's Press, 1995.

Greer, Germaine. *The Female Eunuch.* London: MacGibbon and Kee, 1970.

Greer, Germaine. "My Mailer Problem." *Esquire,* September 1971, 90-93, 214-218.

Gutman, Stanley T. *Mankind in Barbary: The Individual and Society in Norman Mailer.* Hanover, N.H.: University Press of New England, 1975.

Hagar, Jennifer. "Beverly Bentley: A Life in the Theater of Our Times." *P'town Women* (1998), 40--46.

Hamill, Pete. *A Drinking Life: A Memoir.* Boston: Little, Brown, 1994.

Hamilton, Ian. *Robert Lowell: A Biography.* New York: Random House, 1982.

Hayes, Harold, ed. *Smiling Through the Apocalypse: Esquire's History of the Sixties.* New York: McCall, 1969.

Hayman, Ronald. *Sartre: A Life.* New York: Simon and Schuster, 1987.

Hirschhorn, Clive. *Gene Kelly: A Biography.* London: W. H. Allen, 1974.

Howe, Irving. *A Margin of Hope: An Intellectual Autobiography.* New York: Harcourt Brace Jovanovich, 1982.

Jacobson, Dan. "The Jews of South Africa: Portrait of a Flourishing Community." *Commentary* (Jan. 1963), 39-44.

Jumonville, Neil. *Critical Crossings: The New York Intellectuals in Postwar America.* Berkeley: University of California Press, 1991.

Kakutani, Michiko. "Norman Mailer." In *The Poet at the Piano: Portraits of Writers, Filmmakers, Playwrights and Other Artists at Work.* New York: Times Books, 1988, 45-51.

Karnow, Stanley. *Paris in the Fifties.* New York: Times Books, 1997.

Kazin, Alfred. "The Writer as Sexual Show-Off." *New York,* June 9, 1975, 36.

Kingsley, April. *The Turning Point: The Abstract Expressionists and the Transformation of American Art.* New York: Simon and Schuster, 1992.

Knox, Mickey. *The Good, The Bad and the Dolce Vita: The Adventures of An Actor in Hollywood, Paris and Rome.* Preface by Norman Mailer. New York: Nation Books, 2004.

Kostelanetz, Richard, ed. *On Contemporary Literature.* New York: Avon, 1968.

Krassner, Paul. *Confessions of a Raving Unconfined Nut: Misadventures in the Counterculture.* New York: Simon and Schuster, 1993.

Lant, Jeffrey, ed. *Our Harvard: Reflections on College Life by Twenty-Two Distinguished Graduates.* New York: Taplinger, 1982.

Lasch, Christopher. *The Agony of the American Left.* New York: Vintage, 1969.

Leeds, Barry H. *The Structured Vision of Norman Mailer.* New York: New York University Press, 1969.

Leeming, David. *James Baldwin: A Biography.* New York: Knopf, 1994.

Lennon, J. Michael, ed. *Conversations with Norman Mailer.* Jackson: University Press of Mississippi, 1988.

Lennon, J. Michael. *Norman Mailer. A Double Life.* London: Simon and Schuster, 2013.

Liebling, A. J. "The Morest." In *A Neutral Corner: Boxing Essays.* New York: Simon and Schuster, 1990, 181-90.

Lindner, Robert. *The Fifty Minute Hour* (1955). New York: Bantam, 1956.

_____. *Prescription for Rebellion* (1952). New York: Grove Press, 1962.

_____. *Must You Conform?* New York: Holt, Rinehart and Winston, 1955.

Lucid, Robert F., ed. *Norman Mailer: The Man and His Work.* Boston: Little, Brown, 1971.

Lukas, J. Anthony. *The Barnyard Epithet and Other Obscenities. Notes on the Chicago Conspiracy Trial.* New York: Harper and Row, 1970.

Lynn, Kenneth, "One-Round Writer?" *Commentary,* March, 1983.

MacShane, Frank. *Into Eternity: The Life of James Jones, American Writer.* Boston: Houghton Mifflin, 1985.

McGinley, Maggie, *Understanding Norman Mailer.* South Carolina: University of South Carolina Press, 2017.

Mailer, Thomas. *Newhouse.* New York: St. Martins, 1994.

Mailer, Adele. *The Last Party: Scenes from My Life with Norman Mailer.* New York: Barricade, 1997.

Mailer, Norris Church. *A Ticket to the Circus. A Memoir.* New York: Random House, 2010.

Mailer, Susan. *In Another Place. With And Without My Father Norman Mailer.* Virginia: Northampton House Press, 2019.

Mallory, Carole. "Norman Mailer: The Power of Sex." *M*, February 1990, 79-83, 146-148.

--------. *Loving Mailer.* Beverly Hills: Phoenix, 2009.

Manso, Peter. *Mailer: His Life and Times.* New York: Simon and Schuster, 1985.

_____, ed. *Running Against the Machine.* Garden City, N.Y.: Doubleday, 1969. McAuliffe, Kevin. *The Great American Newspaper: The Rise and Fall of the "Village Voice."* New York: Scribner's, 1978.

McDowell, Edwin. "Little, Brown Rejects New Norman Mailer Novel." *The New York Times*, October 6, 1983, 32.

Meredith, Robert. "The Forty-Five-Second Piss: A Left Critique of Norman Mailer and *Armies.*" *Modern Fiction Studies* 17 (Autumn 1971), 433-49.

Merrill, Hugh. *Esky: The Early Years of "Esquire."* New Brunswick, N.J.: Rutgers University Press, 1995.

Merrill, Robert. *Norman Mailer.* Boston: Twayne, 1978.

Miller, James. *"Democracy is in the Streets": From Port Huron to the Siege of Chicago.* New York: Simon and Schuster, 1987.

Millett, Kate. *Sexual Politics.* Garden City, N.Y.: Doubleday, 1970.

Mills, Hilary. *Mailer: A Biography.* New York: Empire, 1982.

Nobile, Philip. *Intellectual Skywriting: Literary Politics and "The New York Review of Books."* New York: Charterhouse, 1974.

Page, Tim, ed. *The Diaries of Dawn Powell.* South Royalston, Vt.: Steerforth, 1995.

Pilati, Joe. "Mailer for Mayor: On the Steps of City Hall", *Commonweal,* May 16th, 1969.

Plimpton, George. *Shadow Box.* New York: Putnam's, 1977.

_____. *Truman Capote.* New York: Doubleday, 1997.

Podhoretz, Norman. *Breaking Ranks: A Political Memoir.* New York: Harper and Row, 1979.

_____. *Doings and Undoings.* New York: Farrar, Straus, & Giroux, 1964.

_____. *Ex-Friends: Falling Out with Allen Ginsburg, Lionel and Diana Trilling, Lillian Hellman, Hannah Arendt, and Norman Mailer.* New York: Free Press, 1999.

_____. *Making It.* New York: Random House, 1967.

Poirier, Richard. *Norman Mailer.* New York: Viking, 1972.

_____. *The Performing Self.* New York: Oxford University Press, 1971.

Polsgrove, Carol. *It Wasn't Pretty, Folks, But Didn't We Have Fun: "Esquire" in the Sixties.* New York: Norton, 1995.

Posner, Gerald. *Case Closed: Lee Harvey Oswald and the Assassination of JFK*. New York: Random House, 1993.

Preston, Charles, and Edward A. Hamilton, eds. *Mike Wallace Asks: Highlights from 46 Controversial Interviews*. New York: Simon and Schuster, 1958.

Ramsey, Roger. "Current and Recurrent: The Vietnam Novel." *Modern Fiction Studies* 17 (Autumn 1971).

Richman, Alan. "No Longer Such a Tough Guy, Norman Mailer Frets Over His Shaky Career As A Filmmaker." *People,* October 5th, 1987.

Robins, Natalie. *Alien Ink: The FBI's War on Freedom of Expression*. New York: William Morrow, 1992.

Rodman, Selden. *Tongues of Fallen Angels*. New York: New Directions, 1974.
Rollyson, Carl. *Lillian Hellman: Her Legend and Her Legacy*. New York: St. Martin's, 1988.

_____. *The Lives of Norman Mailer*. New York: Paragon House, 1991.

Rosenbaum, Ron. "The Trouble with Tough Guys." *Mademoiselle*, November 1987, 112, 115, 284.

Ruas, Charles. "Norman Mailer." In *Conversations with American Writers*. New York: Knopf, 1984, 18-36.

Schultz, John. *Motion Will Be Denied: A New Report on the Chicago Conspiracy Trial*. New York: William Morrow, 1972.

Schumacher, Michael. *Dharma Lion: A Biography of Allen Ginsberg*. New York: St. Martin's, 1992.

Sloan, James Park. *Jerzy Kosinski: A Biography*. New York: Dutton, 1996.

Smith, Dinita. "Tough Guys Make Movie." *New York*, January 12, 1987, 32-37.

Solotaroff, Robert. *Down Mailer's Way*. Urbana: University of Illinois Press, 1974.

Stern, Sydney Ladensohn. *Gloria Steinem: Her Passion, Politics, and Mystique*. New York: Birch Lane, 1997.

Stratton, Richard. "Norman Mailer: The Rolling Stone Interview." *Rolling Stone,*
Jan. 2 and Jan. 16, 1975.

Sukenick, Ronald. *Down and In: Life in the Underground*. New York: William Morrow, 1987.

Toback, James. "At Play in the Fields of the Bored." *Esquire,* December, 1968.

Torres, Jose, with Bert Sugar. ...*Sting Like a Bee: The Muhammad Ali Story*. New York: Abelard Schuman, 1971.

Thompson, Hunter S. *The Proud Highway: Saga of a Desperate Southern Gentleman, 1955-1967*. Edited by Douglas Brinkley. New York: Villard, 1997.

Trilling, Diana. *The Beginning of the Journey: The Marriage of Lionel and Diana Trilling*. New York: Harcourt Brace, 1993.

_____. *Claremont Essays*. New York: Harcourt Brace, 1964.

_____. *We Must March, My Darlings: A Critical Decade*. New York: Harcourt
   Brace Jovanovich, 1978.

Vidal, Gore. *Palimpsest: A Memoir*. New York: Random House, 1995.

_____. *Rocking the Boat*. Boston: Little, Brown, 1962.

Von Hoffman, Nicholas. *Citizen Cohn*. New York: Doubleday, 1988.

Wakefield, Dan. *New York in the Fifties*. Boston: Houghton Mifflin, 1992.

Wald, Alan M. *The New York Intellectuals: The Rise and Decline of the Anti-Stalinist
   Left from the 1930s to the 1980s*. Chapel Hill: University of North Carolina
   Press, 1987.

Weatherby, W J. *James Baldwin: Artist on Fire*. New York: Dell, 1990.

Weber, Bruce. "Mailer's Flight to Ancient Egypt." *Harper's Bazaar*, May 1983,
   96, 104, 160-161.

Wenke, Joseph. *Mailer's America*. Hanover, N. H.: University Press of New
   England, 1987.

West, James L. W. *William Styron: A Life*. New York: Random House, 1998.

Wilson, Rosalind Baker. *Near the Magician: A Memoir of My Father, Edmund
   Wilson*. New York: Grove Weidenfeld, 1989.

Winters, Shelley. *Shelley, Also Known as Shirley*. New York: Ballantine Books,
   1980.

Woodley, Richard. "A Literary Ticket for the 51ˢᵗ State." *Life*, May 30, 1969,
   71-73.

Wright, William. *Lillian Hellman: The Image, the Woman*. New York: Simon and
   Schuster, 1986.

Wreszin, Michael. *A Rebel in Defense of Tradition: The Life and Politics of Dwight
   Macdonald*. New York: Basic Books, 1994.